Dissent on Aadhaar

Dissent on Aadhaar

Big Data Meets Big Brother

Edited by
REETIKA KHERA

Orient BlackSwan

DISSENT ON AADHAAR: BIG DATA MEETS BIG BROTHER

ORIENT BLACKSWAN PRIVATE LIMITED

Registered Office
3-6-752 Himayatnagar, Hyderabad 500 029, Telangana
e-mail: centraloffice@orientblackswan.com

Other Offices
Bangalore, Bhopal, Chennai, Guwahati,
Hyderabad, Jaipur, Kolkata, Lucknow,
Mumbai, New Delhi, Noida, Patna, Visakhapatnam

First published by Orient Blackswan Private Limited 2019
Reprinted 2019 (twice)

029608

ISBN 978-93-5287-542-9

Typeset in
Minion Pro 11/13
by Shine Graphics, Delhi

Printed in India at
Yash Printographics, Noida

Published by
Orient Blackswan Private Limited
3-6-752, Himayatnagar, Hyderabad 500 029
e-mail: info@orientblackswan.com

Contents

Figures and Tables

Figures

Tables

Abbreviations

ABBA : Aadhaar-Based Biometric Authentication
AEPS : Aadhaar Enabled Payment System
AFSPA : Armed Forces Special Powers Act
BJP : Bharatiya Janata Party
BPL : Below Poverty Line
CIDR : Central Identities Data Repository
CIS : Centre for Internet and Society
CJI : Chief Justice of India
CMC : Computer Maintenance Corporation
CSC : Common Service Centre
DBT : Direct Benefits Transfer
DBTL : Direct Benefits Transfer of Liquefied petroleum gas
DSL : Digital Subscriber Line
EMV : Europay Visa Mastercard
IHDS : India Human Development Survey
iSPIRT : Indian Software Product Industry Roundtable
JAM : Jan Dhan–Aadhaar–Mobile
KYC : Know Your Customer
LPG : Liquefied Petroleum Gas
MDM : Mid-Day Meal
MIS : Management Information System
MLA : Member of Legislative Assembly
MNIC : Multipurpose National ID Card
MoRD : Ministry of Rural Development
NDA : National Democratic Alliance
NFSA : National Food Security Act
NIDAI : National Identification Authority of India
NIU : National Information Utility
NGO : Non-Governmental Organisation
NIC : National Informatics Centre

NIPFP	:	National Institute of Public Finance and Policy
NPR	:	National Population Register
NREGA	:	National Rural Employment Guarantee Act
NSAP	:	National Social Assistance Programme
NSS	:	National Sample Survey
OMR	:	Optical Mark Recognition
OTP	:	One-Time Password
PAN	:	Permanent Account Number
PDS	:	Public Distribution System
PIL	:	Public Interest Litigation
PMJDY	:	Pradhan Mantri Jan Dhan Yojana
POS	:	Point of Sale
RBI	:	Reserve Bank of India
RFID	:	Radio Frequency Identification
RTI	:	Right to Information
SCOSTA	:	Smart Card Operating System Standard for Transport Application
SDG	:	Sustainable Development Goal
SECC	:	Socio-economic Caste Census
SFinGe	:	Synthetic Fingerprint Generator
SRDH	:	State Resident Data Hub
SSA	:	Social Security Administration
SSN	:	Social Security Number
SSP	:	Social Security Pensions
TADA	:	Terrorist and Disruptive Activities (Prevention) Act
TAG-UP	:	Technology Advisory Group on Unique Projects
TOR	:	The Onion Router
UID	:	Unique Identity
UIDAI	:	Unique Identification Authority of India
UPA	:	United Progressive Alliance
VA	:	village accountant
VCLP	:	Vidhi Centre for Legal Policy
VPN	:	Virtual Private Network
VSAT	:	Very Small Aperture Terminal

Foreword

Over the past decade or so, the complex issue of digital identity, commonly referred to as Aadhaar, has invited considerable debate from all corners of society in India. On the one hand, we have seen a blitzkrieg of sorts from the government, with ample support from the media, favouring the unique identity project, and arguing that it can help in many ways, for example, by bringing millions out of poverty. On the other hand, vociferous naysayers have tried to prove that Aadhaar is nothing short of a tool of exclusion, pushed down the throats of a powerless electorate. They are concerned that the collection of sensitive biometric and demographic data would lead to unnecessary profiling and the creation of a surveillance state, which would, in turn, violate the fundamental right to privacy.

Unsurprisingly, there is a lot of noise when the subject of Aadhaar is brought up. Everyone has an opinion. Everyone is jostling for space. And everyone wants to be the only audible person in the room. In this crowded environment, it becomes difficult to separate the signal from the noise. This book attempts to do precisely that, by gathering together the opinions of people trained in law, economics, policy, technology, finance, and offering, as a result, a bouquet of essays that identify the many weaknesses of the Aadhaar project. In doing so, it presents a comprehensive picture of the challenges that India has faced with this digital identity initiative, and that it will continue to face going forward, after the law has received constitutional blessings from the Supreme Court of India. I am deeply honoured and delighted to have been invited to write the foreword to this book, which I believe is an invaluable contribution to the academic literature around the subject.

While I am no expert on the technology around Aadhaar, I have been following the legal developments over the past few years closely, the constitutional aspects of the right to privacy and related issues being of particular interest to me. It started as an unlegislated and unregulated policy where sensitive identity-related—demographic and biometric—information was obtained from citizens. It was then retroactively legislated through a controversial money bill (on grounds that the law pertained to government spending and appropriation, and which, consequently, did not require approval from the Rajya Sabha—or upper house—in order to be legislated). The law did not go unchallenged; first, a nine-judge constitutional bench of the Supreme Court of India was entrusted with adjudicating upon, primarily, whether the right to privacy was a fundamental right, and later, a five-judge constitutional bench on whether Aadhaar had come about through lawful means, and whether it was being used for legal purposes.

The *Aadhaar case*—as it has come to be colloquially referred—saw one of the longest hearings ever in the history of the Supreme Court, spanning several days, weeks and months, with lengthy submissions made by lawyers, bureaucrats, technologists and academics, among others. Every day of the hearing in the Court was followed with bated breath, with the public anxious to know which way the Court would eventually swing.

The decision of the constitutional bench finally came in September 2018—*(Justice (Retd) KS Puttaswamy & Ors v. Union of India, WP (C) 494/2012, judgment dated 26 September 2018, Supreme Court of India)*—and the outcome was a majority verdict, albeit with some riders, in favour of Aadhaar as a form of digital identity, and the law creating Aadhaar and regulating its use. The majority bench granted some relief in favour of the citizens. For example, the Court observed that children's Aadhaar, or UID numbers, could be used only with parental consent and not be demanded of them (although, it ignored the question of 'coercion as consent'). On the issue of exiting Aadhaar, the Court said that a person could exit the Aadhaar system upon reaching majority. Alternately, since enrolment in the system was voluntary, those who specifically refused to give consent for enrolment could exit from the Aadhaar scheme. Similarly, the majority agreed that making Aadhaar mandatory 'in the name of checking money laundering or black money is grossly disproportionate'. On the issue of surveillance, the majority judgment, while ignoring the *potential* of surveillance, directed that metadata be deleted after six months. Through all this, though, even if one acknowledges that there were some concessions made to the people (over the state), the majority judgment still falls short, for dealing inadequately, or not at all, with fundamental issues that were at the heart of the case, such as identity and dignity.

For that, instead, we have to turn to the solitary dissent that emerged from one corner of the Court. Justice D. Y. Chandrachud chose to disagree with the rest of his brethren on the bench, and struck down the entire idea of Aadhaar and the legislation as unconstitutional. His opinion, besides being a landmark contribution to our jurisprudence, discussed issues of vital importance, such as dignity, autonomy and self-determination. It is unfortunate that his bold dissent did not, in any measure, prevent the legislation from going through. But as Chief Justice Charles Evan Hughes (1862–1948) of the United States Supreme Court once wrote, '[A] dissent in a court of last resort is an appeal to the brooding spirit of law, to the intelligence of a future day…'

In contrast, the majority judgment did not offer a sufficiently nuanced discussion on the interface between identity and dignity so as to convince its audience of the necessity of Aadhaar. The underlying justification offered by the majority for having a biometric identification was the need to grant an identity. Justice A. K. Sikri, for example, wrote, 'Aadhaar gives identity to those persons who otherwise may not have such identity. In that sense, it recognises them as residents of this nation and in that form gives them their dignity.' But I remain concerned that the Court failed to satisfactorily consider the challenges of granting such identity to the most deserving, either on account of technological limitations, or the quality of governance, or even simpler social concerns of accessibility (for example, how can a nonagerian who cannot walk, and who does not have the strength to submit a fingerprint for documentation, stake their legitimate claim to the old-age pension granted by the state?). For all the talk around the 'benefits' of Aadhaar, there remains a real concern that a large-scale use of Aadhaar for the purposes of authentication is likely to lead to large populations of society remaining excluded from social sector benefits, particularly manual labour and senior citizens.

With this judgment, the Court has effectively made a distinction between the haves and the have-nots; those who are privileged, as against those who are in need of state assistance. My own reservations with Aadhaar and the judgment have been echoed by many others, and can be found in quality opinions in this collection as well. In my view, Aadhaar was falsely marketed as a panacea for the poor and impoverished. Over the years, as the project was operationalised and scaled throughout the country, many case studies increasingly pointed to facts that suggested that the poor were not *beneficiaries*, as originally intended, but rather, the *victims* of the Aadhaar project. Instead of serving as an inclusive tool, and being used to increase access to social, political and civil rights, Aadhaar had become an instrument of exclusion. Stories abound as to how the state proactively used the lack of a digital identity to deny basic services to its citizens, and thus deprived millions of their rightful benefits—benefits which had been designed precisely for such populations.

As the net of Aadhaar widened, the state made Aadhaar a necessary prerequisite for seeking any kind of benefit, whether it was scholarships for economically weaker sections of society, or compensation for victims of natural disasters, reimbursement of health expenses for persons with debilitating diseases, and so on. A slew of official notifications were issued, over 130 of them. The notifications were issued under Section 7 of the Aadhaar Act, 2016, which mandates that individuals should produce their Aadhaar (or the Aadhaar number) to access social services, subsidy, and benefits, wherever funds are drawn from the Consolidated Fund of India.

The Supreme Court, in its majority judgment, chose to keep this problematic Section 7 of the law untouched. This decision has created a gaping chasm between different sections of our society. This judgment has made it clear that those who are receiving, or who wish to receive benefits from the state (in any form, be it cash or kind), can continue to do so only if they sign up to the Aadhaar scheme. They do not have the luxury of refusing to be a party to the identity project, for the risk is that by refusing to consent to signing up for Aadhaar, they will be deprived of basic socio-economic rights. Aadhaar is now, by law, a necessary prerequisite for anyone who seeks to receive any entitlements from the state. By corollary, assuming that such state entitlements are essential for the survival and sustenance of such persons, the question of them 'consenting' to Aadhaar no longer exists. As a result, everyone who lives below the poverty line, for example, and who relies on state benefits for say, pensions, subsidies or scholarships, no longer has any choice. The right to privacy remains elusive and unaffordable for this stratum of society. From now on, only those who are privileged can continue to enjoy the privilege of privacy, for they are not expected to solicit the state for its largesse. Those who are not so fortunate must forego any fundamental right to privacy they might have imagined they possess. The protections that the state grants them thereafter are, unfortunately, undefined and clouded, leaving a prospective beneficiary at the mercy of the state from now on.

While this split between the privileged and the rest is the central concern, the judgment does not tackle many peripheral (but important) questions with satisfaction either. Take, for example, the arguments raised around Aadhaar allowing the creation of a surveillance state. The majority judgment's opinion can be captured in the following observation made, based on statements made by the Attorney General and the UIDAI's representative, that:

> [N]o State would be interested in any mass surveillance of 1.2 billion people of the country or even the overwhelming majority of officers and employees or professionals. The very idea of mass surveillance by state, which pursues what an ANH [Aadhaar number holder] does all the time and based on Aadhaar, is an absurdity and an impossibility.

In observing thus, the Court, unfortunately, brushed aside the consequences of the seeding of Aadhaar in various databases, which allows information about an individual (that was otherwise stored in different silos) to be combined to create complete profiles of persons. The question of whether this act of creating a profile through converged data would lead to the violation of the right to privacy remained largely unanswered.

The other major concern with the majority judgment is its treatment of the Aadhaar Act as a Money Bill. While extensive arguments during the course of the hearing were made against permitting the Aadhaar Act to be considered as a Money Bill, the majority judgment decided otherwise. Arguably, the Aadhaar Act is a law that defines a digital identity and creates the architecture to deal with the data that comes along with such identity. The law does not solely deal with the allocation of resources for Aadhaar, or indeed, otherwise relate to the financial disbursements, receipts and obligations, as envisioned by Article 110 of the Constitution of India. Had its status as a Money Bill been reversed by the Supreme Court, the trajectory of the law would have been very different. The law would effectively have had to have been struck down completely, and been sent back to Parliament, and specifically to the Rajya Sabha, which would have played its legislative role in assessing the concerns with the law. Instead, the law continues to stand today, with the amendments proposed by the upper house ignored entirely. In concluding that the Aadhaar Act was constitutionally valid, the Court relied on the doctrine of 'pith of substance'—its view was that the heart of the law lay in the delivery of benefits, services and subsidies from the Consolidated Fund of India, which made it, in pith and substance, a Money Bill. On the other hand, in his opinion, Justice Chandrachud concluded that declaring the Aadhaar Act to be a Money Bill was illegal and unconstitutional, noting:

> The Rajya Sabha has an important role in the making of laws. Superseding the authority of the Rajya Sabha is in conflict with the constitutional scheme and the legitimacy of democratic institutions. It constitutes a fraud on the Constitution.... That would constitute a subterfuge, something which a constitutional court cannot countenance.

In the context of all these concerns, this book offers an intelligent, reasoned and wide-ranging counterview to the majoritarian position taken by the three arms of the state. In doing so, it reminds us of the importance for a debate on the role of the state in protecting the marginalised and the poor, and demands a constant re-evaluation of state actions following an assessment of their impact on every aspect of society. Even the slightest disregard for society can have dangerous consequences for the health and conscience of the state. This book, therefore, comes as a timely reminder of such questions, and I am confident that you, the reader, will find it as incisive and thought-provoking as I did.

JUSTICE (Retd) AJIT PRAKASH SHAH
November 2018

Acknowledgements

Writing acknowledgements is hard. As with other collaborative work, the book benefits from more people than I can thank adequately. Apart from those who shaped this book, there were those who helped understand the full import of the Aadhaar project—and resist it.

Among those who are not in the book but have influenced it are many lawyers—young and senior—whose legal work has been an inspiration. There were the tireless student volunteers who documented, in several field surveys, the many failings of Aadhaar. People in the media gave us a patient hearing and managed to create space for views that challenge the government narrative. Concerned citizens from across the country kept us informed of worrying Aadhaar-related developments, which we could investigate further. Many strangers helped in different ways—some hosted me in their homes; unsuspecting students who would invite me for talks were co-opted for field visits; readers (of my opinion pieces) who wrote in or called to thank me for raising their issues (which made it easier to cope with ill-informed trolls); insights gleaned from Twitterfolk.

For the book itself, which is like most of my earlier 'research for action' work, I should start by thanking the publishers for coaxing me to send a book proposal, even though I was not initially convinced of the value of such a book. I thank all the contributors for agreeing to be part of it, cooperating with deadlines and being gracious about the delay. For thoughtful comments and helpful suggestions on earlier drafts, I thank Arudra Burra, Rajesh Jha, Simona Sawhney, Aakash Solanki and Anmol Somanchi. Anmol has done a lot more than comment on the book—research at the early stages, organising and participating in various field studies, preparing the name and subject index, and much else. Anshika Jain provided excellent research assistance for the book through a large part of its journey.

Usha Ramanathan has been very important—she helped me understand the many ramifications of the Aadhaar project, think about how to resist it and kept us cheerful through it all. Jean Drèze, apart from volunteering framing advice for the book and the many issues it raises, helped plan it, pointed out the gaps, offered comments many times over and made me think harder about the arguments. And finally, in advance, my thanks to all the readers who, I hope, will give us a fair hearing on Aadhaar.

Introduction

Reetika Khera

Since 2010, over the course of my research, I have met scores of people across states whose lives have been grievously disrupted by Aadhaar.

As early as 2011, in Ratu (Ranchi district), we encountered our very first Aadhaar victim. An old man was being forced to open a new bank account because the government wanted to route his pension to an Aadhaar-linked bank account instead of the local post office. The helpful banking correspondent had to turn him back because one key document was missing. A few minutes later, we saw him squatting by the roadside on the way home, which was about a kilometre away. We stopped to ask him why, and he said he could not walk any further—he was too exhausted from the excursion.

Later, in East Godavari, the 'pioneer' district in linking the Public Distribution System (PDS) to Aadhaar, at a PDS outlet, I met Jyothi, a young Dalit mother of twins. For some reason, which no one was able to explain to her, the new system would not allow her to draw her rations any more. As she described the condition of her hungry twins, despite herself, she broke down.

Most recently, in December 2017, I met Kapil and Savitri Paikra in Surguja (Chhattisgarh). Kapil Paikra has been bedridden since 2009 after a bad road accident. His PDS rations have been discontinued as he has not given his Aadhaar number. He has never been able to enrol for Aadhaar as he has been bedridden since before Aadhaar was initiated. Savitri asked us, 'Can I carry his bed to the Aadhaar enrolment centre?'

These are just three people of many in whose name the Aadhaar project is being rolled out. Their stories are symptomatic of a much larger problem, and there is plenty of evidence of it, even in the government's own data. Yet, the official narrative continues to push the line that Aadhaar empowers the poor.

Packaged as a welfare-enhancing initiative of the second United Progressive Alliance (UPA-2) government in India, an enormous amount of public money was spent to saturate the public discussion with the message that Aadhaar was good for the poor, that it would lead not only to a more inclusive system of welfare, but also greater 'efficiency' in welfare delivery.

Over the years, the project has reinvented itself—as a welfare-enhancing technocratic initiative, a project for financial inclusion, an administrative aid against terrorism and better tax administration, and most recently, a big data opportunity. While this helped create 'buy-in' for the project from various segments of society, it has also meant that critical voices from different spheres have become involved in the Aadhaar debate. Many have been raising uncomfortable questions about the 'Unique Identity' (UID) project. Some have questioned its role in welfare, others on the legal aspects, yet others on technology. There have been contributions on the implications of the UID project for privacy, civil liberties and the possibility of surveillance and tracking, and how this affects the functioning of a democracy.

Yet I noticed that those writing about these *other* weaknesses of the Aadhaar project tended to end their critique with a line about how we must make it work because it is helping the poor and disadvantaged people, or (at least) it has the potential to help them. Those raising technical concerns seem unaware of the privacy and civil liberty concerns. It appeared that we (the dissenters from different quarters) were operating in silos which did not speak to each other. There was little engagement *across* fields.

That is why I felt that it may be worth putting together a book that brought all these silos under one cover. This book is an attempt in that direction, with contributions from the fields of law, technology, finance, economics and social policy. What has emerged over the past few years is that it is not just the technology that is broken, the law is broken too, and Aadhaar is also breaking India's meagre yet precious welfare state.

What is Aadhaar?

On 28 January 2009, the Government of India constituted the Unique Identification Authority of India (UIDAI) through a Gazette notification, with the Planning Commission as the nodal agency within the government. Later that year, Nandan Nilekani was appointed as the Chairperson of the UIDAI. The main aim was to 'generate and assign UID to residents'. In mid-2010, the UID project was given a brand name, 'Aadhaar' (meaning 'foundation' in some Indian languages) and a logo. Over time, the brand name Aadhaar has come to be used more or less universally (in this book 'Aadhaar' and 'UID' are used interchangeably). The Aadhaar project came to be seen as one of the flagship schemes of the second UPA (UPA-2) government.

The idea behind Aadhaar was to provide each Indian resident a unique number, the uniqueness of which is guaranteed by biometric identification (and demographic details if need be). At the time of enrolment, people must provide the following demographic information: name, gender, date of birth, parent's (or husband's) name, residential address and any other information that the government may prescribe (barring caste, religion and a few other sensitive attributes). Along with this, they are required to submit three biometrics also—photographs, 10 fingerprints and both iris scans. These are stored in the UIDAI's Central Identities Data Repository (CIDR). For the purpose of generating a unique number, the UIDAI does a one-on-n match, that is, each new enrolee's details are matched against each existing person in the CIDR who has been issued a unique number. This is supposed to guarantee uniqueness.

By September 2010, the UIDAI had begun issuing Aadhaar numbers to Indian residents. With the impending threat of making Aadhaar compulsory for welfare programmes, and an incentive-based private agency led enrolment model, enrolment picked up quickly even though there was no legal framework guiding the project. This legal vacuum has serious consequences because a law would have defined the rights of ordinary people vis-à-vis the state (for example, give clarity about why their data was being collected and what they could do if it is compromised). Over 80 crore Indian residents were enrolled into the database by 2015.

Since 2012, however, several concerned citizens began approaching the courts challenging the project. Between September 2013 and October 2015, the Supreme Court issued six interim orders to restrain or prevent the government from making the use of Aadhaar compulsory for any service. Unfortunately, the 2015 orders (in August and October), which allowed only voluntary use for six schemes, have been interpreted, by the government as a license to make Aadhaar compulsory for those schemes. Nearly seven years into full-fledged operation, in March 2016, the Indian government passed the Aadhaar (Targeted Delivery of Financial and Other Subsidies, Benefits and Services) Act (or, Aadhaar Act).

Initially, Aadhaar was projected as a *voluntary* facility for all residents. Though in the UPA-2 years, the use of Aadhaar spread rapidly, its spread was more or less confined to 'welfare' applications. This changed dramatically in 2016 after the Aadhaar Act was passed. Since then, it is being made compulsory for many services. For instance, women in labour have delivered babies at the doorstep of hospitals after they were denied admission for lack of Aadhaar. What started as a voluntary ID gradually became compulsory and there is a danger of it becoming the *only* ID for certain uses. Compulsory Aadhaar is a very different thing from a voluntary Aadhaar.

Why Aadhaar?

An early profile of Nandan Nilekani, the main promoter of Aadhaar, had noted, 'He is known as a great salesman, but he sells softly, blithely, by making it seem almost an imposition to have to explain the benefits of his product' (Parker 2011).

Perhaps this explains the many narratives to justify the Aadhaar project. Perhaps appealing to various constituencies was a strategy to create maximum buy-in for the project. Some of these narratives are outlined below.

The Welfare Façade

The most forceful framing of Aadhaar was as an enabler of welfare. Identity and inclusion were the twin objectives that proponents used to sell the idea to the Indian public. The early media blitz (in the national and international press) was focused on the 'transformational' potential of Aadhaar. The claim was that having an Aadhaar number would enable inclusion. Non-existent ('bogus', 'duplicate', 'ghost') beneficiaries were everywhere, according to the UIDAI narrative. A centralised database with a unique number associated with each person would sanitise beneficiary databases of such non-existent beneficiaries. By ensuring 'inclusivity' and corruption-free implementation, it would be a 'game-changer' for welfare in India.

Further, some of those concerned with the poor performance of welfare programmes felt that Aadhaar would facilitate a transition to cash transfers. Cash transfers, they felt, were a better option than some existing in-kind forms of social support as these were believed to be less prone to corruption. India has 'in-kind transfers' such as subsidised grain through the PDS or free meals for pre-school and school-going children, and cash transfers such as social security pensions. Though cash was not explicitly pushed by the UIDAI, the early welfare claims and Nilekani's 2009 book (*Imagining India*) betrayed some indications of this. For instance, 'interoperability' and 'portability' (that is, welfare benefits that can be claimed anywhere, especially important for migrants) were projected as desirable and only possible within the Aadhaar eco-system.[1] Aadhaar, it was claimed, would eliminate middlemen and thus, corruption also.

Are Digital IDs the Future?

Internationally, the role of digital IDs for growth and development has been stressed considerably in recent years. For instance, according to the World Bank, 'Lack of identity is an impediment for poor people to exercise their basic democratic and human rights… Digital identification can help overcome barriers to participation.' The narrative that was pushed in India mirrors international rhetoric: millions of Indians are without IDs, more often than not, these happen to be the poor, the lack of an ID deprives them of access to government services and a new ID such as Aadhaar is therefore necessary. Indeed, the proponents of Aadhaar regularly refer to it as the equivalent of the Social Security Number (SSN) in the United States of America.

No doubt IDs play a facilitating role in many ways, but it is worth bearing in mind that many countries without a national ID continue to provide good public services. A cursory look around the world suggests that national IDs are neither a necessary, nor a sufficient condition 'for poor people to exercise their basic democratic and human rights'.

The United Kingdom is a useful example—it does not have a national ID (not even paper-based) and its proposed biometric 'Identity Project' was ultimately scrapped when the Conservative Party came to power. Like Aadhaar, the attempt was to introduce not just *any* national ID, but a digital biometric ID. There are many parallels between the UK's Identity Project and the Aadhaar project in India—for example, how the case for such an ID was over-sold, the scale of the problems that it could solve were exaggerated, the costs and technological issues were understated and so on. Eventually, in the case of the UK, timely public debate ensured that the project was scrapped. There are other examples of such ID projects being initially heralded as transformative and revolutionary, but eventually being scrapped—Australia's anti ID-card campaign in 1987 is legend (Davies 1996).

Enabling Financial Inclusion

Aadhaar, by providing an identity document (or rather, a number) was to enable financial inclusion (narrowly understood as the opening of bank accounts, into which benefits in the form of cash could be deposited). There are many barriers to financial inclusion in India—lack of documents for Know Your Customer (KYC), limited reach of the banking system, costs of servicing new customers, etc. The lack of KYC documents was singled out as the main cause of financial exclusion, and Aadhaar was again projected as the best way forward. Combined with 'banking correspondents' who would act as extension counters of banks in areas where regular bank branches were not financially viable was another way in which Aadhaar was supposed to improve financial inclusion.

Over the years, the Reserve Bank of India (RBI) and the Indian government have taken various measures to increase access to the formal banking system. These measures included the opening of 'basic saving bank deposit' (also known as 'no frills' or 'zero-balance') accounts, simplification and relaxation of KYC norms, etc. For instance, in 2008–09, the Ministry of Rural Development (MoRD) decreed that wage payments related to the National Rural Employment Guarantee Act (NREGA) could only be made through bank accounts and NREGA 'job cards' were declared adequate KYC for opening no-frills or zero-balance accounts. In 2013, after some back-and-forth on the issue, the RBI declared Aadhaar as a valid document for KYC.

As a result of all these initiatives, between 2005–06 and 2015–16, the proportion of women who had a bank or post office account that they used themselves rose from just 15 per cent to 53 per cent. It is no doubt true that a large number of people have opened bank accounts using Aadhaar. What is not clear is how many of these people already had accounts. Another potential contribution of Aadhaar is a reduction in the cost of acquiring new customers. Here again, good data is hard to come by. It is hard to tell from the available data the extent to which the improvements in financial inclusion can be attributed to Aadhaar alone, as opposed to a secular rise and other government and RBI initiatives.

Data, the New Oil

Most recently, the Aadhaar project is revealing itself as a mega 'data mining' project. In the words of its promoter Nilekani, 'Data is the new oil' and as someone on Twitter put it, 'and Aadhaar is the drill to get it'. This also explains the zeal for digital IDs. What is not clear is whether Aadhaar is reinventing itself as a tool for mining personal data or just shedding its scales.

To the extent that Aadhaar *is* like the SSN, it is worth recalling that in the US the SSN played a crucial role in helping to build credit histories of individuals, a development associated with the rise of the credit and insurance industries. Both these industries have a chequered history of exploiting personal information for profiteering (O'Neil 2016).

An important development in 2016–17 has been that while regular biometric authentication is not being extended beyond specific applications (not yet, at least), there is a concerted and single-minded focus on 'seeding'—the practice of storing the Aadhaar number permanently—in public and private databases. From cradle to grave, the government wants people to leave their digital (Aadhaar) footprint in every database. Seeding the UID number in different databases opens the door for profiling of individuals—something that is key for the credit-rating and insurance industries.

A Surveillance Infrastructure

The discussion on digital IDs and the facilitating role they can play in data mining naturally leads us to the surveillance potential—intended or unintended—of the Aadhaar project. The spectre of surveillance has generally been evoked in the context of government surveillance. The fact of, and dangers from, corporate surveillance are only now beginning to emerge in the public debate (see Schneier 2015). Corporate surveillance refers to the use of our personal data for the purposes of targeted advertising and, as the revelations by Christopher Wylie in early 2018 about Facebook and Cambridge Analytica show, even in manipulating elections.

The proliferation in the compulsory applications of Aadhaar since 2016 will create the opportunity for both types of surveillance. When the same number is stored permanently in numerous databases in the country, tracking people and creating profiles of people by pulling in data from different sources becomes easier than ever before. Where and how I travel (air versus train), what I spend my money on (books, or clothes, or food), who I meet or talk to—all this information can be pooled together to create a profile of me, to target products on the one hand, and to red-flag me on the other. For instance, frequent trips to Jharkhand by train and by road would be useful information for companies operating in that state and could equally red-flag me on the government's radar as a visitor to a state affected by Maoist violence.

The government asserts that since UIDAI itself collects and keeps very little information, the question of profiling, tracking and surveillance does not arise. This is disingenuous because as the Aadhaar number is linked with numerous databases, including many government databases, it is very easy for the government to pull in information from various sources. Another defence that the government puts forward is that metadata (which is what UIDAI primarily deals in) alone prevents collation of an individual's data from different sources. What they do not acknowledge is that metadata can reveal a lot (for instance, information on the most frequently called number is as revealing as information on what the conversations were about). Further, data mining techniques are now sophisticated enough to match individuals across databases with greater accuracy (even when they were originally anonymised metadata). Having a unique identifier across databases will make that task much easier. In the world of algorithmic decision-making, frequent trips to rural Jharkhand are equally likely to be classified as those of a field researcher as they are to be classified as a Maoist supporter's. When the auto-correct feature on our phones regularly makes mistakes, can we trust Artificial Intelligence (in moments of exasperation, 'natural ignorance' seems to describe these techniques better) with decisions that are fundamental to people's existence?

Aadhaar Concerns

The previous section focused on the many narratives justifying the need for Aadhaar and the inadequacies of those narratives. Beyond the questions about official narratives, there are five fundamental concerns with a project such as Aadhaar.

Manufacturing Elite Consensus

Nilekani, who was charged with the rollout of the project, was well aware of the possibility of resistance to the project if a fair debate was allowed. When asked about his strategy to deal with the 'opposition' to Aadhaar, he makes the startling revelations that they employed three strategies: 'do it quickly' (that is, do not give people time to comprehend the implications of the project), 'do it below the radar' and 'create a coalition that wants Aadhaar' (outsiders who bat for the project). The strategy was to make it big swiftly, so that rollback would seem impossible. Manufacturing elite consensus to mute any possible challenges was essential to achieve this. From the very beginning, perception management through advertisements, branding, etc. has been a part of the project's strategy to manufacture elite consensus in favour of Aadhaar.

Aadhaar meant so many things to so many different constituencies, that everyone bought into it. What is increasingly clear is that welfare was just the sugar-coating on the darker aspects of the UID project—its potential as a tool of government and corporate surveillance.

'Labelling' was an important way to shape perceptions. In the early years, those who questioned the Aadhaar project were labelled as 'anti-technology' or Luddites. More recently, those who raise difficult questions have been called 'vested interests'. Any dissenting voice then easily came across as reactionary or inclined to conspiracy theories. The media strategy to create Aadhaar's brand image includes 'damage control'. Though critical voices were not entirely suppressed, after a critical opinion was published, newspapers would 'make amends' by publishing gushing editorials soon after. After the *Wall Street Journal* questioned estimates on LPG savings, it prompted a response from the government in *Indian Express* (George and Subramanian 2016). Soon after, an episode of 'Walk The Talk' with Nandan Nilekani (who had left UIDAI by then) appeared. The interview completely ignored the 'retraction' of savings estimates and instead provided a platform to repeat the discredited figures. The interview itself looked suspiciously like an attempt to whitewash any damage from the retraction.

Planting convenient stories at crucial junctures is an oft-used strategy. Close on the heels of important government announcements of Aadhaar-linking, stories of 'fake' school enrolments, 'ghost' teachers, 'bogus' ration cards, etc. discovered due to Aadhaar appeared, to create the impression that the decision was justified. One report claimed that nearly one crore fake job cards had been deleted, whereas follow-up investigations reveal that there was little substance in these stories. Manipulating headlines is another commonly used strategy (for instance, the use of creative accounting techniques such as putting the *cumulative* savings figure for several years in the headline).

Another element that fuels the propaganda is 'sponsored research'. The most telling example of this is an almost entirely fabricated 'potential savings' due to Aadhaar, put out in a World Bank report (Drèze and Khera 2018). Apart from the World Bank, several philanthropists such as the Omidyar Network are funding large research projects on Aadhaar in India. Omidyar is known to have a business interest in 'fintech' (Solodkiy 2016), a sector that will likely receive a big boost due to Aadhaar. Similarly, the Bill and Melinda Gates Foundation, with an interest in (private) health insurance, also works on Aadhaar.

One result of the concerted 'media strategy' of the UIDAI, since its inception, is that the favourable impression in people's minds is hard to dislodge, in spite of the growing evidence of exclusion, denial and hardship.

Undermining Parliamentary Processes

After its creation by an executive order in 2009, the project operated in a legal vacuum until 2016. The National Identification Authority of India (NIDAI) Bill 2010 brought to Parliament by the UPA-2 government in December was sent to the Parliamentary Standing Committee on Finance. The Committee submitted its report in December 2011 after wide consultations. Its verdict was damning. The Committee felt that the project was 'riddled with serious lacunae'; it had 'been conceptualized with no clarity of purpose and leaving many things to be sorted out during the course of its implementation'. In the end, the Committee urged the government to reconsider the UID scheme:

> In view of the afore-mentioned concerns and apprehensions about the UID scheme, particularly concerning the contradictions and ambiguities within the Government on its implementation as well as its implications, the Committee categorically convey their unacceptability of the National Identification Authority of

> India Bill, 2010 in its present form... The committee would, thus, urge the Government to reconsider and review the UID scheme as also the proposals contained in the Bill in all its ramifications and bring forth a fresh legislation before Parliament. (Government of India 2011: 35)

In spite of the Committee's damning verdict, the project continued unabated, reaffirming the Committee's indictment of it as an 'overbearing' project. The only concession that the government made was with respect to the recommendation to undertake a feasibility study, 'which ought to have been done before approving such an expensive scheme'.

The Planning Commission commissioned the National Institute of Public Finance and Policy (NIPFP) to undertake a cost-benefit analysis for the project. The NIPFP report claimed that linking seven welfare programmes to UID would lead to huge savings, with an internal rate of return of 50 per cent. When it was pointed out that the NIPFP study was based on faulty assumptions (Khera 2013), the authors of the report conceded that:

> [A] 'full-fledged cost benefit analysis of Aadhaar' is difficult for two reasons: first, many gains from Aadhaar are difficult to quantify because they are intangible; and second, even if in specific schemes there may be tangible benefits, the information available on those schemes does not permit a precise quantification of those benefits. (Chandrashekharan et al. 2013)

The most egregious violation of the parliamentary process, however, was the passage of the Aadhaar Act as a Money Bill. Under increasing public pressure to enact a law, the National Democratic Alliance (NDA) government that came to power in 2014 rammed an Aadhaar Bill through Parliament in 2016. It was brought to Parliament as a 'money bill', allowing it to effectively bypass the Rajya Sabha, where the party of the day did not have a majority. Informed legal opinion on this is not only that its classification was wrong, but also that the Speaker's decision to classify it as such is open to judicial review. To be classified as a money bill, the Aadhaar Bill ought to have contained 'only provisions' that deal with matters listed in Article 110 of the Constitution. In fact, to the extent that the Aadhaar Bill contained the matters listed in Article 110, those provisions of the Aadhaar Bill were 'incidental to the Act's core purpose' (Parthasarathy 2017). After the passage of the Act, the government issued notifications which were making it near impossible for anyone to survive without Aadhaar. Since the final hearings began in January 2018, the government has had to relent slightly (for example, by extending deadlines, sometimes indefinitely), but it has continued to exploit the ambiguity it has created regarding the mandatory nature of Aadhaar to exert pressure to link it to all kinds of services.

The Right to Privacy Challenge

The main challenge to the Aadhaar project in the Supreme Court is on the grounds that it violates the Right to Privacy, a fundamental right under the Constitution of India. In a bizarre turn of events in 2015, the Government of India even challenged whether indeed the right to privacy was a fundamental right (bizarre, because several decades of jurisprudence had firmly established the right to privacy as a fundamental right).

The Aadhaar project is a privacy hazard from several angles—data security, bodily integrity due to the use of biometrics, personal integrity and personal data mining. While *any* centralised database creates a data security vulnerability, a unique number ('key'), such as Aadhaar linking all the data silos, *magnifies* those vulnerabilities. Of course, this is precisely what creates massive commercial possibilities from personal data mining—information on nature and frequency of travel, who we meet or talk to, what we buy and so on, has great value for targeted advertising and other decision-making algorithms that are being used in more and more spheres. Centralised and inter-linked databases also enable tracking, profiling, leading to self-censorship, which endangers our freedom. The mining of personal data, thus, clashes in a fundamental way with civil liberties, a clash that lies at the heart of the Aadhaar debate.

The Aadhaar project, given how it is being implemented, has serious repercussions for democratic practice. By linking all aspects of our lives (air and train travel, bank transactions, mobile usage, employment and health records, etc.), the UID project is creating a mass surveillance infrastructure which facilitates tracking and profiling of ordinary citizens. We know that private entities easily hand over our data to government agencies—for example, mobile companies to the National Security Agency in the US, Google to governments requesting data on its users and so on (Schneier 2015). Profiling and surveillance are known to lead to self-censorship (Greenwald 2015). Self-censorship of thought and actions severely hampers free thought and expression, stifling dissent. Such tools of control have no place in a democracy.

Technocratic Tyranny in Welfare

The use of Aadhaar in welfare programmes (those that it was supposed to help) is fast turning into a 'weapon of mass destruction'. What are brushed aside as teething problems or rare implementation issues, are routine—not rare—occurrences: people have been shut out of their pensions, PDS rations, hospital services, savings, mobile connections, etc. In Jharkhand alone, the use of Aadhaar has been made compulsory in the PDS and has resulted in the deaths of over a dozen people after they were denied PDS rations due to Aadhaar-related failures.

Earlier, to get any social benefits, people needed to meet the eligibility criteria for that scheme. There were many hurdles along the way: learning about the existence of such schemes, figuring out eligibility criteria, running from pillar to post to understand application procedures, gathering supporting documents, etc. What Aadhaar has done is to add a few new hurdles at the finishing line, pushing it out of people's reach again.

The first new hurdle is getting the Aadhaar number. While it is true that there is only a tiny fraction now that does not have Aadhaar, the tiny fraction can add up to a large absolute number *and*, as bedridden Kapil Paikra's case illustrates, it can be those who are the most in need of state support.

The second new hurdle is 'seeding'. Seeding (or linking) the Aadhaar number with each new scheme for which it is made compulsory is not as small a demand as it seems: a single trip can be cumbersome for the elderly; in many cases, the task cannot be accomplished in one trip. This problem is well illustrated by the old pensioner in Ratu, who we met in the opening paragraphs above, or of Jyothi, in whose case nobody at the Mandal level was able to figure out what had gone wrong during the transition from the old to the new system.

The third hurdle is Aadhaar authentication at the time of drawing their benefits. This fails for a variety of reasons—connectivity issues, electricity supplies, biometric authentication failures, etc. Authentication by the beneficiary *herself* means that people like Olasi Hansda, who lives alone and is immobile, and who could earlier send a neighbour to fetch rations, are simply excluded. For others, it means increased transaction costs in terms of repeated visits, longer waiting times, etc.

Solove (2001) argues that the privacy problem that arises with databases is inadequately captured by George Orwell's 'Big Brother' metaphor where 'privacy is invaded by uncovering one's hidden world', leading to 'inhibition, self-censorship, embarrassment, and damage to one's reputation'. He argues that a more accurate metaphor is 'The Trial' by Franz Kafka, which characterises the problem as 'the powerlessness, vulnerability and dehumanization created by the assembly of personal information'. The anecdotes listed above amply demonstrate that precisely these problems have arisen from the use of Aadhaar in welfare. Importantly, writing about the use of technology in welfare administration in the US, Eubanks (2017) proposes that as rights began to be enshrined in law and political will teetered, the response was to 'unleash' technology to contain rising costs.

There are several technology pieces of the Aadhaar project that are worth scrutinising. The UIDAI has always emphasised the robustness of their technology. However, serious questions have arisen about biometrics (how reliable and secure they are), security of the CIDR, data security (for example, encryption standards, who has access to it, etc.), and processes (the display of Aadhaar numbers on government portals or demographic data were available for Rs 500 in Punjab).

In the push for using biometrics in welfare, the similarity between India and the US is striking. Magnet (2011: 77–83) shows how the incidence of 'duplicate-aid fraud' was exaggerated in order to expand the market for products of the biometrics industry (p. 69). When no substantial savings could be established, savings estimates were manufactured. For instance, any reduction in the number of welfare recipients—even due to other reasons—was attributed to the use of biometrics. Both these problems—exaggerating the incidence of duplicate-aid fraud (the only form of fraud that biometrics can potentially resolve) and fabricated savings due to the use of biometrics—have been documented in the Indian case as well (see chapter 1 of this volume and Drèze and Khera 2018).

Like Eubanks and others, Magnet's assertion is that technology is used to push back on welfare spending. Magnet also documents the fallibility—in terms of failures and 'high-tech racism'—of biometric technology itself.

There is a question of technological readiness in India. For certain services, the government proposes to use Aadhaar to biometrically authenticate each time a service is used (for example, purchase of subsidised grains each month). In a country where electricity supply is erratic, as is mobile and server connectivity, the wisdom and economics of such a move need to be considered.

Furthermore, there are anxieties related to the appropriateness of making such technologies ubiquitous and compulsory. The Aadhaar 'eco-system' demands high digital, technological and legal literacy. Yet, it is being foisted on a society with low levels of literacy (according to the 2011 Census, nearly 30 per cent of the population was not literate). Given the low levels of digital, tech and legal preparedness, this is irresponsible and undemocratic.

Examples of the damage from the compulsion already abound: for example, when mobile phone users were forced to link their Aadhaar numbers, one company (Airtel) opened Airtel Payments bank accounts for those customers *and* further credits (such as cooking gas subsidy, wages earned by working on NREGA projects) to these customers were automatically redirected from their regular bank accounts into the airtel bank account. Both—the opening of Airtel Payments accounts and the redirecting funds—happened without any meaningful consent from the affected persons.

Big Data Meets Big Brother

If 'data is the new oil', seeding the Aadhaar number in as many public and private databases as possible will facilitate extraction of the oil. Making Aadhaar compulsory in increasingly ridiculous applications (such as painting and sports competitions for children) is likely being done to create a digital trail of as many facets as possible of an individual's life. Traditionally, such techniques have been used for targeted advertising.

The new avatar of targeted advertising is 'digital kleptocracy', which is authoritarian as well (Kaiser 2018). Applications that correlate behaviour of individuals across data silos will create business opportunities in credit-rating, health insurance, even marriages, and blue-collar and other hiring, to name just a few. These will be facilitated by the 'data brokering' industry, which tends to emerge in such digital economies. In a speech, Nilekani describes it thus: 'The business models that will emerge in India will...allow people to take their digital wealth and convert that into economic wealth, and that is the trickle-up.'

There is a genuine concern that the social, political and economic interests of large parts of the population—including the variously disadvantaged—are becoming secondary to the demands of Big Data *and* Big Brother.

We have had some glimpses of this already. In April 2017, it was discovered that in contravention of the Aadhaar Act, many state agencies were freely displaying individual Aadhaar numbers along with personal identification information on their websites. The Aadhaar numbers of thousands, possibly millions, were compromised. This 'Data Leaks' scandal coincided with the government insistence on mandatory linking of Aadhaar with Permanent Account Number (PAN), mobile phones and bank accounts. These two incidents generated a lot of public interest and debate, especially on social media. There was a sudden proliferation of what was labelled 'anti-Aadhaar' (a term used to identify anyone who questioned Aadhaar) sentiment on social media. For the first time in seven years, the proponents of Aadhaar seemed to be losing control over the carefully curated narrative. The 'elite consensus' appeared to be slipping away. Around this time, a handful of anonymous trolls appeared on Twitter attacking the anti-Aadhaar handles. Soon after, the trolls were exposed and traced to members of iSPIRT. iSPIRT is an association for nurturing software start-ups and includes several prominent members of the UIDAI team. The most prominent of the trolls exposed was, in fact, the head of iSPIRT.

The most revealing aspect of the ugly Twitter war was that it provided an indication of the extent to which businesses, such as those involved in iSPIRT, are invested in the Aadhaar project. Why else would a person with close links to Aadhaar's founder risk his reputation and good standing in the industry? As the welfare mask of Aadhaar slowly fell off, some business interests openly petitioned the Supreme Court in 2018 pleading that the Aadhaar project be kept alive to safeguard their business interests.

Similarly, also related to the 'Data Leaks' in 2017, the Center for Internet and Society (CIS), an independent research organisation, published a report that merely documented what had already been reported widely and cautioned against the vulnerabilities of the Aadhaar eco-system. CIS was being a good citizen. The publication of the report led to CIS being served legal notices by government agencies. This was not the only incident of whistleblowers being punished. At least three other such incidents have been reported (in each case, different vulnerabilities in the Aadhaar eco-system were exposed). The 'chilling effect' is very much in evidence already in the Aadhaar project: several of the whistleblowers' contributions since then are quite subdued.

Outline of the Book

In the summer of 2010, three functionaries of the UIDAI met me to explain how 'transformational' the then government's new initiative, UID or Aadhaar, was for reducing corruption in the PDS and in NREGA. Upon reading their policy documents on PDS and NREGA, I was aghast because they betrayed a complete lack of understanding of the problem they were trying to address and hence, I began writing to warn that *in principle* this technology can do little to help these programmes. Perhaps the visit from the three friendly government folks was to enlist my help in their project of manufacturing elite consent for the Aadhaar project? It was a 'public relations' exercise that went badly wrong because it put Aadhaar on my radar and this book is ultimately a result of that interaction.

The collection begins with two chapters that 'blow the lid', so to speak, on the welfare-related claims. The first is based on a careful examination of the official claims and the 'in principle' possibility of realising such benefits. It also scrutinises recent government claims of savings due to Aadhaar. Most of these savings estimates are akin to rabbits pulled out of a hat (the estimates even multiply like rabbits). It also documents the growing evidence on the disruption in welfare programmes due to the forced integration of Aadhaar in these programmes. For instance, there is mounting evidence that officially entitled people are being struck off welfare rolls, and the reduction in expenditure thus achieved is projected as savings. This, of course, causes immense hardship on the ground. An extreme example of this is the death of nearly two dozen persons since 2017. All of them died due to hunger—in some cases, the family's card had been cancelled because they did not link Aadhaar; in others, it was because biometric authentication failed for few months in a row. There have been a few more deaths since that are directly attributable to the disruption caused by Aadhaar.

The second chapter is based on field reports by Anumeha Yadav, who has reported extensively from the field across many Indian states. Her work examines the human cost of the coercive imposition of Aadhaar in several welfare programmes.

In chapter three, Jean Drèze's explains that Aadhaar as a voluntary facility is very different from a compulsory, coercive Aadhaar. As early as 2010, Drèze had warned of UIDAI's doublespeak, when it says on the one hand that Aadhaar is not compulsory and on the other hand that it can be made compulsory for various benefits or facilities. As he put it, 'This is like selling bottled water in a village after poisoning the well, and claiming that people are buying water voluntarily'. His contribution here explains how the Aadhaar project is fast becoming a dream project for intelligence agencies, and how the Aadhaar Act, 2016 facilitates not just the government's surveillance potential but also corporate surveillance and personal data mining (more on this below).

The fourth chapter discusses the ways in which Aadhaar infringes on privacy. I explain why the usual responses to privacy concerns are inadequate and how the August 2017 privacy judgment provides significant protections.

Many believe that most of the criticisms of Aadhaar can be dealt with by improving the implementation. When the problems with Aadhaar are pointed out, the standard counter is technocratic—that it can be fixed by doing this or that. The measures are either technological or legal or even administrative, and always overlook the social and political context in which the project operates. The belief is that the problems can be 'fixed'.

The next three chapters, on the Aadhaar technology, are written by people who work with related technologies and have observed how they operate in real life situations. Sunil Abraham's chapter shows how the 'fixes'—legal or technological—are not going to help. The Aadhaar project—in its design (for instance, the creation of a centralised database), its choice of technology (such as biometrics)—is fundamentally flawed. His chapter helps bridge worldviews, in terms of values, between a democratic and technocratic society.

L. Viswanath discusses the reliability and suitability of biometrics in an identity project and the weak case for its application in the Aadhaar project. Kiran Jonnalagadda's chapter is important because it goes to the heart of the problem of a technocratic undertaking such as Aadhaar. It makes explicit the social context in which such technologies operate, and how that context is distinct from the worldview of the technocrat (where the messiness of the real world is rarely acknowledged, and is mostly just wished away).

The next four chapters are by lawyers, all of whom have been involved in some way with the cases in the Supreme Court. The first of these is an overview of the project and its ramifications by Shyam Divan, a senior advocate in the Supreme Court, who has argued the case since 2013. S. Prasanna's chapter provides an overview of the legal challenges to Aadhaar in the Court, from the different petitions that were pending. There were nearly 30 petitions in the Supreme Court.

Another important development in the courts has been the reference of the privacy matter to a nine-judge Constitution bench in the course of the Aadhaar hearings. Briefly, in July–August 2015, Mr Rohatgi (then Attorney General) was cornered on the question of Aadhaar violating the right to privacy. He requested a nine-judge bench, on the grounds that all judgments after *MP Sharma and Kharag Singh* (that upheld privacy as a fundamental right) would have to be revisited because these two rulings were from larger benches than subsequent ones. The Court agreed, and while it promised urgency in the matter, it was not until July 2017, nearly two years later, that the nine-judge bench was constituted. The landmark privacy judgment was delivered in August 2017. Gautam Bhatia's chapter helps understand the importance of that judgment (not just for the Aadhaar matter) and cautions us about its actual implementation.

Consent, especially informed consent, is a particularly weak point of the Aadhaar project. The lack of it is best demonstrated in the way children are being forced to enrol into the Aadhaar database. Kritika Bhardwaj outlines the nature of the problem insofar as children are concerned. Importantly, her contribution discusses the idea of 'informational privacy', which is an area of growing concern in the age of extensive economic activity based on mining personal data.

The next two chapters (by Usha Ramanathan and M. S. Sriram) highlight another significant development that is not fully understood yet: the rise of quasi-government entities—not quite government, and not quite private. Usha Ramanathan's contribution explains how government entities are morphing into hybrid entities, with the consequence that accountability is weakened. She documents the commercial entities involved in the project and the fallout of their involvement. In a data-driven economy, the government emerges as a customer. Some of these features of government are also the theme of M. S. Sriram's chapter. He examines the promise of Aadhaar, and the betrayal of it, from the lens of financial inclusion. Going further, his article highlights a new genre of the conflict of interest.

The last two chapters in the book look at the Aadhaar project in international comparative perspective. Aadhaar is often compared with America's SSN. Srujana Bej uses a legal lens to examine the argument, comparing the legal framework that governs the SSN and its uses with that of the Aadhaar project. Two big differences between them are that the SSN was the result of a law which created a variety of entitlements and the SSN has repeatedly rejected the use of biometric information (even photographs). It appears that the closest approximation of the SSN is the PAN, not Aadhaar.

Finally, Gus Hosein and Edgar Whitley look at the Aadhaar 'eco-system' in a comparative perspective. What constitutes a good 'digital identity', why digital identities may be necessary and does Aadhaar meet those requirements? The authors, key members of the London School of Economics and Political Sciences' influential and path-breaking report on The Identity Project, bring some of that experience into comparative focus.

* * *

Unfortunately, this collection excludes many important voices on the subject—and there are many now! Even among those who have been included, this book is hardly a fair representation of all their Aadhaar-related work. This is especially true of Usha Ramanathan—she has done and written enough to fill another book (or two) herself—she promises that she is 'working on it'.

This collection does not privilege academic or theoretical knowledge over the practitioners' knowledge. If anything, it is the reverse. It is perhaps worth mentioning also that many of those who have contributed to this book have never met each other—indeed, even I have not met all of the contributors! The Aadhaar project has helped create this community of dissenters, who have been drawn together by virtue of (initially) being lone voices in their respective fields. In that sense, we owe the project for fostering new friendships in unlikely quarters.

Note

1. The latter is not true—portability and interoperability of cash transfers only require access to a modern banking system.

References

Chandrashekaran, Sumathi, Shekhar H. Kumar, Ila Patnaik, Smriti Parsheera, Madhavi Pundit, Ajay Shah, and Suyash Rai. 2013. 'Response to "A Cost-Benefit Analysis of UID"'. *Economic and Political Weekly* 48 (10), 9 March, pp. 78–80.

Davies, Simon. 1996. 'On Campaigns of Opposition to ID Card Schemes'. Privacy International. Available at https://privacyinternational.org/sites/default/files/2017-12/ID%20CardSchemes.pdf (accessed 4 September 2018).

Drèze, Jean, and Reetika Khera. 2018. 'Aadhaar's $11bn Question'. *Economic Times*, 7 February.

Eubanks, Virgina. 2017. *Automating Inequality, How High-Tech Tools Profile, Policy and Punish the Poor.* New York: St. Martin's Press.

George, Siddarth, and Arvind Subramanian. 2016. 'Clearing the Air on LPG'. *Indian Express*, 2 April.

Government of India. 2011. 'The National Identification Authority of India Bill, 2010, Forty Second Report'. Standing Committee on Finance (2011–12), Fifteenth Lok Sabha, Ministry of Planning. New Delhi: Lok Sabha Secretariat.

Greenwald, Glenn. 2015. 'Why John Oliver Can't Find Americans Who Know Edward Snowden's Name (It's Not About Snowden)'. *The Intercept*, 6 April.

Kaiser, Brittany. 2018. 'Facebook Should Pay its 2bn Users for their Personal Data'. *Financial Times*, 9 April.

Khera, Reetika. 2013. 'On the NIPFP Response'. *Economic and Political Weekly* 48 (10), 9 March, pp. 80–81.

Magnet, Shoshana Amielle. 2011. *When Biometrics Fail, Gender, Race, and the Technology of Identity.* Durham and London: Duke University Press.

National Institute of Public Finance and Policy. 2012. 'A Cost-Benefit Analysis of Aadhaar', 9 November.

Nilekani, Nandan. 2009. *Imagining India: The Idea of a Renewed Nation.* New York: Penguin.

O'Neil, Cathy. 2016. *Weapons of Math Destruction, How Big Data Increases Inequality and Threatens Democracy.* New York: Crown.

Parker, Ian. 2011. 'The I.D. Man'. *New Yorker*, 3 October.

Parthasarathy, Suhrith. 2017. 'What Exactly is a Money Bill?' *The Hindu*, 27 February.

Schneier, Bruce. 2015. *Data and Goliath, The Hidden Battles to Collect your Data and Control your World.* New York: W.W. Norton & Company.

Solodkiy, Vladislav. 2016. 'Why Zuckerberg, Gates and Omidyar are Investing in Fintech for the Poor'. *Forbes*, 27 October.

Solove, Daniel. 2001. 'Privacy and Power: Computer Databases and Metaphors for Information Privacy'. *Stanford Law Review* 53 (6), Julu, pp. 1393–462.

———. 2008. *Understanding Privacy*. Cambridge: Harvard University Press.

1

Impact of Aadhaar in Welfare Programmes*

*Reetika Khera***

> A little learning is a dangerous thing;
> drink deep, or taste not the Pierian spring:
> there shallow draughts intoxicate the brain,
> and drinking largely sobers us again.
>
> Alexander Pope (1709)

Pope aptly describes the origins and evolution of the Unique Identity (UID) project (widely known as 'Aadhaar'), that was initiated to provide each resident of India a unique number linked to his or her biometrics. Among other things, it was meant to lead to greater inclusion into welfare programmes, reduce corruption in them and remove middlemen from the delivery mechanism.

Based on evidence of the *source* of corruption in programmes such as the National Rural Employment Guarantee Act (NREGA), Public Distribution System (PDS), Social Security Pensions (SSP), etc., and the proposed use of UID in them, it is clear that *a priori*, there is a very limited role for Aadhaar in improving their implementation (Khera 2011). Despite these early warnings,

---

* A previous version of this chapter was published as Reetika Khera, 2017, 'Impact of Aadhaar on Welfare Programmes', *Economic and Political Weekly,* vol. 52, no. 50, pp. 61–70.

** I thank Anshika Jain, Siddhartha Pradeep and Monika Yadav for research assistance, John Harriss for crucial inputs and Jean Drèze for numerous discussions and rounds of comments.

the government continued to push for Aadhaar-integration in these programmes. This chapter looks at the impact of Aadhaar-integration primarily in NREGA, PDS and SSP. The case of the Liquefied Petroleum Gas (LPG) subsidy and the proposed application of Aadhaar in the Mid-Day Meal (MDM) scheme are also discussed briefly.

What emerges is as follows: one, the extent of corruption in these programmes varies, but even where it is high, there has been a decline predating Aadhaar-integration (for example, in NREGA and PDS). Two, Aadhaar-integration cannot solve the major forms of corruption that persist (primarily 'quantity fraud'). Three, far from improving the implementation of these programmes, there are signs that Aadhaar-integration causes serious damage. Four, based on their own data, the government's savings estimates due to Aadhaar-integration are highly questionable.

In a nutshell, the gains are limited and tentative whereas the damage is certain and possibly substantial. Given this, the government's decision to make Aadhaar mandatory for a range of welfare programmes is cause for alarm. The 'right to privacy' challenge to the Aadhaar project has received a lot of attention, but the 'right to life' challenge to it has thus far not been adequately highlighted. This paper attempts to fill that gap.

Lack of an ID

The proponents of the UID project claimed that a large number of Indians were denied welfare benefits because people did not have any identity documents. This assertion, not really supported with evidence, provided the initial justification for the project.[1] If, as the government claimed, the coverage of existing forms of ID was incomplete, then those could have been expanded to ensure wider coverage. This option was rejected on the grounds that existing databases were seriously flawed.

The Unique Identification Authority of India (UIDAI) was set up to organise enrolment and generation of Aadhaar numbers.

Apart from the National Population Register (NPR), there are two ways of enrolling for an Aadhaar number from the UIDAI directly: one, using a proof of ID and a proof of address from a list (including passports, ration cards, voter IDs, etc.) drawn up by the UIDAI;[2] two, using the 'introducer' system. This was set up keeping in mind people who were lacking in pre-existing IDs.

According to a response to a Right to Information (RTI) query in 2015, only 0.03 per cent of Aadhaar numbers were issued through the introducer system. The rest were issued to those who submitted two IDs or through the NPR, raising questions about the basic premise of the Aadhaar project.

Note also that the UIDAI used those very IDs to enrol for Aadhaar that it had rejected as error-ridden or flawed. This circularity went largely unnoticed. It has serious implications for the reliability of the Aadhaar database. Independent of biometric data (fingerprint, photograph and iris scans), the accuracy of demographic data (for example, name, date of birth, etc.) in the Aadhaar database is especially important now as it is becoming the basis for claiming benefits. There has been no independent audit of the database, so we do not know to what extent there are errors, but media reports regularly highlight them and their fallout.

The promoters of UID also succeeded in creating the impression that Aadhaar would guarantee access to benefits, end the '*mai-baap sarkar*' (state as lord and master) culture and enable people to assert their rights vis-à-vis state structures. Here again, the UIDAI was misinformed. Exclusion is largely the result of a weak 'targeting' mechanism (identification of the poor) and the imposition of stringent caps on coverage (arising from budgetary constraints). For instance, in the PDS, statewise central commitment was fixed at the poverty rate estimated using National Sample Survey (NSS) data from 1993–94 until the passage of the National Food Security Act (NFSA) in 2013. Caps were applied in several schemes (such as pensions and housing). The possession of an additional ID cannot solve the problem of exclusion, unless these caps are relaxed or identification methods improve. Instead, as discussed below, Aadhaar is slowly becoming a tool of exclusion, the last hurdle after all the prior eligibility hurdles have been crossed. For some, even enrolling for Aadhaar has not been easy.

Corruption

Another justification for the Aadhaar project was its purported role in reducing corruption in welfare programmes such as NREGA, PDS and pensions. Fraud in these programmes can be broadly categorised as 'eligibility fraud', 'identity fraud' and 'quantity fraud' (see Table 1.1).

Eligibility fraud refers to inclusion of persons who do not meet official eligibility criteria, for example, by presenting fudged supporting documents. Quantity fraud takes the form of eligible persons receiving less than their entitlements, for instance by under-selling in the PDS (people are forced to sign off on more than what they actually get); in MDM, it could refer to dilution of prescribed nutrition norms (for example, not following the menu at all, or giving watery *dal*).

Identity fraud refers to cases where one person's benefits are claimed fraudulently by another. In the PDS, an official may defraud the system by getting a ration card in the name of a non-existent person or dead person ('ghosts'), or getting two cards when they are entitled to only one ('duplicates'). In the MDM scheme, identity fraud can take the form of inflated attendance (where costs are booked for more children than are actually being served meals).

In programmes such as NREGA and SSP, which provide support in cash rather than kind, one big protection against identity fraud comes from using the banking system to transfer funds. This eliminates, by and large, the possibility of identity fraud so long as banking norms are observed.[3]

Biometric technology, to the extent that it is reliable, can help eliminate identity fraud, but cannot help in reducing quantity fraud or eligibility fraud. There is limited evidence on the magnitude of each type of fraud, but available evidence suggests that quantity fraud is the bigger problem (Khera 2011, 2015 and Muralidharan et al. 2018). Therefore, contrary to the government's understanding, Aadhaar can only play a marginal role in reducing corruption.

Aadhaar in Welfare

For the PDS, NREGA, SSP and the MDM scheme, three broad themes are examined: recent evidence on corruption, the government's claims about Aadhaar's contribution to improved implementation of these schemes, and the emerging evidence on disruption due to Aadhaar-integration.

Aadhaar-integration is planned in two ways. One, 'Aadhaar-seeding' refers to adding a data field for the Aadhaar number to the software (Management Information System, MIS) that is used to administer these programmes. This is supposed to be a simple one-off activity, yet it is not quite as simple as it sounds. For each scheme, each entitled person needs to be informed of what is needed, a range of supporting documents may be required, the number may not be correctly entered, etc. Further, in many cases, re-enrolment of biometrics has been necessary as fingerprints or iris scans become outdated. In programmes with universal coverage, Aadhaar-seeding can help with eliminating identity fraud by weeding out 'bogus' beneficiaries (for example, dead, non-existent persons, etc.). Once 100 per cent Aadhaar-seeding is achieved, beneficiaries in the MIS without Aadhaar numbers are deemed to be bogus and are deleted.

Two, Aadhaar-Based Biometric Authentication (ABBA) refers to the practice of installing a Point of Sale (POS) machine equipped with a fingerprint reader and authenticating a person each time she accesses her entitlements. For instance, at the time of purchase of PDS grain each month, any one person listed on the ration card needs to authenticate themselves; similarly for pensions, elderly persons must go to the point of delivery (for example, post office or Gram Panchayat office) to authenticate themselves. ABBA performs the role of signatures (in the earlier pre-Aadhaar days). ABBA on POS machines is currently a monthly activity, so each of its associated technologies (correct Aadhaar-seeding, mobile connectivity, electricity, functional POS machines and UIDAI servers and fingerprint recognition) need to work for a person to get her entitlement (see Table 1.1).

Public Distribution System

The PDS provides subsidised ration (mainly wheat and rice) to entitled households through a network of PDS outlets. Corruption has been a serious problem: identity fraud (duplicates, ghosts, non-existent, etc.), quantity fraud (under-selling) and eligibility fraud and exclusion errors have plagued the PDS. According to one estimate, half of the poorest did not have a Below Poverty Line (BPL) ration card in the early 2000s (Drèze and Khera 2010). There are other problems in the PDS too (such as over-charging, quality of grain) that are not as well documented.

According to NSS data, all-India leakages declined from 54 per cent (in 2004–05) to 42 per cent (in 2011–12, the latest year for which estimates of corruption are available) and from 49 per cent to 32 per cent, according to India Human Development Survey (IHDS) data (Drèze and Khera 2015a). The reduction in leakages was remarkable in a handful of states such as Chhattisgarh, Odisha, etc. For instance, in Chhattisgarh, leakages declined from 50 per cent in 2004–05 to around 10 per cent in 2011–12.[4]

With the passage of the NFSA in 2013, the coverage of the PDS was to be expanded to 75 per cent of the population in rural areas and 50 per cent in urban areas. The Act also mandated the drawing up of a fresh list of entitled households. Two categories of households were created: 'priority', with a per capita entitlement of 5 kg per person per month and 'Antyodaya', 35 kg per household per month.

Initial evidence from field surveys suggests that the roll-out of the NFSA has led to a further reduction in leakages. In states like Madhya Pradesh and West Bengal, early evidence suggests that the gains from the roll-out of the NFSA have been dramatic: entitled households now get more than 95 per cent of their entitlements in these states (Drèze and Khera 2015b; Drèze et al. 2016).

Close on the heels of the implementation of the NFSA, orders for Aadhaar-integration in the PDS were issued on 7 November 2014. Different states are at different stages of accomplishing this. A handful of states (Andhra Pradesh, Jharkhand, Rajasthan and Telangana) have already moved to a more or less 100 per cent Aadhaar-integrated PDS, including the use of POS machines with ABBA each month. The effects of Aadhaar-integration are perhaps best documented in the PDS.

Identity Fraud

The extent of identity fraud before the roll-out of the NFSA was not documented. The government relied, at best, on anecdotal evidence of 'ghosts' and 'duplicates' to make its case for Aadhaar-integration. After the roll-out of the NFSA, the evidence suggests that there is hardly any identity fraud in those states that used Socio-economic Caste Census (SECC) data, such as Bihar, Jharkhand and West Bengal. The SECC itself, if anything, suffered from exclusion errors (for example, some hamlets were not covered or individuals in households did not get enumerated). In other states which did not use SECC, we still do not know the extent of identity fraud.

As mentioned earlier, in programmes with universal coverage, 100 per cent Aadhaar-seeding can help detect identity fraud by linking each person's Aadhaar numbers to their name in the PDS database. (Those names or cards that are without an Aadhaar number can be deleted.)

The government claimed that Rs 14,000 crore have been saved in the PDS due to 'deletion of 2.33 crore ration cards up to 2016–17 and better targeting of beneficiaries' (Government of India 2017). Questions answered in Parliament, however, suggest that these claims are bogus. This is partly because *all* the deletions are due to ineligibility—the government treats 'ineligible cards', or 'eligibility fraud', as bogus.[5] Digitisation or Aadhaar-integration cannot eliminate eligibility fraud. Eligibility is determined by the criteria notified by states (such as living in a mud house, or caste status, etc.). Aadhaar does not provide this information. Moreover, most of the deletions pre-date Aadhaar-integration orders; by April 2016, only half of all ration cards had been Aadhaar-linked, raising further questions about Aadhaar's role in detecting these 'bogus/ineligible' cards.

Quantity Fraud

Quantity fraud in the PDS refers to under-selling. In the manual system, cardholders were told to sign off ('authenticate') on full purchase even though they may be given less (say, 32 kg instead of 35 kg). With the introduction of the POS machine and ABBA, the register has been replaced with the POS, but under-selling continues more or less as before. Several field studies in Delhi, Gujarat, Rajasthan and Jharkhand confirm this.

One form of quantity fraud that ABBA may help with is the 'skipping' of months. In some states (such as Bihar and Jharkhand), apart from taking a cut each month, dealers also siphon off entire months' worth of rations. Similarly, in many states, dealers could divert 'leftover' rations to the open market.[6] The introduction of ABBA can put an end to skipping and leftovers. Skipping used to be rampant in several north Indian states, but there is evidence of a decline in recent years, before Aadhaar was introduced (Drèze et al. 2015).

Exclusion, Denial and Higher Transaction Costs

In a handful of states, ABBA is mandatory each month, at a POS machine installed at the ration shop. ABBA is contributing to exclusion from the PDS in a number of ways. One, families or individuals without Aadhaar numbers cannot register, so they cannot get the rations to which they are legally entitled. In Delhi, for instance, without Aadhaar, names are not included on the NFSA card. Central government directive requires that as long as any one member's Aadhaar number is linked, everyone listed on the ration card will get grain. While Jharkhand follows this rule, in Delhi and Andhra Pradesh, the quantity of ration provided is according to the number of Aadhaar numbers that are linked to the ration card. Missing Aadhaar numbers mean ration is cut.

Two, outright exclusion can also be because no member of the family is 'POS-able' (a POS-able person is one who is Aadhaar-linked and whose fingerprints are recognised by the POS machine). Biometric failures have been recorded in states using Aadhaar and non-Aadhaar biometrics (for example, in Gujarat).

These failures have been admitted to in Parliament as well: for instance, on 17 March 2017, the government stated that in Rajasthan in February 2017, '78% of NFSA beneficiaries have been provided wheat through POS transactions' and it is claimed there that there were alternate arrangements (such as One-Time Password, OTP) for the others. In August 2016, the government admitted that 'the disruption in the Aadhaar authentication services in Rajasthan...were on account of "inadequate server capacity of the Rajasthan Government", "insufficient lease-line capacity", "poor mobile signal at POS devices", "incorrect seeding of Aadhaar numbers in PDS database"', etc. (Government of India 2016)

Official data from Rajasthan show that, from July 2016 to June 2017, 25–30 per cent of one crore cardholders in the state (accounting for 12–35 per cent of allotted grain) did not buy grain from PDS outlets. Earlier studies show that demand for PDS grain is high, and that eligible households would not purchase PDS grain only under very compelling circumstances (such as an entire family being out in a particular month).

Table 1.1: Role of Aadhaar in Curbing PDS Corruption

Type of fraud	*Examples*	*Can Aadhaar help?*
Identity fraud	Duplicates, ghosts	Yes
Quantity fraud	Underselling, skipping months	Partially
Eligibility fraud	Government employee, owner of four-wheel vehicle are selected	No
Overcharging	Charge Rs 2/kg instead of Re 1/kg, not returning small change	No
Quality fraud	Replace PDS grains with lower quality	No

Source: Compiled by Author.

Apart from outright exclusion, ABBA is leading to sporadic denial of ration and higher transaction costs. For example, only those members whose Aadhaar number is seeded in the PDS database can withdraw rations. Technology failures (such as connectivity, failure of fingerprint authentication, server issues, etc.) also contribute to these problems.

A recent survey of 900 households in rural Jharkhand corroborates the findings that when ABBA works for entitled households, it comes with higher transaction costs and little protection against quantity fraud—'pain without gain'. Those who are excluded by ABBA tend to be the most vulnerable—elderly who cannot walk, widows with young children, etc. (Drèze et al. 2017).

National Rural Employment Guarantee Act

The NREGA was passed in 2005 and guarantees 100 days of work (per household) to any adult willing to work. As per the Act, at least 60 per cent of total expenditure is on wages and the rest on material. Corruption is observed in both wage and material expenditure.

In 2008, the central government made it mandatory for wages to be paid into bank and post office accounts. The move from cash payments to bank payments led to a sharp reduction in corruption. NSS data suggests that between 2007–08 and 2011–12, wage corruption declined from 44–58 per cent to 22–32 per cent (Imbert and Papp 2015). Using IHDS data for 2011–12, Drèze (2014) finds that the decline is even more impressive. Less than 5 per cent of NREGA work in government records was not confirmed by respondents. As with the PDS, the decline in wage corruption predates Aadhaar-integration.

This suggests that, contrary to government rhetoric, there are other methods of reducing corruption in these programmes. In NREGA, the dramatic reduction in wage corruption is because of separation of the implementing agency (for example, the Panchayat) and the payment agency (banks and post offices). Even with payments into accounts, wage corruption can continue in three forms: extortion (forcibly taking wages once labourers have withdrawn it from their account), collusion (workers allow corrupt functionaries to use their job card and account to inflate work on muster rolls and sharing embezzled funds with them) and deception (operating the workers account without his/her knowledge). Extortion and collusion can be characterised as 'quantity fraud' where ABBA cannot help. Deception is a form of identity fraud where ABBA can help. Two caveats: one, we do not know the size of deception in total wage corruption; two, once wage corruption through deception is blocked, those who were using it may resort to extortion and collusion.

Savings

In the NREGA, Rs 7,633 crores are assessed to have been saved up to 31 December 2016 due to Aadhaar-integration (Government of India 2017). In a news report, the Secretary, Rural Development was cited saying that, 'With the use of IT, Aadhaar, leakages have come down'. A right to information (RTI) query enquired about the methodology used to 'arrive at the assessment (qualitative and quantitative) on decrease in leakages'. The response stated that 'Mahatma Gandhi NREGA has been covered under Direct Benefit Transfer and savings are in terms of increasing the efficiency and reducing the delay in payments etc.' In other words, there was no *estimate* of savings, as initially reported.

Similarly, after a news report stated that in 2016–17, 94 lakh 'fake' job cards (approximately 8 per cent of total job cards) had been deleted, an RTI reply revealed that out of all deleted job cards, only 12.6 per cent were classified as 'fake' or 'duplicate'. The rest were deleted for other reasons, such as change of address, surrender of job card, etc. Nearly 60 per cent were deleted due to 'other' reasons. This could include, though that information is not provided in the RTI response, those who did not submit their Aadhaar numbers.[7] Thus, there is as yet no credible evidence of a reduction in leakages due to Aadhaar in NREGA.

Disruption

While the gains from Aadhaar-integration are dubious, it has led to several new problems in the implementation of NREGA. Demand for work can only be registered through the MIS, and the MIS requires the Aadhaar number of an applicant to proceed. Further, for payments to be processed, correct Aadhaar-seeding in the MIS and at banks is required. This has led to hardship, especially for those who are unaware of these requirements. It has been nobody's business to inform NREGA workers of what is required of them. The administrative arrangements for this are inadequate (for example, the task of seeding and routine NREGA work fall on the same person), so the programme has suffered from a slowdown.

In some cases, the re-engineering of NREGA to make it Aadhaar-compliant has meant that workers' job cards are deleted. In others, wrong seeding has led to delays in payment (even non-payment) of wages. Adding to the confusion, due to multiple waves of enthusiasm over 'financial inclusion' over the years, some workers have ended up with several accounts. The bank account in the NREGA MIS may be different from the one that is Aadhaar-seeded. For these reasons, wages are either seriously delayed, rejected, or even 'lost'. The MIS shows that the worker has been paid, but when workers enquire at the bank, their account has not been credited.

Social Security Pensions

The National Social Assistance Programme (NSAP) provides SSP for the elderly, single women and disabled persons. The central government contributes Rs 200 per person per month and most states top up this pension with a state contribution. The pension payment mechanism varies from state to state—for example, in Odisha, pensions are paid in cash at the Gram Panchayat each month whereas other states use money orders, post office accounts, bank accounts, etc. (Drèze and Khera 2017). Corruption appears to be less of a problem in pensions (Bhattacharya et al. 2015).

An administrative constraint that opens the door to identity fraud is that states do not have a system for keeping lists updated (additions due to births and marriage, deletion due to death or migration). This means that in states where payments are made through bank accounts, the pension keeps getting credited, but not withdrawn, until family members try to close the account. In such cases, the extra credits (based on the date of death in the death certificate) cannot be encashed by family members, and are supposed to be reversed.

Where pensions are given in cash, anecdotal evidence suggests that the disbursing functionary may continue the pension for a few extra months on sympathy grounds (for example, to help the family tide over death ceremony expenses), or may siphon off the money for some months, or may honestly strike off the name to accommodate someone on the pension waitlist.

As with other schemes, numbers on identity fraud in pensions are hard to come by. The PEEP Survey conducted in 10 states verified pension lists covering 3,789 pensioners and found only one case of duplication (Drèze and Khera 2017).

Savings or Exclusion?

The government claimed that Aadhaar-integration saved Rs 399 crores up to 31 December 2016. At a given level of benefits, a reduction in government expenditure in any particular transfer scheme can be on two counts—removal of ghosts and duplicates ('efficiency'); and a fall in the number of genuine beneficiaries ('shrinkage'), for instance, if they do not link their Aadhaar numbers when required.

Across welfare schemes, the government has been treating *any* reduction in expenditure as 'savings', even when it comes from shrinkage. This is true for SSP as well; for instance, in Rajasthan, when pensioners were 'mistakenly' recorded as dead, this was presented as Aadhaar-enabled savings.

In Jharkhand too, pensioners' names have been deleted because they did not complete Aadhaar-seeding formalities or pensions stopped due to seeding errors. Studying 100 pensioners, selected from 10 randomly-selected villages from five blocks of Ranchi district in February 2017, Biswas (2017) finds that 84 per cent of her respondents receive pensions, but irregularity in payments was a big issue. The remaining 16 per cent were not receiving it due to Aadhaar-related issues.

Hardship

The most heart-wrenching stories of hardship have been documented in SSP. In a village of Surguja District (Chhattisgarh), apart from seven elderly persons whose pension had stopped due to biometric and other technical failures, all pensioners have to travel 9 km to collect their pension to reach the nearest point with connectivity (Paikra 2017).

Abraham et al. (2017) report very high failure rates in fingerprint and iris authentication among pensioners (14.4 per cent and 17.4 per cent for iris and fingerprints respectively in Andhra Pradesh) in 2015–17.

Mid-Day Meals

The MDM scheme is one of India's most successful social policies, with far-reaching benefits in terms of school attendance, child nutrition and learning achievements, among others (Drèze and Khera 2017). The most pressing problems in the implementation of the MDM—improving menus, providing safe storage and cooking spaces, timely release of funds—cannot be resolved by Aadhaar-integration. Yet, in 2017, the Ministry of Human Resource Development made it mandatory to enrol or provide Aadhaar numbers in order to remain eligible for school meals.

Inflated Attendance as Identity Fraud

The rationale for Aadhaar-integration was widely questioned. The only possible justification for using ABBA in the midday meal scheme is to check 'inflated attendance', a form of identity fraud. If attendance inflation exists, it could be for two reasons: to make up the shortfall in allocations to be able to provide food according to the menu or to siphon off funds. In such cases, administrators who fudge records should be punished, not children. Moreover, there are better options to prevent attendance inflation. For instance, teachers can be instructed to SMS the number of children each day, and the Block office can make surprise checks to a handful of schools to verify this.

What is the evidence on inflated attendance in the MDM scheme? Monika Yadav (2017) matched the number of children that are recorded in the government database with those reporting having MDM in the IHDS in 2011–12. Government records report that out of 143 million children enrolled in school, 105 million had been served school meals. Using IHDS data, she finds that between 100–07 million children report enjoying school meals. This suggests that the number of children for whom expenditure is being claimed (roughly) matches the number of children who actually enjoy school meals.

A Glimpse of Future Disruption

Currently, the government only wants to ensure that children enrol for Aadhaar by making it compulsory for MDMs. Even the push towards enrolment is likely to be hugely disruptive—it will likely derail not just the MDM programme, but also educational activities in schools. Teachers and (over-stretched) school administration will be forced to make arrangements for Aadhaar enrolment. Once that is done, Aadhaar-seeding will waste their time.

ABBA in schools has not yet been fully operationalised. If the government proposes to move towards daily ABBA before serving meals in the future, the move will cause further damage. The technology failures discussed earlier (connectivity, authentication failures) can arise here too, resulting in a waste of time, and exclusion.

Some glimpses of what lies ahead were visible in a residential school for tribal children in Jharkhand, where ABBA had started. Out of 232 enrolled children, 190 were Aadhaar-linked. Out of these, the online real-time portal was showing that only 132 students were present, whereas a headcount at the school resulted in about 230 children being counted. Thus, out of the 190 who were registered, not all were being recognised by the machine. Similar numbers came up at other residential schools in the area. In yet others, due to lack of electricity, the machine was not being used, teachers complained of time wasted due to the slowness of the system.

Other Claims

There are several other claims that do not stand up to scrutiny. Some of these are briefly discussed below.

LPG Subsidy

The government's boldest claims with respect to savings due to Aadhaar relate to the LPG subsidy. In 2013–14, the government initiated a 'Direct Benefits Transfer' (DBT) pilot in 300 districts, whereby the subsidy would be credited into a person's Aadhaar-seeded bank account. Barnwal (2015) uses data from this pilot to estimate *potential* savings, using per unit subsidy and the reduction in LPG purchase that followed the DBT. He admits that the reduction might be due not only to lower leakages but also to 'shrinkage', that is, low UID penetration and poor access to banks which ends up 'completely excluding genuine beneficiaries' (p. 19). Taking his work further, George and Subramanian (2015) claim that USD 2 million, or approximately Rs 14,000 crore, had been saved due to Aadhaar-integration.[8]

According to Clarke (2016), however, George and Subramanian (2015) misattribute savings to Aadhaar: the period under study saw three major policy initiatives in LPG and a 'connection regularization initiative' was the main reason for removal of invalid connections, not Aadhaar-seeding. Similarly, LPG savings after 2014 result from other government initiatives (including PAHAL, GiveItUp, etc.) and a reduction in international oil prices (CAG 2016).

There are two further questions about the reliability of these estimates. First, Cabinet Secretariat minutes for November 2015 record a savings of merely Rs 91 crore due to Aadhaar-integration. Two, George and Subramanian (2016) *themselves* clarified that what they were referring to was 'potential' savings rather than 'actual' savings.[9] In short, there is absolutely no evidence that actual Aadhaar-enabled savings in the LPG subsidy are anywhere near the initial projections, still routinely quoted by government sources.

Elimination of Middlemen

Among the early stated aims of the UID project was the elimination of 'middlemen' who were seen as the main source of corruption. For instance, this referred to ration dealers in the case of the PDS, or the postman who delivered money orders to pensioners. As noted earlier, the corruption of the middleman in these schemes is being dealt with by other means (such as, by bringing greater accountability in the system).

Meanwhile, the Aadhaar project has spawned its own new army of middlepersons, some of whom are also corrupt. This includes enrolment agents, seeding agents, persons managing kiosks (such as E-Mitra in Rajasthan, Pragya Kendras in Jharkhand), data entry operators in government offices and so on.

Concluding Remarks

The Aadhaar project began without much understanding of the problem that it was expected to solve. In spite of early warnings about the possible damage it might cause, the project has been scaled up and in the official narrative, it is a great success. This paper takes a hard look at the evidence on these issues.

Available evidence does not substantiate any significant gains from Aadhaar-integration in welfare programmes. On the contrary, it has inflicted considerable pain. Apart from (supposedly) one-time costs of enrolment and Aadhaar-seeding, people are now faced with higher transactions costs on a monthly basis (for example, in pensions and the PDS), and in a significant minority of cases, also face exclusion and denial. Even when it works, people suffer from considerable indignities.

Aadhaar-integration has also facilitated over-centralisation of administrative controls. If a person does not get authenticated, there is no easy or accessible redress available. Even with the best of intentions, POS machine operators may not be able to ascertain the meaning of a particular error message (there are over 50 error codes!) and guide affected persons on what to do. An error in the system (such as wrongly entered entitlements) can only be corrected at far-off servers. In this and other ways, Aadhaar-integration has reduced transparency and accountability in the system and added to a sense of disempowerment.

Another damage is the 'displacement' effect. Privileging Aadhaar over all other technologies that have a proven record of improving administration displaces efforts to scale up those technologies. For instance, in Bihar, the uploading of NFSA ration card lists (very important to enhance transparency and reduce the arbitrary power of PDS dealers) was delayed. Under pressure from the central government, the short-staffed food department had to focus on Aadhaar-seeding rather than uploading NFSA lists. Abandoning experiments with smart cards, in lieu of ABBA, for last-mile authentication is another example.

The use of Aadhaar is an admission of 'governance' failure. The government has failed to hold to account the minority who indulged in corrupt practices. Instead, by deploying untested and fragile technology, the victims of corruption are paying the price.

Notes

1. Low rates of birth registration would be mentioned in passing, but according to the Civil Registration System data, over 80 per cent of births of children under five were registered in 2009. According to National Family Health Survey data, the corresponding figure for 2015–16 is 80 per cent.
2. The full list includes the documents that can be produced for children (Government of India n.d.).
3. This is not always the case—for example, labourers may not always be given their passbooks, overburdened banks may rely on 'middlemen' (such as sarpanches or panchayat secretaries) to facilitate bulk withdrawals on behalf of workers, etc.
4. The reduction in leakages in these states before the NFSA was largely driven by PDS reforms (see the literature cited in Drèze and Khera 2017).
5. The 22 November 2016 answer is worth quoting at length:

   The exercise of *deletion of bogus/ineligible cards and inclusion of eligible families is a continuous process* and State/UT Governments are to periodically carry out the same. As per the information received from State/UT Governments, *as a result of the continuous exercise of reviewing the list of Ration Cards, a total of 2.33 crores ration cards have been deleted during the period 2013 to 2016* [upto 16-11-2016]. (Emphasis added.)

6. Leftover rations refer to that part of the stock that remains unsold at the end of the month because cardholders did not claim it. In many states, there is a 'carryover' facility, that is, beneficiaries could claim missed rations in subsequent months, so it is quite likely that the share of leftovers was quite small.

7. There was tremendous pressure to achieve 100 per cent Aadhaar-seeding in the NREGA MIS. In order to meet these targets, anecdotal evidence suggests that field-level functionaries simply deleted job cards of those who failed to give Aadhaar numbers.
8. This figure is also in Government of India 2017.
9. Alternate estimates are more conservative: only 3 per cent reduction, compared with the government's claim of 24 per cent (Clarke 2016; Lahoti 2016). Interestingly, when government estimates were challenged in the Supreme Court (in the Shantha Sinha petition), the government chose to ignore these questions.

References

Abraham, Ronald, Elizabeth Bennett, Noopur Sen, and Neil Buddy Shah. 2017. 'State of Aadhaar Report 2016–2017', IDInsight. Available at http://stateofaadhaar.in/wp-content/uploads/State-of-Aadhaar-Full-Report-2016-17-IDinsight.pdf (accessed 4 September 2018).

Barnwal, Prabhat. 2015. 'Curbing Leakage in Public Programs with Biometric Identification Systems: Evidence from India's Fuel Subsidies'. Job Market Paper. Available at https://web.archive.org/web/20161104180349/http://www.med.uio.no/helsam/english/research/news-and-events/events/conferences/2015/vedlegg-warsaw/subsidy-leakage-uid.pdf (accessed 4 September 2018).

Bhattacharya, Shrayana, M. M. Jos, S. K. Mehta, and Rinku Murgai. 2015. 'From Policy to Practice: How should Social Pensions be Scaled up?' *Economic and Political Weekly* 50 (14), 4 April, pp. 60–67.

Biswas, Sambhavna. 2017. 'In Jharkhand, the Elderly Struggle for Meagre Pensions'. *The Wire*, 18 April. Available at https://thewire.in/government/jharkhand-pensions-aadhar (accessed 4 September 2018).

Clarke, Kieran. 2016. 'Estimating the Impact of India's Aadhaar Scheme on LPG Subsidy Expenditure', International Institute of Sustainable Development, 16 March. Available at https://www.iisd.org/gsi/news/estimating-impact-indias-aadhaar-scheme-lpg-subsidy-expenditure (accessed 4 September 2018).

Comptroller and Auditor General of India. 2016. 'Implementation of PAHAL (DBTL) Scheme', Ministry of Petroleum and Natural Gas, Government of India. Available at http://www.cag.gov.in/sites/default/files/audit_report_files/Union_Comme (accessed 4 September 2018).

Drèze, Jean. 2014. Learning from NREGA. *The Hindu*, 23 August. Available at http://www.thehindu.com/opinion/op-ed/learning-from-nrega/article6342811.ece (accessed 4 September 2018).

Drèze, Jean, Jessica Pudussery, and Reetika Khera. 2015. 'Bihar on the Move'. *Food Security* 50 (34), 22 August, pp. 44–52.

Drèze, Jean, Nazar Khalid, Reetika Khera, and Anmol Somanchi. 2017. 'Aadhaar and Food Security in Jharkhand: Pain without Gain'. *Economic and Political Weekly* 52 (50), 16 December, pp. 50–60.

Drèze, Jean, Prankur Gupta, Reetika Khera, and Isabel Pimenta. 2016. 'Food Security Act, How are India's Poorest States Faring?' *Ideas for India*, 29 June.

Drèze, Jean, and Reetika Khera. 2010. 'The BPL Census and a Possible Alternative'. *Economic and Political Weekly* 45 (9), 27 February, pp. 54–63.

———. 2015a. 'Understanding PDS Leakages'. *Economic and Political Weekly* 50 (7), 14 February, pp. 39–42.

———. 2015b. 'Thought for Food'. *Outlook*, 31 August.

———. 2017. 'Recent Social Security Initiatives in India'. *World Development* 98, pp. 555–72.

George, Siddharth, and Arvind Subramanian. 2015. 'JAM Trinity'. *New York Times*, 2 April.

———. 2016. 'Clearing the Air on LPG'. *Indian Express*, 2 April. Available at https://indianexpress.com/article/opinion/columns/clearing-the-air-on-lpg-direct-benefit-transfer-subsidies/ (accessed 4 September 2018).

Government of India. n.d. Available at https://uidai.gov.in/images/commdoc/valid_documents_list.pdf (accessed 4 September 2018).

———. 2010a. 'Financial and Executional Guidelines for Aadhaar related IEC Activities', dated 10 November, no. A/12025/V/E/2010-UIDAI, Planning Commission. Available at https://uidai.gov.in/images/commdoc/financial_and_executional_guidelines_for_aadhaar_related_iec.pdf (accessed 4 September 2018)

———. 2010b. 'Office Memorandum dated 17 February', no A-11016/15/10-UIDAI, Planning Commission. Available at https://uidai.gov.in/images/commdoc/Media_Awareness.pdf (accessed 4 September 2018)

———. 2016. Unstarred question 2556, Rajya Sabha, 9 August.

———. 2017. Starred question No 384, Rajya Sabha, 7 April.

Imbert, Clement, and John Papp. 2015. 'Estimating Leakages in India's Employment Guarantee: an Update', Working Paper. Research Institute for Compassionate Economics.

Khera, Reetika. 2011. 'The UID Project and Welfare Schemes'. *Economic and Political Weekly* 46 (9), 26 February, pp. 38–44.

———. 2015. 'UID: From Inclusion to Exclusion'. *Seminar* 534, August, pp. 78–81.

Lahoti, Rahul. 2016. 'Questioning the Phenomenal Success of Aadhaar-linked Direct Benefit Transfers for LPG'. *Economic and Political Weekly* 51 (52), 24 December.

Muralidharan, Karthik, Paul Niehaus, and Sandip Sukhtankar. 2018. 'Balancing the Costs and Benefits of Aadhaar'. *LiveMint*, 6 March. Available at https://www.livemint.com/Opinion/qFeWbHCXPq1wNZ43wfk3RP/Balancing-the-costs-and-benefits-of-Aadhaar.html (accessed 4 September 2018).

Paikra, Vipul. 2017. 'In Chhattisgarh's Kardana, Biometric Failures are Depriving Old Villagers of their Pension'. *The Wire*, 24 April. Available at https://thewire.in/politics/in-chhattisgarhs-kardana-village-biometric-failures-are-depriving-old-villagers-of-their-pension (accessed 4 September 2018).

Yadav, Monika. 2017. 'Midday Meals Scheme: Are Corruption Claims Exaggerated?'. *Ideas for India*, 31 July. Available at http://www.ideasforindia.in/topics/governance/midday-meals-scheme-are-corruption-claims-exaggerated.html (accessed 4 September 2018).

2

On the Margins of Aadhaar*

The Living Dead, and Food 'Disruptions'

Anumeha Yadav

It was a humid July evening. A few lights had come on in the village. Hukum Singh's hut lay in complete darkness. The 80-year-old farm worker sat on a stone slab at the entrance of the hut, in a white shirt and dhoti. Inside, Singh's wife, Kamla Devi, a farm worker in her late 70s, lay on a plastic sheet on the floor of the hut, unwell and in pain.

Five months earlier, the Rajasthan government had declared both Hukum Singh and Kamla Devi dead. The elderly couple received small amounts of pensions under the National Social Assistance Programme. When the government made it mandatory to switch from post office accounts to bank accounts linked to Aadhaar, Singh and Devi, both of whom could not walk without assistance, failed to open such a bank account in time to continue receiving their pensions.

Hukum Singh told me that when he went to open an Aadhaar-linked bank account, his fingerprints did not work in 'Bhamashah', a database that the Rajasthan government had created, building on Aadhaar infrastructure. After this, the government officials had declared the elderly couple dead and stopped their pension of Rs 750 per person per month in February 2016.

Five months after being declared dead, Hukum Singh was not sure how to get their pension started again. The couple had made unsuccessful attempts to be recognised as still alive. 'When

* Originally published as a series of articles under the title 'Identity Project' at *Scroll.in*.

someone said, "Pensions have come", I spent Rs 200 to hire a vehicle for Kamla and me to get there and register ourselves as living', he recounted. 'Officials in Bhim and Barar did not listen to us. We cannot afford to go there again and again.' Kamla Devi passed away a few days later, on 1 August 2016. In her last seven months, she had been cut off her only source of sustenance to buy essentials food and medicines.

Power of Disruption

Since the launch of the Unique Identification, or Aadhaar project, in 2009, bureaucrats heading the Unique Identification Authority of India (UIDAI), the agency that issues Aadhaar identity numbers and manages the database, have presented it as a scheme for the India's 'indigent and the marginalised' (Sharma 2011). They claimed that matching the biometrics of a resident in real time with the data stored in centralised Aadhaar servers would stop pilferage in public schemes by ensuring that no one gets the same benefits twice. It was argued that Aadhaar would allow for payments to happen at the 'doorsteps' of beneficiaries through a network of banking correspondents and micro-ATMs. Technological entrepreneurs employed on contract with UIDAI argued that obtaining digital identities through Aadhaar makes systems 'presenceless', and allows people to 'go anywhere, anytime and avail the services' they were entitled to (iSPIRT Foundation 2015).

Nandan Nilekani, a billionaire software entrepreneur and the former chairperson of the UIDAI, had described the transition to the biometrics-based system as a 'period of disruption', in which it would be 'up to individual players to take advantage' (Abrar 2015).

The term 'disruption' has acquired a positive connotation in the software industry, that a fledgling, lower-cost technology, if adopted on large scale in a short period, may displace older, more established players. But the scaling up of Aadhaar in the absence of infrastructure and legal safeguards relied on it being foisted upon the mass welfare schemes, which serve as a safety net to the poorest and most vulnerable.

Following several challenges in court to the Aadhaar project on its legal validity and on privacy grounds, in October 2015, the Supreme Court ordered that the use of Aadhaar to access public benefits like pensions and provident fund was voluntary, not mandatory.

Rajasthan government had started the process of 'seeding' (or linking) Aadhaar numbers of pension beneficiaries to bank accounts in March 2015. It did not pause to offer pensioners like Kamla Devi and Kalu Singh any choice in enrolling into the biometrics database even after the court orders. At the state and district level, citizens were presented with the 'choice' of either enrolling or going without essential government services, in this case their pensions, from the beginning.

In 2015, when the government started linking pensions to Aadhaar, Rajasthan had 68.6 lakh pension beneficiaries in the old age, widows and disabled categories who get monthly pensions of Rs 500 and Rs 750. By June 2016, the state claimed that it had saved Rs 600 crore by stopping pensions for 3.5 lakh, and cancelling pensions for 7 lakh beneficiaries, of whom 2.97 lakh pensioners were declared dead, and 1.7 lakh as 'duplicates'.

In Rajasthan, the disruption came at a huge cost to the elderly, women and the disabled. The names of several thousands of pension beneficiaries like Hukum Singh and Kamla Devi were simply struck off lists if they failed to open a bank account or enrol in Aadhaar, or if E-Mitras, the local e-governance service providers, linking online details of beneficiaries with their Aadhaar numbers made errors while doing so.

In Kushalpura panchayat, Hukum Singh and Kamla Devi were among 44 pensioners who were declared dead. Of these, 25 were still living. In Bhim Block (Rajsamand district), where Kushalpura panchayat is located, officials had cancelled pensions for 3,749 persons, recording 1,799 as dead. After several protests and a door-to-door by the Mazdoor Kisan Shakti Sangathan, a grassroots campaign, the names of 1,308 of 1,799 beneficiaries wrongly classified as 'dead' or having migrated were reinstated and their pensions resumed.

Hindi daily *Dainik Bhaskar*'s team of reporters estimated that more than 1 lakh of Rajasthan's 2.97 lakh pensioners had been incorrectly declared dead, after the newspaper's district reporting teams went door to door with lists of the 'dead' in a few sample villages in 28 of 33 total districts. They found that more than half of those declared dead were still living.

Almost a year later, in August 2016, when I visited Bhim panchayat, the site of the first ground verification by local activists, the government had paid arrears to just 33 of more than 29,000 people whose pensions had been wrongly stopped or cancelled. It was another year before the Bhim administration paid back all 1,308 pensioners whose pensions were wrongly stopped pension arrears of over Rs 6 lakh. After continued protests, the government had to reinstate 5 lakh persons whose pensions had been wrongly stopped or cancelled all over the state.

In the state capital Jaipur, Ravi Jain, a director in the Department of Social Justice and Empowerment, told me that the claims that people were wrongly recorded as dead were exaggerated. He said that to correct the errors, the government offered to organise more enrolment camps for residents.

He described these instances of people not receiving pensions or being declared dead as 'teething problems' that would get corrected as the Aadhaar infrastructure was fully rolled out.

Rajasthan's old and infirm continued to bear the burden of the biometric experiments.

Early Signs

The effects of the experimentation on people's food entitlements were even more stark.

On 11 March 2016, as the National Democratic Alliance pushed for passing the Aadhaar (Targeted Delivery of Financial and Other Subsidies, Benefits, and Services) Act, the Finance Minister Arun Jaitley argued in parliament that over 99 crore persons—99 per cent of India's adult population and 67 per cent of children—had already enrolled in Aadhaar. 'The earlier we implement the idea, the better it would be in the overall interest of the country', he argued.

While the central and state government pushed to speed up Aadhaar-Based Biometric Authentication (ABBA), central Rajasthan was gripped by a severe drought for a second consecutive year, which worsened the condition of small farmers and wage workers. At such a time, the top-down, hasty transition threatened to cut off the most vulnerable citizens from even the meagre social support of food rations under the National Food Security Act (NFSA).

Under the new ABBA system, ration beneficiaries were asked to place a finger on a small Point of Sale (POS) machine, which would use the internet to match their biometric information against the data stored on Aadhaar servers. Only after their identity was authenticated in this manner were they allowed to buy the subsidised grains that they were legally entitled to get under the food law.

Five technologies need to work together for biometric authentication to be successful—the POS device, internet connectivity, biometrics, the National Informatics Centre server, and the UIDAI servers. When even one failed, it disrupted some of the poorest citizens' access to food grains.

The day after Jaitley made his statement in parliament, on a hot afternoon in March in Daulatpura village in Masuda Block in Ajmer district, as the fair price shop owner Abdul Aziz tried to figure the snags in the machine, a large crowd waited behind him (Yadav 2016a).

Only two beneficiaries had successfully verified their fingerprints in two hours that day on the POS machine to get their quota of grains. Mithia Ghisa, a farm worker, said it was his sixth attempt that month to buy food grains from the fair price shop. Hanja Devi, a frail 68-year-old woman who needed a stick to walk, had trekked four kilometres to the fair price outlet from her village Karanpura for the third time in three days. In her weathered hands, she held a yellow 'Antyodaya' card given by the government to the poorest of the poor category, but the machine was repeatedly rejecting her fingerprints and her claim to buy 35 kg of wheat.

In Shankar Nagar in Ajmer city, urban workers were less patient. A group of construction workers broke the POS machine when they could not authenticate their fingerprints even after trying for two hours. The long wait and repeated trips to authenticate successfully meant the loss of a day's wage for the workers. Ajmer district's Food and Civil Supplies Department officials responded by registering a first information report with the police against the workers.

In Ajmer district, officials deleted 62,251 ration cards between 1 January and 18 March 2016, saying they were weeding out fake beneficiaries in order to achieve their target of higher seeding levels (or Aadhaar-linking) of ration cards. But they did not follow any mechanism, such a public hearing, to verify whether it was really a fake or 'ghost' beneficiary who was being cut off food security, or a genuine low-income or landless family.

The Rajasthan government had made ABBA mandatory at ration shops in December 2015, three months before the Aadhaar law was even introduced, and when ration Aadhaar-seeding had been completed for less than half of its ration card holders.

The authentication would work for only those members of a household who had obtained Aadhaar, and whose details had been seeded correctly. In many cases, even families did not know which member's details had been linked and found out only after different members of the household, including children, tried their luck on the machines.

As per government records, in Ajmer district, 4.6 lakh of 8.68 lakh (or, only 52 per cent) ration cards had been linked with Aadhaar till March 2016.

The government was aware that nearly half the ration beneficiaries in Ajmer would be rejected by the POS machines, and yet it had gone ahead with asking ration card holders to submit their fingerprints compulsorily every month.

Bureaucrats justified this saying unless government pressured people to enrol and get all members' details seeded, no beneficiaries would do it on their own. In Rajasthan, a person was required to additionally seed their details in 'Bhamashah'.

High Failure Rates

While the promise of 'doorstep delivery' of benefits did not come true, the forced linking with Aadhaar threw up absurd situations.

Santosh Devi, a goat-herder with two small children, faced a peculiar problem when the POS machine read her fingerprints as that of Rukma Devi, a farm worker of the neighbouring Baral village. Local agents in Jawaja block could not tell if it was a seeding- or biometrics-capturing error. The E-Mitra, the local e-governance service provider, advised Santosh Devi that her husband Ram Singh, a deaf and mute construction labourer working 430 km away in Ahmedabad, come back home and try with his fingerprints, for the family to continue to get subsidised grains.

The Aadhaar Act lacks a block- or district-level grievance redressal process. Block-level officials dismissed instances of ration card holders saying the grains card was 'locked from above', and that the workers would have to go to the district office in Ajmer, 60 km away, to get it working again.

Six months after Rajasthan started using Aadhaar verification for the distribution of Public Distribution System (PDS) grain, Hansraj Yadav, the additional director of UIDAI in Rajasthan, admitted that biometric authentication did not work for 10–15 per cent of users. He explained this as because of errors while capturing fingerprints, and also changes in fingerprints through cuts, abrasion, etc.

From December 2015 till May 2016, out of a total of over 98 lakh ration beneficiaries, only 44 lakh (or, 45 per cent) could get their rations after being verified by POS machines, showed Rajasthan government data accessed by Mazdoor Kisan Shakti Sangathan (Yadav 2016b).

Officials in Rajasthan's department of information technology and communication, who were supervising the electronic PDS, corroborated that only 45 per cent of beneficiaries in the state could get their rations using POS machines and argued that the figure would improve with time. They said they were conducting camps to educate panchayat functionaries on how to correctly put fingers on the machine, to wash hands before using the machines, and to try and stick to using only the mobile number registered in Aadhaar databases so that a one-time password may be sent for authentication in case fingerprints did not work.

This logic offered by Rajasthan's local officials was similar to the recourse adopted by Jharkhand authorities in 2011 in Ramgarh, a pilot district for testing the use of Aadhaar in the Mahatma Gandhi National Rural Employment Guarantee scheme (NREGA), that provides 100 days of work to any rural household willing to do manual work. In Ramgarh, when Adivasi rural workers failed to verify their identity through their weathered hands, banking correspondents sent them back without wages, with only a prescription to use skin-softening creams (Yadav 2012).

A year on, in Rajasthan, in June 2017, only 70.6 per cent of ration card holders were able to procure their rations from the rations outlets using the new system, according to the website of the Government of Rajasthan (Khera 2017).

Inappropriate Technology

While administrators continued to have faith in the Aadhaar-based biometric authentication system, arguing that it would start showing better results as time went by, a previous system of fingerprint authentication launched by the Gujarat state government that had created a database of the biometrics of ration card holders in 2010 had thrown up similar problems.

The Gujarat system was not the same as Aadhaar, but was founded on the same idea that biometrics can help eliminate theft in social welfare delivery by ensuring only real beneficiaries accessed their benefits. But government data showed the system was not functioning smoothly, and there was nearly 30 per cent fingerprint authentication failure.

In November 2016, when I travelled to Gujarat to report on this six-year-old system, of 1.2 crore ration cards linked with the state biometrics database, only 83.7 lakh cards recorded transactions the previous month, in October 2016. Of these 83.7 lakh cards, fingerprint authentication failed for 24.6 lakh cards—nearly one in three families.

In the villages of Koli Adivasi in Panchmahal district, 125 km east from Ahmedabad, where nearly 85 per cent of the district's population is rural and there is poor infrastructure, ration card holders recounted problems of day-long power cuts, irregular electricity, network connectivity issues, and repeated trips to get their rations. Government records showed that in October 2016, fingerprint authentication in Panchmahal failed for nearly one-third of the 234,702 ration beneficiaries who attempted it.

In the state capital Gandhinagar, officials gave two reasons for the failures. 'One, there are network connectivity issues', said Ronak Mehta, deputy secretary in the state department of food, civil supplies and consumer affairs. 'Two, fingerprint authentication often does not work for those who do hard work with their hands, like farm workers, construction workers'. Sumi Kapadia, an official in the project management unit of the department, said nearly 15–20 per cent of all transactions failed solely because fingerprints did not match on account of skin abrasions, and in the case of the elderly, because of unclear fingerprints. 'The fingerprint problems magnify in winter months as the skin becomes rough and dry', she said. 'But the villagers are impatient. They are not willing to wait even an hour to get their fingerprints authenticated.'

Ration card holders complained that the dealer pilfered food grains even after doing biometric authentication. The fingerprint authentication system helped the government check and authenticate if a beneficiary was who she claimed to be. But it had done nothing to stop the ration shop dealer from pilfering a part of grain entitlements, referred to as 'quantity fraud'. The system had little mechanism to strengthen transparency and accountability at the local level.

Next, I travelled to Chhattisgarh to Dhamtari and Raigarh, the two pilot districts for the implementation of ABBA in the PDS in 2016. Chhattisgarh has one of the best functioning PDS among all states. It is credited for the successive election victories of Chief Minister Raman Singh, who is called '*chaawal wale baba*' (rice man).

Two field surveys in 2010 recorded that over 90 per cent genuine beneficiaries were getting ration grains (Puri 2012).

This is attributed to a series of reforms the state government undertook after 2004, of broadening the coverage of the PDS, making it nearly universal, simplifying entitlements to make sure everyone knew how much grain they should be getting, a higher level of community vigilance.

Chhattisgarh officials said that after ration cards under the NFSA were seeded, the government had detected 3 lakh duplicate cards out of 58.4 lakh cards (that is, 5 per cent), reinforcing what earlier studies had found—that much of the grain was already reaching actual beneficiaries and duplication was not a serious issue. State officials said they felt this showed that ABBA was not necessary to ensure better delivery of grains. The state government had, however, introduced Aadhaar in ration shops at the behest of the Centre.

State National Informatics Centre officials said 1 lakh out of 3 lakh transactions using fingerprint authentication did not go through—a failure rate as high as 30 per cent. They attributed the failures primarily to network connectivity problems and skin abrasions on fingers.

With fingerprint authentication failing for even genuine cardholders, Chhattisgarh came up with an innovative workaround—ration shop owners were asked to take photographs of such people before giving them food rations. This photograph was stored in the government's server as a deterrent to ration dealers, that in case of a complaint, the government may check if grains were given to the right beneficiaries.

But the photograph also complicated people's lives. Earlier, a person unable to go to the ration shop because they were working or travelling could leave the ration card with a relative or a neighbour to collect their grains in their absence. After ABBA was made mandatory, a beneficiary had to go in person to collect the grains, as the authentication requires providing biometric scans or a photograph.

As in the case of pensions, this was especially difficult for those who were unwell, the disabled, and the elderly. Officials said that after they received reports that the elderly and the disabled found it difficult to access ration shops under the new system, the Chhattisgarh government proposed to allow a system of 'friendly families', where ration card holders could provide a one-time biometric authentication to add other neighbours or relatives, who could collect grains on their behalf. The government proposed to give the district collector the powers to waive off biometrics authentication entirely, in special cases.

For Whose Benefit?

Two successive prime ministers—Manmohan Singh and then Narendra Modi—pushed Aadhaar, arguing it would help improve delivery of social schemes. In several states, the required infrastructure was absent and it was not clear when the infrastructure would be ready. Even if the infrastructure was put in place, there was no evidence that Aadhaar was an appropriate system for welfare.

A previous scheme in Gujarat showed biometric authentication did not work for lakhs of manual workers and the elderly. In Gujarat, the technological fix of the biometric database had failed to reduce leakages in the PDS as fingerprint authentication was ineffective in preventing either the wrongful exclusion of the poor or quantity fraud by dealers. Yet, the Centre was imposing a scaled up, centralised biometric authentication system even in states like Chhattisgarh, which had already fully computerised the PDS years ago, and had streamlined delivery by other measures including community monitoring. Recording high biometric failures and not wanting to turn away people from ration shops, the Chhattisgarh government was looking for ways around Aadhaar.

In pilots on wages of manual workers in NREGA and later in social security pensions, the effects had been even more devastating. But not letting the evidence come in the way to weaken its faith in Aadhaar, the union government introduced ABBA next in nutrition schemes for pregnant women and children in the Integrated Child Development Services schemes, and also had started collecting it from those seeking medical treatment at government health facilities at the end of 2016.

The claims of efficiency and convenience through use of Aadhaar did not reflect on the ground. Across states, Aadhaar was disrupting welfare delivery and causing distress to the poor. But mandating the use of Aadhaar in the PDS, among other social schemes, the government had achieved at least one goal—it had created a database holding the demographic and biometric information of 80 per cent of India's population.

Aadhaar project's creators were now talking of building new data businesses and companies. In a foreword to a Credit Suisse report on the Indian banking sector, Nandan Nilekani noted that the use of Aadhaar 'digital footprints' of residents would open up a USD 600 billion business opportunity (Nilekani 2016).

New businesses, built on the backs of the poor who were coerced to get Aadhaar to get pensions and ration grains in the first place, were in the making.

References

Abrar, Peerzada. 2015. 'India is Going through a Technological Disruption'. *The Hindu*, 11 October. Available at http://www.thehindu.com/business/Industry/interview-with-nandan-nilekani-cofounder-infosys/article7747561.ece (accessed 1 September 2017).

iSPIRT Foundation. 2015. Available at https://www.youtube.com/watch?v=x4_1Fv9Dc2M (accessed 1 September 2017).

Khera, Reetika. 2017. 'Impact of Aadhaar in Welfare Programmes'. *Economic and Political Weekly* 50 (52), 16 December, pp. 61–70.

Nilekani, Nandan. 2016. 'The Coming Revolution in Indian Banking'. *Indian Express*, 20 July. Available at http://indianexpress.com/article/opinion/columns/the-coming-revolution-in-indian-banking-2924534/ (accessed 1 September 2017).

Puri, Raghav. 2012. 'Reforming the Public Distribution System: Lessons from Chhattisgarh'. *Economic and Political Weekly* 47 (5), 4 February.

Sharma, R. S. 2011. 'UIDAI Clarifies on Aadhaar'. *The Hindu*, 15 September. Available at http://www.thehindu.com/opinion/op-ed/uidai-clarifies-on-aadhaar/article2453509.ece (accessed 1 September 2017).

Yadav, Anumeha. 2012. 'To Pass Biometric Authentication, Apply Vaseline or Boroplus on Fingers Overnight'. *The Hindu*, 15 December. Available at http://www.thehindu.com/opinion/op-ed/To-pass-biometric-identification-apply-Vaseline-or-Boroplus-on-fingers-overnight/article12450793.ece (accessed 1 September 2017).

Yadav, Anumeha. 2016a. 'Rajasthan Presses on with Aadhaar after Fingerprint Readers Fail: "We'll Buy Iris Scanners"'. *Scroll.in*, 10 April. Available at https://scroll.in/article/806243/rajasthan-presses-on-with-aadhaar-after-fingerprint-readers-fail-well-buy-iris-scanners (accessed 1 September 2017).

———. 2016b. 'Six Months after Rajasthan Introduced it, Only 45% of Beneficiaries used Aadhaar at Ration Shops'. *Scroll.in*, 11 June. Available at https://scroll.in/article/809661/six-months-after-rajasthan-introduced-aadhaar-at-ration-shops-only-45-beneficiaries-accessed-food (accessed 1 September 2017).

3

A Unique Identity Dilemma*

Jean Drèze

It is easy to see why India's Unique Identity (UID) project, also known as Aadhaar, has caught the imagination of many administrators, economists and policy-makers. Identity verification is a routine problem in India and Aadhaar sounds like a foolproof solution. The idea is really smart and the technology is cutting-edge. After the initial hurdle of universal enrolment, numerous applications are possible: monitoring the attendance of government employees, linking multiple databases, fighting tax evasion, facilitating the portability of social benefits and much more. When ace promoter Nandan Nilekani was appointed to lead the project, the happy fate of Aadhaar appeared to be sealed.

Voluntary or Compulsory?

And yet, Nilekani's sales pitch left one question unanswered: is Aadhaar voluntary or compulsory? The initial claim was that Aadhaar was a voluntary facility. Indeed, this is how many of the sceptics were swayed. Yet this claim was clearly hollow: how could Nilekani, or the Unique Identification Authority of India (UIDAI), assure us that Aadhaar was voluntary when they had no control over its applications? The UIDAI's real position was: 'we provide the number, it is up to the government to decide what to do with it'.

---

* This chapter draws on four previously published articles: 'Unique Identity Dilemma', *Indian Express*, 19 March 2015; 'The Aadhaar Coup', *The Hindu*, 15 March 2016; 'Hello Aadhaar, Goodbye Privacy', *The Wire*, 24 March 2017; 'Dissent and Aadhaar', *Indian Express*, 8 May 2017.

This raised the possibility that Aadhaar would become mandatory for various social programmes such as the National Rural Employment Guarantee Act (NREGA) and the public distribution system (PDS). In fact, it quickly became clear that the Indian government was keen to impose Aadhaar on a whole series of schemes—almost anything that involved identity verification. That suited the UIDAI very well, since it led people to rush to Aadhaar enrolment centres. Indeed, the UIDAI's claim that Aadhaar was a voluntary facility posed a problem—how would enrolment be fast-tracked? The government's imposition of UID as an eligibility condition for social benefits provided a neat answer.

And so, a tacit understanding quickly emerged that while Aadhaar was voluntary in principle, it was due to become essential for anyone who wanted to function—use a mobile phone, get a driving licence, transfer property, have a civil marriage or just get paid as a NREGA worker. In short, frankly speaking, it was compulsory.

This should have called for a reassessment of the whole project, because there is a world of difference between a voluntary Aadhaar and a compulsory Aadhaar. Providing Indian residents with a convenient way of identifying themselves would certainly be doing a great service to millions of people who lack adequate identity documents. But imposing Aadhaar as an all-purpose identity proof is another matter.

The Aadhaar Coup

It took the Supreme Court to put an end to this doublespeak. In March 2014, the court ruled that 'no person shall be deprived of any service for want of Aadhaar number in case he/she is otherwise eligible/entitled'. This was a very sensible interpretation of what it would really mean for Aadhaar to be voluntary. Throughout the proceedings, incidentally, the government stood by the claim that Aadhaar was a voluntary facility. The Supreme Court did nothing more than to clarify the implications of that claim.

It is important to note that Aadhaar could work wonders as a voluntary facility. A certified, verifiable, all-purpose identity card would be a valuable document for many people. But the UIDAI has never shown much interest in the Aadhaar card, or in developing voluntary applications of Aadhaar. Instead, it has relentlessly pushed for Aadhaar being used as a mandatory identification number in multiple contexts, and for biometric authentication with a centralised database over the internet. That is a very different ball game.

The Supreme Court order caused consternation in official circles, since it ruled out most of the planned applications of Aadhaar. The Aadhaar Act 2016 is the government's counter-attack. Under Section 7, the Act gives the government sweeping powers to make Aadhaar mandatory for a wide range of facilities and services. Further, Section 57 enables the government (and even private entities) to impose Aadhaar identification in virtually any other context, subject to the same safeguards as those applying to Section 7.

In concrete terms, the Act allows the government to make Aadhaar authentication compulsory for salary payments, old-age pensions, school enrolment, train bookings, marriage certificates, getting a driving licence, buying a SIM card, using a cybercafé—virtually anything. Judging from the experience of the last few years, the government will exercise these powers with abandon and extend Aadhaar's grip to ever more imaginative domains. Indeed, Aadhaar was always intended to be 'ubiquitous', as Nandan Nilekani, former Chairman of the UIDAI, himself puts it.

Why is this problematic? Various concerns have been raised, from the unreliability of biometrics to possible breaches of confidentiality. But the main danger is that Aadhaar opens the door to mass surveillance. Most of the 'Aadhaar-enabled' databases will be accessible to the government even without invoking the special powers available under the Act, such as the blanket 'national security' clause. It will be child's play for intelligence agencies to track anyone and everyone—where we live, when we move, which events we attend, whom we marry or meet or talk to on the phone. No other country, and certainly no democratic country, has ever held its own citizens hostage to such a powerful infrastructure of surveillance.

If this sounds like paranoia, think again. Total surveillance is the dream of intelligence agencies, as we know from Edward Snowden and other insiders. The Indian government's own inclination to watch and control dissenters of all hues has been amply demonstrated in recent years. For every person who is targeted or harassed, thousands fall into line. The right to privacy is an essential foundation of the freedom to dissent.

Mass surveillance threatens to halt the historic expansion of civil liberties and personal freedom. For centuries, ordinary people have lived under the tyranny of oppressive governments. Compulsion, arrests, executions, torture were the accepted means of ensuring their submission to authority. It took long and harsh struggles to win the freedoms that we enjoy and take for granted today—the freedom to move about as we wish, associate with whoever we like, speak up without fear. No doubt these freedoms are still elusive for large sections of the populations, especially Dalits and those who live under the boot of the security forces. But that is a case for expansion, not restriction, of the freedoms we already have.

The Aadhaar Act asks us to forget these historic struggles and repose our faith in the benevolence of the government. Of course, there is no immediate danger of democracy being subverted or civil liberties being suspended. Only a simpleton, however, would fail to anticipate Aadhaar being used as a tool of mass surveillance. And mass surveillance per se is an infringement of democracy and civil liberties, even if the government does not act on it. As Glenn Greenwald aptly puts it in his book *No Place to Hide*, 'history shows that the mere existence of a mass surveillance apparatus, regardless of how it is used, is in itself sufficient to stifle dissent'.

The champions of Aadhaar downplay these concerns for the sake of enabling the government to save some money. Wild claims are being made about Aadhaar's power to plug leakages. In reality, Aadhaar can only help to plug specific types of leakages, such as those related to duplication in beneficiary lists. Further, recent experience has shown that Aadhaar can easily play havoc with fragile programmes such as NREGA and the PDS. I have seen some of this damage at close range in Jharkhand, where Aadhaar was supposed to prove its mettle. Aadhaar applications (in the PDS, NREGA, and even the banking system) have had poor results in Jharkhand and caused much disruption. For instance, job cards and ration cards have been cancelled on a large scale for the sake of achieving '100 per cent Aadhaar seeding'. And compulsory biometric authentication at ration shops has severely disrupted recent progress with PDS reforms in Jharkhand.[1]

Eight years after it was formed, the UIDAI has failed to produce significant evidence of Aadhaar having benefits that would justify the risks. Instead, it has shown a disturbing tendency to rely on public relations, sponsored studies and creative estimates of 'Aadhaar-enabled savings'. To my knowledge, there has been no serious evaluation of any of the Aadhaar applications so far. Worse, some failed experiments have been projected as successes through sheer propaganda—business correspondents in Ratu (Jharkhand) and 'direct benefit transfer' of kerosene subsidies in Kotkasim (Rajasthan) are just two examples.

No doubt Aadhaar, if justified, could have some useful applications. Given the risks, however, the core principle should be 'minimum use, maximum safeguards'. The government has shown its preference for the opposite—maximum use, minimum safeguards. The Aadhaar Act includes some helpful safeguards, but it does nothing to restrain the use of Aadhaar or prevent its misuse as a tool of mass surveillance. And even the safeguards protect the UIDAI more than the public.

The wizards of Aadhaar are fond of telling us that we are in the thick of a 'revolution'. With due respect for their zeal, a coup would be a more appropriate term. The Aadhaar Act enabled the government to evade Supreme Court orders and build an infrastructure of social control. Further, it did so by masquerading as a money bill, pre-empting any serious discussion of these issues. This undemocratic process reinforces the case for worrying about Aadhaar.

Hello Aadhaar, Good-bye Privacy

The tussle between the Supreme Court and the Indian government on these matters is far from over. On 24 August 2017, a nine-judge bench of the Supreme Court unanimously affirmed that privacy is a fundamental right. Predictably enough, this order sent Aadhaar's public relations machine into damage control mode. After denying the right to privacy for years, the government promptly changed gear and welcomed the judgment. Ajay Bhushan Pandey, CEO of the UIDAI, suddenly asserted that 'the Aadhaar Act is based on the premise that privacy is a fundamental right'. He also clarified that the judgment would not affect Aadhaar as the required safeguards were already in place.

The fact of the matter is that Aadhaar, in its current form, is a major threat to the fundamental right to privacy. The nature of this threat, however, is poorly understood.

Types of Private Information

There is a common perception that the main privacy concern with Aadhaar is the confidentiality of the Central Identities Data Repository (CIDR). This is misleading for two reasons. One is that the CIDR is not supposed to be inaccessible. On the contrary, the Aadhaar Act puts in place a framework for sharing most of the CIDR information. The second reason is that the biggest danger, in any case, lies elsewhere.

To understand this, it helps to distinguish between three different types of private information: biometric information, identity information and personal information. The first two are formally defined in the Aadhaar Act, and protected to some extent. Aadhaar's biggest threat to privacy, however, relates to the third type of information.

In the Aadhaar Act, biometric information essentially refers to photograph, fingerprints and iris scan, though it may also extend to 'other biological attributes of an individual' specified by the UIDAI. The term 'core biometric information' basically means biometric information minus photograph, but it can be modified once again at the discretion of the UIDAI.

Identity information has a wider scope. It includes biometric information but also a person's Aadhaar number and the demographic characteristics that are collected at the time of Aadhaar enrolment, such as name, address, date of birth, phone number, and so on.

The term 'personal information' (not used in the Act) can be understood in a broader sense, which includes not only identity information, but also other information about a person, for instance where she travels, whom she talks to on the phone, how much she earns, what she buys, her internet browsing history, and so on.

Coming back to privacy, one obvious concern is the confidentiality of whatever personal information an individual may not wish to be public or accessible to others. The Aadhaar Act puts in place some safeguards in this respect, but they are restricted to biometric and identity information.

Identity Information can be Shared

The strongest safeguards in the Act relate to core biometric information. That part of the CIDR, where identity information is stored, is supposed to be inaccessible except for the purpose of biometric authentication. There is a view that, in practice, the biometric database is likely to be hacked sooner or later. Be that as it may, the UIDAI can at least be credited with trying to keep it safe, as it is bound to do under the Act.

That does not apply, however, to identity information as a whole. Far from protecting your identity information, the Aadhaar Act puts in place a framework to share it with 'requesting entities'. The core of this framework lies in Section 8 of the Act, which deals with authentication. Section 8 underwent a radical change when the draft of the Act was revised. In the initial scheme of things, authentication involved nothing more than a Yes/No response to a query as to whether a person's Aadhaar number matches her fingerprints (or possibly, other biometric or demographic attributes). In the final version of the Act, however, authentication also involves a possible sharing of identity information with the requesting entity. For instance, when you go through Aadhaar-based biometric authentication to buy a SIM card from a telecom company, the company typically gains access to your demographic characteristics from the CIDR. Even biometric information other than core biometric information (which means, as of now, photographs) can be shared with a requesting entity.

The foundational shift that occurred between the National Identification Authority of India Bill 2010 (NIDAI) and the Aadhaar Act 2016 on this matter is clear from their respective definitions of authentication:

> **NIDAI 2010:** The Authority shall respond to an authentication query with a positive or negative response or with any other appropriate response *excluding any demographic information and biometric information.*
>
> **Aadhaar Act 2016:** The Authority shall respond to an authentication query with a positive, negative or any other appropriate response *sharing such identity information excluding any core biometric information.* (emphases added)

Quite likely, this little-noticed change in Section 8 has something to do with a growing realisation of the business opportunities associated with Aadhaar-enabled data harvesting. 'Data is the new oil', the latest motto among the champions of Aadhaar, was not part of the early discourse on unique identity—at least not the public discourse.

Section 8, of course, includes some safeguards against possible misuse of identity information. A requesting entity is supposed to use identity information only with your consent, and only for the purpose mentioned in the consent statement. But who reads the fine print of the terms and conditions before ticking or clicking a consent box?

There is another important loophole: the Aadhaar Act includes a blanket exemption from the safeguards applicable to biometric and identity information on 'national security' grounds. Considering the elastic nature of the term, this effectively makes identity information accessible to the government without major restrictions.

Mining Personal Information

Having said this, the proliferation and possible misuse of identity information is only one of the privacy concerns associated with Aadhaar, and possibly not the main concern. A bigger danger is that Aadhaar is a tool of unprecedented power for mining and collating personal information. Further, there are few safeguards in the Aadhaar Act against this potential invasion of privacy.

An example may help. Suppose that producing your Aadhaar number (with or without biometric authentication) becomes mandatory for buying a railway ticket—not a far-fetched assumption. With computerised railway counters, this means that the government will have all the details of your railway journeys, from birth onwards. The government can do exactly what it likes with this personal information—the Aadhaar Act gives you no protection, since this is not 'identity information'.

Further, this is just the tail of the beast. By the same reasoning, if Aadhaar is made mandatory for SIM cards, the government will have access to your lifetime call records, and it will also be able to link your call records with your travel records. The chain, of course, can be extended to other 'Aadhaar-enabled' databases accessible to the government—school records, income-tax records, pension records, and so on. Aadhaar enables the government to collect and collate all this personal information with virtually no restrictions.

Thus, Aadhaar is a tool of unprecedented power for the purpose of mining personal information. Nothing in the Aadhaar Act prevents the government from using Aadhaar to link different databases, or from extracting personal information from these databases. Indeed, many state governments (aside from the central government) are already on the job, under the State Resident Data Hub (SRDH) project, which 'integrates all the departmental databases and links them with Aadhaar number', according to the SRDH websites. The Madhya Pradesh website goes further, and projects SRDH as 'the single source of truth for the entire state'—nothing less. The door to state surveillance is wide open.

What about private agencies? Their access to multiple databases is more restricted, but some of them do have access to a fair amount of personal information from their own databases. To illustrate, Reliance Jio is in possession of identity information for more than 100 million Indians, harvested from the CIDR when they authenticate themselves to buy a Jio SIM card. This database, combined with the records of Jio applications (phone calls, messaging, entertainment, online purchases and more) is a potential gold mine—a dream for 'big data' analysts. It is not entirely clear what restrictions the Aadhaar Act imposes, in practice, on the use of this database.

In short, far from being 'based on the premise that privacy is a fundamental right', Aadhaar is the antithesis of the right to privacy. Perhaps further safeguards can be put in place, but Aadhaar's fundamental power as a tool for mining personal information is bound to be hard to restrain. The very foundation of Aadhaar needs to be reconsidered in the light of the recent Supreme Court judgment on the right to privacy.

Aadhaar Propaganda

The power of Aadhaar as a tool of mass surveillance is all the more worrying as the Indian government has already shown an ominous propensity to stifle dissent. Many people and institutions are now anxious not to get on the wrong side of the government. Non-Governmental Organisations (NGOs) are afraid that their registration might be cancelled if they antagonise the authorities. Vice-chancellors and principals are unable to stand up for their students' right to hold public meetings on sensitive issues. Newspapers treat the government with kid gloves, especially on security matters. Investigative agencies target or spare opposition leaders at the government's bidding. Nationalism is confused with obedience to the state. With Aadhaar immensely reinforcing the government's power to reward loyalty and marginalise dissenters, the embers of democracy are likely to be further smothered.

How did we get there, with so little resistance? One answer is that we have been numbed by a series of lies, myths and fictions about Aadhaar.

The first lie, discussed earlier, was that Aadhaar is a voluntary facility. Today, we know that this was just doublespeak. Soon, it will be virtually impossible to live in India without Aadhaar. And if you cannot live without Aadhaar, in what sense is it voluntary? As a columnist aptly put it, Aadhaar must be 'the biggest bait-and-switch in history'.

Another early fiction was that the purpose of Aadhaar is to help welfare schemes. As discussed in chapter 1 of this volume, the truth is closer to the reverse: welfare schemes have been used to promote Aadhaar (by creating mass dependence on it), irrespective of the consequences. As it happens, the consequences so far have been disastrous. If the name of a worker employed under the NREGA is spelt differently in his job card and Aadhaar card, he is at risk of not being paid. If an old widow's age happens to be understated on her Aadhaar card, she may be deprived of the pension that keeps her alive. For the PDS, Aadhaar is a calamity: in Jharkhand and Rajasthan, large numbers of people are deprived of their food rations every month due to problems related to Aadhaar-Based Biometric Authentication (ABBA), according to the government's own data.

Third, Aadhaar was endowed with mythological powers as a weapon against corruption. Many people fell for the simplistic claim that Aadhaar would 'ensure that the money goes to the right person'. In reality, Aadhaar can prevent only some types of corruption, mainly identity fraud. If a contractor fleeces the government by over-invoicing, Aadhaar does not help. Nor does it help when a dealer gives people less than their due under the PDS. Sometimes, Aadhaar can make things worse, by disrupting fragile systems and creating confusion. For all we know, it may even create new varieties of identity fraud. Even if Aadhaar proves effective in curbing various forms of corruption, it is not the magic bullet that had been announced.

Fourth is a series of bogus claims about Aadhaar-enabled 'savings'. Most of the savings figures have no solid basis. Instead, they acquire an aura of plausibility by repetition. A common pattern is that an official press note mentions a savings figure, say, from a closed-door presentation at the Prime Minister's Office, newspapers quote that figure without verification, sundry commentators repeat it, and it becomes part of the Aadhaar lore. These dubious figures are then added up to produce an awesome grand total. Some of them are worse than gas—for instance, when Aadhaar-related glitches deprive people of their entitlements and the shortfall is counted as 'savings'.

Fifth, the technology was claimed to be flawless. Today, there is growing evidence that this is not the case. In ideal conditions, ABBA seems to work most of the time. But often the conditions are far from ideal, causing immense inconvenience. And even the ideal-condition success rates may not be good enough if ABBA is to serve as a common tool of identity verification. In a recent interview, Nandan Nilekani stated that 'this is a system which works perfectly in 95 per cent of cases'. That does not sound reassuring: In many contexts, a 95 per cent success rate is far from adequate.

Sixth, there is an ambiguity about the relation between Aadhaar and citizenship. Aadhaar, we are told, is for all residents, whether they are citizens or not. Sure, that is what the Aadhaar Act says. But then, why has enrolment been stalled in Assam? And why is Aadhaar enrolment in Assam being linked to the National Register of Citizens? Aadhaar deprivation could easily be used there as a weapon against illegal migrants, or communities branded as illegal migrants.

Finally, as discussed earlier, the confidentiality of the identity information collected at the time of Aadhaar enrolment is a myth. The initial draft of the Aadhaar Act did protect that information, but the final version does not. On the contrary, it creates a framework that enables the government to share or sell that information, except for the core biometrics, with any 'requesting entity'. A vast collection of lucrative Aadhaar applications is now being built on the back of this information sharing facility. This is almost as big a bait-and-switch as the claim that Aadhaar is voluntary.

All this raises an interesting question: if the government misled the public to no end on this subject, can we trust it not to misuse the formidable powers of Aadhaar? The problem, however, is deeper. Even if it is not misused, the very existence of a huge infrastructure of surveillance is bound to stifle dissent. This ought to be a major concern for anyone committed to democratic rights and civil liberties.

Note

1. For further discussion, see Drèze et al. 2017, and earlier work cited there.

Reference

Drèze, J. P., N. Khalid, R. Khera, and A. Somanchi. 2017. 'Aadhaar and Food Security in Jharkhand: Pain without Gain?'. *Economic and Political Weekly* 52 (50), 16 December, pp. 50–60.

4

Aadhaar and Privacy*

Reetika Khera

After the privacy judgment,[1] the obvious question that has arisen is: what is the relevance of the judgment for the Aadhaar project? Privacy is interpreted in different, equally valid ways by different sets of people. Many of these meanings find their way into the privacy judgment. This chapter enumerates some of the ways in which the Aadhaar project infringes on privacy and how the privacy judgment deals with these concerns.

Privacy Concerns with Aadhaar

For instance, when computer scientists use the word privacy, they tend to interpret it from a narrow 'data security' perspective. Lawyers in the Supreme Court have been highlighting many other aspects of it too: civil liberties, bodily integrity, personal integrity, etc. This resulted in groups talking past each other: for example, the solutions that the computer scientists propose (stronger standards for data security, including encryption) are not satisfactory to those who highlight the civil liberties aspects of privacy. Some of the dimensions of privacy are enumerated below to enable a more constructive conversation on the issue.

---

* This chapter builds on Reetika Khera, 2017, 'The Different Ways in which Aadhaar Infringes on Privacy', *The Wire*, 19 July. Available at https://thewire.in/government/privacy-aadhaar-supreme-court (accessed 4 September 2018).

Personal Integrity

A second privacy concern is the more colloquial understanding of the term, from the 'personal integrity' point of view. Here, it is the discomfort from information about our lives being available to people or institutions with whom we do not wish to share it. One may be comfortable discussing one's personal life with someone, but not financial matters. One may be comfortable doing it today, but not tomorrow.

Everyone—rich or poor, man or woman, rural or urban—sets boundaries regarding what they share with others about their lives. These boundaries may vary by person (for example, in Delhi's buses and in the metro, I often blush when I hear young college students openly discussing their love interests). What is seen as a privacy concern varies from person to person (financial matters, food preferences, shopping habits, sexuality, medical history, and so on) and it also varies over time.

A playful representation of this concern is an Aadhaar joke that has been doing the rounds for a few years now, where the life of a person ordering a pizza for home delivery is laid bare before the telephone operator. She has access to his health records (so advises him against red meat), his financial records (so insists on a cash payment at the time of delivery), etc.

Bodily Integrity

Some contend that the Aadhaar project gathers biometric information and that is a violation of bodily integrity.[2] Further, the giving of biometrics is associated with crime. To this, Aadhaar supporters say, visa applications to some countries also require submission of biometrics. The government responded by saying that the Registration Act collects biometrics. This response is inadequate because it ignores that such usage comes with stringent legal restrictions on usage, and 'purpose limitation' (see Sections 57, 78 and 91 of the Registration Act).

Data Integrity

Possibly the narrowest view of privacy is the technical—'data security'—point of view. The focus is on what data need to be secure (the Aadhaar number, or demographic information or biometrics), whether data stored in the Central Identities Data Repository (CIDR) is secure (encryption standards, probability of hacking), and what would the consequences of data breaches be (some people ask what is the harm if an Aadhaar number is publicly displayed), etc.[3] The response of the Unique Identification Authority of India (UIDAI) and others is that data are encrypted using the highest standards and that access is severely restricted (Sinha 2017).[4] Experts, however, believe that for centralised databases, the question is not whether it can be hacked, but when. For instance, Bruce Schneier told Pranav Dixit: 'When this database is hacked—and it will be—it will be because someone breaches the computer security that protects the computers actually using the data' (Dixit 2017).

The very feature that is a data scientist's dream come true is a nightmare for a data security expert and also from the civil liberties point of view. Databases linked to each other with a unique 'key' (Aadhaar-seeding will accomplish that), though not necessary for data mining, will reduce costs substantially. But inter-linked databases also magnify the vulnerabilities. There can be a domino effect. Access one number and you have access to a full profile of my life.

Another source of worry is that the creation of centralised databases also means a loss of control over one's data. This is an especially pertinent worry in the times of big data and data mining.

Centralised and Inter-linked Databases and Surveillance

What sets Aadhaar apart from other examples (the Registration Act or the Social Security Number) that are brought up in this debate is that our biometric and demographic data are being stored in a *centralised database* and a unique number is associated with our biometric and other information. Further, this unique number is being 'seeded' (added as a new data field) with every possible—public and private—database in the country.

Why is that a problem? Today, information about my life is stored in different data silos—train travel, air travel, bank account, mobile phone, employment history, health and so on. The only person who can easily construct a full picture of my life from these disjointed data silos is I. This is because only I have the access to these disconnected data silos.

If the Aadhaar number is 'seeded' into every database, it integrates these data silos. Aadhaar becomes the bridge across the hitherto disconnected data silos with information about my life. I lose control over who can reconstruct a profile of my life. People in government (who I have not authorised) will be able to profile me, by pulling in information from various databases using that single identifier. Just the possibility of such profiling is likely to lead to self-censorship and, as many have documented, is likely to stifle dissent.

When this concern is raised, the government has attempted to obfuscate the issue. For instance, the CEO of UIDAI, Ajay Bhushan Pandey, tried to assure us that 'No one can build Aadhaar users' profile'. However, he misinterprets profiling. What he is actually talking about is 'identity fraud', rather than profiling in the civil liberties sense mentioned above. Similarly, in an interview to Vir Sanghvi, Nandan Nilekani chose to interpret surveillance in the limited sense of 'physical tracking' through GPS, etc. However, the civil liberties interpretation of surveillance is wider as it involves keeping an eye on all the activities of a person (shopping, recreation, travel, communications, etc).

In a nutshell, the concern is with the creation of a centralised database where we do not have control of our own data and an 'eco-system' where a single identifier (the Aadhaar number) links databases. It becomes an infrastructure for profiling and surveillance. This is the fourth and most significant aspect of 'privacy' in the Aadhaar debate. As Senior Advocate Divan warned the Supreme Court, the Aadhaar project is 'an electronic leash' to keep people under control.

Personal Data Economy

There is a fifth dimension of privacy that Aadhaar endangers. Among the supporters of Aadhaar are entrepreneurs and technocrats who want to use technology to 'do good'. They view this as a great resource for data mining and machine learning.

The idea is that when an Aadhaar eco-system is in place (that is, you can see people's lives in different spheres), you can learn useful things: for instance, some suggest that it may 'enable macro level analysis from high frequency micro level data, econometric analysis, epidemiological studies, automatic discovery of latent topics and finding both predictive and causal relationships across multiple domains of the economy' (Banerjee 2017), whereas others believe it will allow data mining for 'improvement in credit rating infrastructure' (*The Hindu* 2014).

This is what Nilekani means when he says, 'India will be data rich before being economically rich' (*ET Now* 2017). Such views are also implicit in the writings of other philanthropist groups such as the Omidyar Network (Bhadra 2017), and Bill and Melinda Gates Foundation (Radcliffe and Bakhshi 2016).

The objection is the creation of a 'personal data economy', which will monetise information about people's personal life ahead of creating adequate digital and legal literacy and safeguards around these issues (see European Commission 2009).

Inadequate Responses

Often, the attempt is to dodge these questions. To the extent that these concerns have been addressed, the responses have been inadequate. A brief summary of the responses and why they are not sufficient follows.

Privacy is an Elitist Concern

Some believe that privacy (in the sense of a loss of personal integrity) is an elitist concern. This sentiment was exemplified in veteran journalist Shekhar Gupta's tweet (2017), 'Crores of rural and urban poor see Aadhaar as tool of empowerment. They don't even know elite anti-Aadhaar echo chambers exist & they don't care.' Such frivolous comments trivialise the debate on privacy.

Some argue that the Hindi word for privacy, 'nijta', is not a colloquially used term. This is presented as a proof that privacy may not matter to (at least) Hindi-speaking Indians. Can this really be interpreted as a lack of concern with privacy? People may not have the same language as us to articulate their privacy concerns, but that does not mean they do not care for it.

In line with such arguments, in the Supreme Court, the Attorney General suggested that Indians do not care about privacy, why else would we find train passengers sharing their life histories? Let us just pause for a minute here. This is a case of a person willingly sharing information about their lives. Perhaps one is more willing to share details with a stranger (whom one is not going to encounter again), which one would not share with people with whom we have more intimate relationships. To counter such frivolous (real or fictional) anecdotes, here is another: on a recent shared taxi ride with two friends, the driver received a call and he felt uneasy continuing his conversation because we were around. He said he would call back. That, to me, is nothing but an expression of valuing one's privacy.

The best response though is in the privacy judgment (pp. 215–21). In Justice Chandrachud's words, the submission that 'the right to privacy is an elitist construct…is unsustainable', it 'betrays a misunderstanding of the constitutional position', 'that the poor need no civil and political rights' and that these rights are 'subservient to socio-economic rights' 'has been categorically rejected in the course of constitutional adjudication by this Court'. The Court emphasised that 'Every individual in society irrespective of social class or economic status is entitled to the intimacy and autonomy which privacy protects.'

You are Already being Surveilled

It is true that we are tracked (for example, the smartphone does that), profiled and our personal data are being monetised (Google and Facebook are good examples of this). Indeed, smartphones, CCTVs, Google and Facebook do violate our privacy in some or all of the ways listed above. But here are four reasons why this is not a satisfactory response.

One, none of these is as all-encompassing as the Aadhaar project is. The way the Aadhaar project is unfolding, it will be the biggest brother of them all.

Two, there is a genuine element of consent with many of these—for example, Facebook may be a great surveillance tool, but it can only know about my banking transactions or travel if I share that information there. One can even walk away from Facebook. But this is not an option in the case of banking or lifeline forms of social support (such as rations, pensions, etc.). There is a strong element of coercion.

Three, there are technologies such as encryption, The Onion Router ('TOR'), Virtual Private Network (VPN), etc. and search engines such as 'DuckDuckGo', browsers such as Firefox to protect ourselves (partially at least) from such surveillance (Schneier 2015).

Four, to say that because we are already being tracked, profiled and surveilled, we should not be questioning the Aadhaar project, is akin to saying that since we have been robbed in the past, we should sleep with our doors and windows open.

I have Nothing to Hide

This is another common response to the realisation that the Aadhaar project is creating an all-seeing surveillance infrastructure. Only those who are doing something wrong would be worried about the linking of their Aadhaar number to various databases. This is a specious argument. An excellent response to this comes from Glenn Greenwald in a TedTalk: he invited those who feel they have nothing to hide to share their password with him. More recently, 'All India Bakchod' (a group of Indian humorists) said that if they were about to die, the only thing they would want to ensure was that their smartphone is locked. One of them said he would not want anyone to know why he had a meme on his phone which said, 'Aren't you the guy who can't get it up?'

One can go on—at traffic signals, or upon spotting traffic police on the road, even if everything is in order (license, seat belts, speed limit), you may sit up straight. If you know you are in the view of a CCTV camera, you may not behave the way you would if it was not there.[5] This point is made most powerfully in Snowden's interview with John Oliver and 'dick pics'. When Snowden explains to Oliver that it is possible for the National Security Agency to see the nude pictures he might share over email, Oliver asks if his response should be to stop sharing them. Snowden answers with a firm no. Why should one alter his/her behaviour because they are (potentially) being watched? This curtails their freedom to do as they please. Finally, as mentioned earlier, there is also a vast literature of the 'chilling effect' of surveillance.

The Law Can Take Care of This

However, one, the law is either silent or weak on several of these aspects. The safeguards (say, against data breaches) in the Aadhaar Act are weak (see chapter 3 of this volume). For instance, if data is 'leaked', only the UIDAI—not the affected person—is authorised to file an FIR under the Aadhaar Act. Further, the implementation of the law is even worse—for example, publishing UID numbers is punishable by up to three years in jail. Yet, after the 'Aadhaar leaks' scandal in which several state departments and centre ministries were found to be violating the Act, the UIDAI has not filed a single case against anyone. Meanwhile, one department implicated in the 'Aadhaar leaks' scandal—Jharkhand's social welfare department—issued a press note denying the data leak! In a nutshell, the Aadhaar Act is weak, its implementation worse.

A data protection law may provide some protection against such surveillance, but the most important legal protection that has been put in place (for instance, in Europe) is to restrict the collection of data in the first place, and to set stringent conditions that could justify its collection, when it is allowed.

The Privacy Judgment

Informational Privacy and the Digital Economy

When the landmark privacy judgment was delivered, the supporters of Aadhaar were quick to latch on to a short discussion on 'reasonable restrictions in the public interest' and 'legitimate concerns of the state' in Justice Chandrachud's judgment (Supreme Court of India 2017). The Aadhaar supporters have been finding solace in paragraphs such as: 'The legitimate concerns of the state would include for instance protecting national security, preventing and investigating crime, encouraging innovation and the spread of knowledge, and preventing the dissipation of social welfare benefits.'

We have already seen that the state's contention that Aadhaar helps in 'preventing the dissipation of social welfare benefits' is patently false (see chapter 1). 'Encouraging innovation and the spread of knowledge' hints at an acceptance of the claimed potential of data mining techniques, both for profit and welfare activities. Elaborating on the state's 'justifiable reasons for the collection and storage of data', Justice Chandrachud writes: 'Digital platforms are a vital tool of ensuring good governance in a social welfare state. Information technology—legitimately deployed is a powerful enabler in the spread of innovation and knowledge.'[6] This was projected as a green signal for the Aadhaar project.

To pull out these passages amounts to a selective reading of not just the entire 547-page judgment, but is also unfair to Justice Chandrachud's opinion. That includes a detailed critique, and adequate warnings of the dangers from the proliferation of uses of data mining (pp. 246–60). For instance, citing Solove (2008), he states: 'Businesses and governments often aggregate a variety of information fragments, including pieces which may not be viewed as private in isolation to create a detailed portrait of personalities and behaviour of individuals' (p. 251). The centrality of consent, safeguarding the principle of non-discrimination and purpose limitation are also highlighted.

As far as information technology as enabler of innovation and knowledge is concerned, again, some sections of the judgment betray a slightly rose-tinted view of the role of information technology, which is not entirely justified.

It is easy to be swayed by this rosy view of the digital economy and the potential for improvement using, for instance, big data techniques. As Kitchin (2014) puts it, 'the hype and hubris surrounding big data has by far outweighed the critique that has been levelled against it. Funding agencies and corporate

R&D [research and development] departments are queuing up to pump money into big data and data analytics projects and training programmes.'

For instance, there are ethical issues (such as personalised pricing, the use of your contacts to build your credit profile, etc.) with the use of these technologies. A disturbing example of this was highlighted in a Forbes article on how Uber may charge users with low battery higher prices (Chowdhry 2016). The fact that the generation of data has proliferated and its data mining potential has preceded the putting in place of a regulatory framework means that there are some greedy, unregulated entrepreneurs who use these techniques in ethically objectionable ways (O'Neil 2016).[7]

Judges who sit on the Aadhaar bench in the future absolutely must engage with the critical scholarship on Big Data. One such is the widely-acclaimed book, *Weapons of Math Destruction*, by mathematician Cathy O'Neil, who worked with a hedge-fund. Her book documents how data mining is actually being used not for enhancing welfare, but rather to seek out people's vulnerable spots and to exploit them (for example, to push payday loans down their throats, use their health information against them, etc.). Importantly, as a review of the book in *Scientific American* puts it:

> [A]n insidious aspect of WMDs [Weapons of Math Destruction] is the fact that they are invisible to those of us with more power and privilege in this society. As a white person living in a relatively affluent neighborhood, I am not targeted with ads for predatory payday lenders while I browse the web or harassed by police officers who are patrolling 'sketchy' neighborhoods because an algorithm sends them there. People like me need to know that these things are happening to others and learn more about how to fight them. (Lamb 2016)

A small glimpse of this problem was highlighted by a short exchange in the Aadhaar matter in November 2017. The Attorney General submitted that messages were not being sent to mobile phone owners to link their Aadhaar numbers, and Justice Sikri immediately retorted saying that he too was getting them.

The government has been similarly lying about Aadhaar not being compulsory for welfare programmes, but because the judges are not directly affected, they have so far not called out those lies.

While this is not the place to get into a debate about big data, we need to be alert to the big data rhetoric. The submission of privacy is presented as a trade-off to enhance wellbeing, an argument that the privacy judgment rejects.

Consent, Coercion and Dignity

The privacy judgment discusses how even the collection of personal data (say, as the Aadhaar project does) is potentially a violation of our rights and carefully outlines privacy concerns that arise in the age of information. While highlighting the importance of consent or data protection, the judgment suggests that they are aware that consent and data protection laws may not be adequate to address the concerns arising from data generation.

Consent is a weak point (some would even say non-existent) in Aadhaar's architecture. Let me give an example. *After* enrolling NREGA labourers and PDS ration card holders into the Aadhaar database, they are *now* being asked to sign off on consent forms. Who is explaining to them the meaning of consent in this context, what its implications are? We have even seen enrolment forms where the consent box comes pre-ticked! If they do not agree, they can no longer get their entitlements (work and ration). There is no choice. Instead of 'informed consent', we have 'forced consent'. More recently, news appeared of how a telephone company was able to open Airtel accounts for some of their customers who had linked Aadhaar. This resulted in the customers' LPG subsidy being credited to Airtel accounts, and them being forced to use this on Airtel products. The vulnerabilities O'Neil highlights will be magnified manifold in India due to low levels of tech and digital awareness.

In the privacy judgment, Justice Chandrachud's opinion clearly states that 'dignity of the individual' is one of the 'foundational pillars of the Indian Constitution'. Privacy as a fundamental right is justified, among other things, on grounds of protecting human dignity. If that is the case, the obvious undermining of the 'right to life', by denying people their legal or other entitlements (see chapter 1) is a central legal argument against the project.

As explained earlier, the use of Aadhaar in welfare delivery is the antithesis of dignity. The objective of the Aadhaar Act is the efficient delivery of welfare, but in fact, Aadhaar is not only a disruptive force, but also violates dignity in the fulfilment of socio-economic rights. Aadhaar-related starvation deaths have been reported since October 2017, but millions are suffering monthly indignities in accessing rations, pensions and wages due to Aadhaar. It is somewhat remarkable, and also a telling comment on Indian society, that the most obvious legal challenge to the Aadhaar project has received so little attention.

Notes

1. In August 2017, a nine-judge Constitution bench of the Supreme Court ruled that the right to privacy is a fundamental right. For more, see chapter 10 of this volume.
2. This line of argument featured prominently in the PAN-Aadhaar case argued in the Supreme Court by senior advocates Shyam Divan and Arvind Datar in April 2017.
3. Agrawal, Banerjee and Sharma (2017) outline the ways in which a data breach or a privacy breach can occur, and offer some solutions to these problems.
4. They also claim that there have been no security breaches so far (which is only partly true).
5. On the dubious record of forensic science in solving crime, see John Oliver (2017).
6. Digitisation has indeed contributed to better implementation of programmes such as NREGA and PDS, but neither is digitisation synonymous with Aadhaar, nor does it need Aadhaar. Conflating the two has been a constant battle in the debate around Aadhaar. When we question 'Aadhaar', the supporters hear 'technology'.
7. In the light of the privacy judgment, now all eyes are on the data protection laws that are supposed to be drafted by the Srikrishna Committee. But the constitution of the committee itself has been questioned, as it is loaded with persons of similar (pro-Aadhaar) views.

References

Agrawal, Shweta, Subhashis Banerjee, and Subodh Sharma. 'A Computer Science Perspective Privacy and Security of Aadhaar'. *Economic and Political Weekly* 52 (37), 16 September, pp. 93–102.

Banerjee, Subhashis. 2017. 'It's Time to Disentangle the Complex Aadhaar Debate'. *The Wire*, 20 April. Available at https://thewire.in/126115/aadhar-privacy-analysis/ (accessed 11 November 2017).

Bhadra, Subhashish. 2017. 'Why we Invested, Digital Identity Research Initiative'. Available at https://medium.com/positive-returns/why-we-invested-digital-identity-research-initiative-diri-5d26ecc08456 (accessed 11 November 2017).

Chowdhry, Amit. 2016. 'Uber: Users are More Likely to Pay Surge Pricing if their Phone Battery is Low'. *Forbes*, 25 May. Available at https://www.forbes.com/sites/amitchowdhry/2016/05/25/uber-low-battery/#54f4659c74b3 (accessed 4 September 2018).

Dixit, Pranav. 2017. 'India's National ID Program May Be Turning the Country into a Surveillance State'. *BuzzFeed*, 4 April. Available at https://www.buzzfeed.com/pranavdixit/one-id-to-rule-them-all-controversy-plagues-indias-aadhaar?utm_term=.feyGJzAxm#.do6ngyq0B (accessed 11 November 2017).

ET Now. 2017. Available at https://www.youtube.com/watch?v=RmHDv1kwhH0 (accessed 11 November 2017).

European Commission. 2009. 'Data Protection and Privacy Ethical Guidelines'. Available at http://ec.europa.eu/research/participants/data/ref/fp7/89827/privacy_en.pdf (accessed 11 November 2017).

Greenwald, Glenn. 2013. 'Privacy'. Available at https://www.ted.com/speakers/glenn_greenwald (accessed 4 September 2018).

Gupta, Shekhar. 2017. Twitter post, 26 March, 11.06 pm. Available at https://twitter.com/ShekharGupta/status/846242075586805760 (accessed 4 September 2018).

Kitchin, Rob. 2014. 'Big Data, New Epistemologies and Paradigm Shifts'. *Big Data and Society* 1 (1), April–June, pp. 1–12.

Lamb, Evelyn. 2016. 'Review: Weapons of Math Destruction'. *Scientific American*, 31 August. Available at https://blogs.scientificamerican.com/roots-of-unity/review-weapons-of-math-destruction/ (accessed 4 September 2018).

O'Neil, Cathy. 2016. *Weapons of Math Destruction: How Big Data Increases Inequality and Threatens Democracy*. New York: Crown.

Oliver, John. 2017. 'Forensic Science, Last Week Tonight', 1 October. Available at https://www.youtube.com/watch?v=ScmJvmzDcG0 (accessed 11 November 2017).

Radcliffe, Dan, and Pawan Bakhshi. 2016. 'Four Ways to Boost the Impact of India's Direct Benefit Transfers'. Available at http://www.cgap.org/blog/four-ways-boost-impact-india%E2%80%99s-direct-benefit-transfers (accessed 4 September 2018).

Schneier, Bruce. 2015. *Data and Goliath: The Hidden Battles to Collect your Data and Control your World.* New York: W.W. Norton & Company.

Sinha, Sanjeev. 2017. 'How Safe is Your Aadhaar Data and What Security Measures are Taken by UIDAI, Here's All You Need to Know'. *Financial Express*, 14 July. Available at http://www.financialexpress.com/money/how-safe-is-your-aadhaar-data-and-what-security-measures-are-taken-by-uidai-heres-all-you-need-to-know/762884/ (accessed 4 September 2018).

Solove, Daniel. 2008. *Understanding Privacy.* Cambridge: Harvard University Press.

Supreme Court of India. 2017. *Justice KS Puttaswamy (Retd) and Anr vs Union of India and Ors,* Writ Petition (Civil) No. 494 of 2012, 24 August.

The Hindu. 2014. 'Aadhaar Linked Transactions to Improve Credit Rating Infrastructure, Says CIBIL Official', 2 September. Available at http://www.thehindu.com/todays-paper/tp-national/tp-andhrapradesh/aadhaar-linked-transactions-to-improve-credit-rating-infra-says-cibil-official/article6371715.ece (accessed 11 November 2017).

5

SURVEILLANCE PROJECT*

Sunil Abraham

Zero: the probability of some evil actor breaking into the central store of authentication factors (such as keys and passwords) for the internet. Why? That is because no such store exists. The decentralised architecture of the internet means that there is no 'single point of failure'. And, what is the probability of someone evil breaking into the Central Identities Data Repository (CIDR) of the Unique Identification Authority of India (UIDAI)? Greater than zero. How do we know this? One, the central store exists and two, the Aadhaar Act lists breaking into this central store as an offence. Needless to say, it would be redundant to have a law that criminalises a technological impossibility. What is the consequence of someone breaking into the central store? Remember, biometrics is just a fancy word for non-consensual and covert identification technology—technology which empowers the state to identify you by measuring your body. Today this can be done from a distance, since high-resolution cameras can remotely capture fingerprints and iris information.

In other words, on 16 March 2016, when Parliament passed the Aadhaar Act, it was as if Indian lawmakers wrote an open letter to criminals and foreign states saying, 'We are going to collect data to non-consensually identify all Indians and we are going to store it in a central repository. Come and get it!' Once again, how do I know that the CIDR will be compromised at

---

* A previous version of this chapter was published as Sunil Abraham, 2016, 'Surveillance Project', *Frontline*, 15 April.

some date in the future? How can I make that policy prediction with no evidence to back it up? To quote Sherlock Holmes, 'Once you eliminate the impossible, whatever remains, no matter how improbable, must be the truth.' If a backdoor to the CIDR exists for the government, then the very same backdoor can be used by an enemy within or from outside. As Bitcoin guru Andreas M. Antonopoulos has repeatedly reminded us, all centralised databases are honeypots, the question is not if they will be compromised but when they will be compromised. In other words, the principle of decentralisation in cyber security does not require repeated experimental confirmation across markets and technologies.

Zero: the chances that you can fix with the law what you have broken with poor technological choices and architecture. And, to a large extent vice versa, you cannot use good technology to fix bad law. Aadhaar is a surveillance project masquerading as a development intervention because it uses biometrics. Globally informed consent is considered the foundation of privacy and data protection law. When a citizen uses Aadhaar, there is no way of verifying if there was consent since both authentication and identification for subsidies or services do not require the conscious cooperation of the data subject. Unless the citizen has a mobile phone, they will not even be notified of the transaction. There are a variety of ways in which corrupt officials can take advantage of this poor technological choice—they could say (a) the machine is not working; (b) the network is not working; or (c) the CIDR is not working, etc. even if the authentication has been successful. Aadhaar makes the citizen transparent to the state but makes the state completely opaque and unaccountable to its citizens.

There is a big difference between the government identifying you and you identifying yourself to the government. Before UID, it was much more difficult for the government to identify you without your knowledge and conscious cooperation. Tomorrow, using high-resolution cameras and the power of big data, the government will be able to remotely identify those participating in a public protest. There will be no more anonymity in the crowd.

I am not saying that law-enforcement agencies and intelligence agencies should not use these powerful technologies to ensure national security, uphold the rule of law and protect individual rights. I am only saying that this type of surveillance technology is inappropriate for everyday interactions between the citizen and the state. Since we started research on Aadhaar in 2010, we have been warning of the misuse of the surveillance potential of the Aadhaar project. Today, many who dismissed this view have had to change their minds.

Some software engineers believe that there are technical fixes for these concerns; they point to the consent layer in the India Stack developed through a public-private partnership with the UIDAI. But this is exactly what Evgeny Morozov has dubbed 'technological solutionism'—fundamental flaws like this cannot be fixed by legal or technical band-aid. If you were to ask the UIDAI how do you ensure that the data do not get stolen between the enrolment machine and the CIDR, the response would be, 'we use state-of-the-art cryptography'. If cryptography is good enough for the UIDAI, why is it not good enough for citizens? That is because if citizens use cryptography (for example, on smart cards) to identify themselves to the state, the state will need their conscious cooperation each time. That provides the feature that is required for better governance without the surveillance bonus. If you really must use biometrics, it could be stored on the smart card after being digitally signed by the enrolment officer. If there is ever a doubt whether the person has stolen the smart card, a special machine can be used to read the biometrics off the card and check that against the person. This way, the power of biometrics would be leveraged without any of the associated harms to security, privacy, equality, inclusion and dignity.

Zero: this time, for the utility of biometrics as a password or authentication factor. There are two principal reasons for which the Act should have prohibited the use of biometrics for authentication. First, biometric authentication factors are irrevocable unlike passwords, PINs, digital signatures, etc. Once a biometric authentication factor has been compromised, there is no way to change it. Imagine not being able to change your lock after you know the key has been stolen. The security of a system secured by biometrics is permanently compromised. Second, our biometrics are impossible to secure and very easy to steal; for example, we leave our fingerprints on almost every surface we touch.

Also, if I upload my biometric data onto the internet, I can then plausibly deny all transactions against my name in the CIDR. In order to prevent me from doing that, the government will have to invest in CCTV cameras [with large storage] as they do for passport-control borders and as banks do at ATMs. If you anyway have to invest in CCTV cameras, then you might as well stick with digital signatures on smart cards, as the previous National Democratic Alliance (NDA) government proposed the SCOSTA (Smart Card Operating System Standard for Transport Application) standard for the MNIC (Multipurpose National ID Card). Leveraging proprietary smart card standards like EMV (Europay Visa Mastercard) or, better still, equivalent open standards, will ensure harnessing greater network effects thanks to the global financial infrastructure of banks. These network effects will drive down the cost of equipment and afford Indians greater global mobility. And, most importantly, when a digital signature is compromised, the user can be issued a new smart card. As Rufo Guerreschi, executive director of Open Media Cluster, puts it, 'World leaders and IT experts should realise that citizen freedoms and states' ability to pursue suspects are not an "either or" but a "both or neither".' Once a privacy-undermining mass surveillance system has been built, you cannot predict what use it will be put to by a future repressive government, a rogue corporation, criminals or terrorists. The chilling effects on the rights to free speech, association and assembly will be felt as soon as citizens understand the scale of the surveillance.

Near zero: We now move to biometrics as the identification factor. The rate of potential duplicates or 'False Positive Identification Rate' which, according to the UIDAI, is only 0.057 per cent. According to them, only '570 resident enrolments will be falsely identified as duplicate for every one million enrolments'.

However, according to an article published in the *Economic and Political Weekly* by my colleague at the Centre for Internet and Society, Hans Verghese Mathews (2016), this will result in one out of every 146 people being rejected during enrolment when total enrolment reaches 1 billion people. In its rebuttal, the UIDAI disputes the conclusion but offers no alternative extrapolation or mathematical assumptions. 'Without getting too deep into the mathematics', it offers an account of 'a manual adjudication process to rectify the biometric identification errors'.

This manual adjudication determines whether you exist and has none of the elements of natural justice, such as notice to the affected individuals and opportunity to be heard. The architecture of the system allows the government to shirk responsibility when rights are infringed and pass the blame on to an inscrutable black box. Elimination of ghosts is impossible if only machines and unaccountable humans perform this adjudication. This is because there is zero skin in the game. There are free tools available on the internet, such as SFinGe (Synthetic Fingerprint Generator), which allow you to create fake biometrics. The USB cables on the UIDAI-approved enrolment setup can be intercepted using generic hardware that can be bought online. I predicted in 2011 that with a little bit of clever programming, countless number of ghosts can be created which will easily clear the manual adjudication process that the UIDAI claims will ensure that 'no one is denied an Aadhaar number because of a biometric false positive'. This prediction came true this year when the police arrested a gang of criminals that had created a ghost enrolment kit and were selling it along with silicon copies of fingerprints of enrolment officers almost as if they were running a franchise operation.

Near zero: this time for surveillance, which, I believe, should be used like salt in cooking—essential in small quantities, but counterproductive even if slightly in excess. There is a popular misconception that privacy researchers such as myself are opposed to surveillance. In reality, I am all for surveillance. I am totally convinced that surveillance is good anti-corruption technology.

But I also want good returns on investment for my surveillance tax rupee. According to Julian Assange, transparency requirements should be directly proportionate to power; in other words, the powerful should be subject to more surveillance. And conversely, I add, privacy protections must be inversely proportionate to power—in other words, the poor should be spared from intrusions that do not serve the public interest. The UIDAI makes the exact opposite design assumption; it assumes that the poor are responsible for corruption and that technology will eliminate small-ticket or retail corruption. But we all know that the powerful (politicians and bureaucrats, for example) are responsible for most large-ticket corruption.

Why does not the UIDAI first assign UID numbers to all politicians and bureaucrats? Then using digital signatures, why do we not ensure that we have a public, non-repudiable audit trail wherein everyone can track the flow of benefits, subsidies and services from New Delhi to the panchayat office or local corporation office? That will eliminate big-ticket or wholesale corruption. In other words, since most of Aadhaar's surveillance is targeted at the bottom of the pyramid, there will be limited bang for the buck. If surveillance is the need of the hour, we need more CCTVs with microphones turned on in government offices than biometric devices in slums.

One: and zero. In the contemporary binary and digital age, we have lost faith in the old gods. Science and its instantiation technology have become the new gods. The cult of technology is intolerant to blasphemy. For example, Shekhar Gupta recently tweeted saying that part of the opposition to Aadhaar was because 'left-libs detest science/tech'. Technology as ideology is based on some fundamental articles of faith: one, new technology is better than old technology; two, expensive technology is better than cheap technology; three, complex technology is better than simple technology; and four, all technology is empowering or at the very least neutral. Unfortunately, there is no basis in science for any of these articles of faith.

Let me use a simple story to illustrate this. I was fortunate to serve as a member of a committee that the Department of

Biotechnology established to finalise the Human DNA Profiling Bill, 2015, which was to be introduced in Parliament. Aside: the language of the Act also has room for the database to expand into a national DNA database, circumventing 10 years of debate around the controversial DNA Profiling Bill, 2015. The first version of this Bill that I read in January 2013 said that DNA profiling was a 'powerful technology that makes it possible to determine whether the source of origin of one body substance is identical to that of another … without any doubt'. In other words, to quote K. P. C. Gandhi, a scientist from Truth Labs, 'I can vouch for the scientific infallibility of using DNA profiling for carrying out justice.'

Unfortunately, though, the infallible science is conducted by fallible humans. During one of the meetings, a scientist described the process of generating a biometric profile. The first step after the laboratory technician generated the profile was to compare the generated profile with her or his own profile, because during the process of loading the machine with the DNA sample, some of the laboratory technician's DNA could have contaminated the sample. This error would not be a possibility in much older, cheaper and rudimentary biometric technology, for example, photography. A photographer developing a photograph in a darkroom does not have to ensure that his or her own image has not accidentally ended up on the negative. But the Aadhaar promoters are die-hard techno-utopians; if you tell them that fingerprints will not work for those who are engaged in manual labour, they recommend the use of iris-based biometrics. But again, complex technologies are more fragile and often come with increased risks. They may provide greater performance and features, but sometimes they are easier to circumvent. A gummy finger to fool a biometric scanner can be produced using glue and a candle, but to fake a passport takes a lot of sophisticated technology. The data from the field show that even iris-based authentication has unacceptably high failure rates. Therefore, it is important for us to give up our unquestioning faith in technology and start to debate the exact technological configurations of surveillance technology for different contexts and purposes.

One: this time representing a monopoly. Prior to the UID project, nobody got paid when citizens identified themselves to the state. Now the UIDAI will get paid every time this happens and every time citizens wish to update their information in the CIDR. The cost of identification has been passed on to those being identified, we are paying to be surveilled. There will be a consumer-service provider relationship established between the citizen and the state when it comes to identification. The UIDAI will become the monopoly provider of identification and authentication services in India which is trusted by the government. That sounds like a centrally planned communist state to me. Should not the right-wing oppose the Act because it prevents the free market from working? Should not the free market pick the best technology and business model for identification and authentication? Will not that drive the cost of identification and authentication down and ensure higher quality of service for citizens and residents?

Competing providers can also publish transparency reports regarding their compliance with data requests from law-enforcement and intelligence agencies, and if this is important to consumers, they will be punished by the market. The government can use mechanisms such as permanent and temporary bans and price regulation as disincentives for the creation of ghosts. There will be a clear financial incentive to keep the database clean, just like the government established a regulatory framework for digital certificates in the Information Technology Act, allowing for e-commerce and e-governance. Ideally, the Aadhaar Act should have done something similar and established an eco-system for multiple actors to provide services in this two-sided market. For it is impossible for a 'small government' to have the expertise and experience to run one of the world's largest databases of biometric and transaction records securely for perpetuity.

To conclude, I support the use of biometrics. I support government use of identification and authentication technology. I support the use of ID numbers in government databases. I support targeted surveillance to reduce corruption and protect national security. But I believe all these must be put in place with care and thought so that we do not end up sacrificing our constitutional rights or compromising the security of our nation state. Unfortunately, the Aadhaar project's technological design and architecture is an unmitigated disaster and no amount of legal fixes in the Act will make it any better. Our children will pay a heavy price for our folly in the years to come. To quote the security guru Bruce Schneier, 'Data is a toxic asset. We need to start thinking about it as such, and treat it as we would any other source of toxicity. To do anything else is to risk our security and privacy.'

Reference

Mathews, Hans Verghese. 2016. 'Flaws in the UIDAI Process'. *Economic and Political Weekly* 51 (9), pp. 74–78.

6

Aadhaar—Identity or Dystopia?

Viswanath L.

The Aadhaar programme is arguably one of the most disruptive of all government initiatives in the history of independent India. Launched in 2009, the programme was initially conceived as a solution to two problems: one, to provide an identity to the most marginalised sections of society and thereby enable them to stake claim to their rightful entitlements; two, to eliminate fake and ghost identities, which were feared to be the dominant reason for pilferage in government welfare schemes. Undoubtedly, the key to achieving these goals is the success of Aadhaar as a unique, secure and easily verifiable identity.

To answer the question of whether or not Aadhaar can provide a technologically sound system of identity, the present article analyses in detail the possible vulnerabilities at the two ends of the Aadhaar identity system—enrolment and authentication—from two perspectives: one, whether they could potentially dispossess bona fide individuals of their identity, and two, whether the vulnerabilities could be exploited to the extent of making the system redundant.

Enrolment

The Aadhaar enrolment process aims to assign a unique identity number to each resident of India, on the basis of biometric de-duplication. The biometrics identified for this purpose are presently photographs, all 10 fingerprints and iris images of both eyes. Now, biometrics are biological attributes and no two samples can ever be exactly equal, so theoretically there should be no risk. But the ability to differentiate between two sets of biometrics is limited by the resolution of the technology.

The point to be noted is that the Aadhaar database is growing organically, entry by entry. The first person to enrol would have faced no challenge to establish his or her unique identity, but the window is progressively narrowing for every subsequent enrolment. Let us call this the 'enrolment risk'. As there are no reliable means to strike off dead people from the list, the enrolment risk will only keep increasing monotonically and never reach a steady state. An analysis of the results of an experiment conducted by the Unique Identification Authority of India (UIDAI) estimated that as the sample space grows from 1 billion to 1.5 billion, the chances of false positives (that is, possibility of a person being wrongly identified as duplicate) will increase from 1/145 to 1/97 (Mathews 2016: 74). Therefore, at a future point, when the risk becomes insurmountable, the only option would be to add a new biometric to the scheme. Possibly towards this end, the Aadhaar Act, in Section 2, leaves the definition of 'biometric information' open to future extension. So it is clear that the basis of enrolment is a probabilistic (rather than deterministic) measure, hence there will always be people falling through the cracks.

The risk is dramatically heightened for those having partial or poor-quality biometrics. Old people typically have wrinkled fingers; their eyes may be clouded by cataract. It is common for people engaged in manual labour to have completely worn-out fingerprints on some or all fingers. These are only indicative examples but are representative of the complex reality of human society. A Right to Information (RTI) query filed by the author in December 2016 revealed that as on 15 January 2017, a little over 15 crore enrolment applications had been rejected, of which some 6 crore were rejected as 'biometric duplicates' (Viswanath 2017b). This when the total Aadhaar generated for age five and above (for whom biometrics are required to be collected) was a little over 105 crores. The ratio of duplicates to successful identities works out to about 1/17, which is significantly higher than the theoretical estimates noted above. The RTI query further sought specific information regarding enrolment applications (both successful and rejected) with partial or poor-quality biometrics, but the same could not be furnished. Thus, it can only be surmised that there are no reliable means to discern how many of the rejected duplicates are actually genuine cases of multiple enrolments and how many are false flags.

From all the above, it can be deduced that though the Aadhaar Act, in Section 3, states that every resident shall be entitled to obtain an Aadhaar number, the enrolment process offers no means to enforce that right. While there is a provision for 'biometric exceptions', the Enrolment and Update Regulations 2016 contemplate this only for cases where the hands and/or eyes are completely absent or are severely deformed. Relaxing this condition runs the obvious risk of opening the floodgates to fraud. As early as 2012, a racket was busted in Hyderabad, where several fake enrolments had been pushed under the biometric exception category (*Times of India* 2012).

While biometric de-duplication cannot provide a guarantee of identity to each and every individual, the other moot question is whether it can be gamed easily, with the intention of pushing fake entries. The answer is a resounding yes, because there are a myriad ways to create bogus (but unique) biometric profiles. Some illustrative examples could be a person interchanging their left and right hands when scanning fingerprints, or pooling in biometrics from multiple persons. The de-duplication engine can never scale up to filter out such kinds of fraud. Added to the matrix is the fact that enrolment operations are largely outsourced to private contractors, numbering into several thousand. Law enforcement is, therefore, likely to be overwhelmed when the full scale of fraud comes to light.

One such scam was exposed recently in the state of Uttar Pradesh (possibly the tip of the iceberg), where a gang involved in creating thousands of fake Aadhaar entries, against bogus biometrics, was apprehended (*Times of India* 2017a).

The vulnerability of the de-duplication process could be mitigated to some extent only if biometric authentication were enforced at every use of the Aadhaar identity, that is, a person exercising their Aadhaar identity would be required to match their biometrics against the records in the database. But then biometric authentication has its own limitations (more on this below), hence is not feasible to apply everywhere. Alternative methods of using Aadhaar, like through mobile One-Time Password (OTP) authentication or as a physical 'Aadhaar card', have, therefore, been introduced. These alternative methods bring to nought one of the foundational goals of Aadhaar, that of using biometric technology to counter fake and ghost identities. A fake Aadhaar identity, once generated through any means, could be used in perpetuity, validated through one of the non-biometric methods.

One of most high-profile uses of Aadhaar in recent times was its mandatory linkage to PAN cards, ostensibly to weed out duplicate cards that many people were feared to be holding. That the faith in Aadhaar stemmed from biometrics was acknowledged by the Union Finance Minister, Mr Arun Jaitley, on the floor of the Parliament (*Indian Express* 2017). But interestingly, biometric authentication of the Aadhaar number was not sought; rather, only details like name, address, date of birth, etc. were matched between the two databases. The exercise should, therefore, be considered nothing more than a placebo.

Biometric authentication being one of the two pillars on which the premise of Aadhaar as a unique identity stands (the other pillar being biometric de-duplication) was admitted to by the UIDAI in its Sur-Rejoinder filed in the case of *Shanta Sinha & ANR vs. Union of India & ANR*. An extract is given below:

> The possibility of a fraud within the system gets checked the moment a person enrolls into Aadhaar system with his or her biometric information including fingerprints and iris scan whereby every time the said person authenticates, the response will confirm that he or she is the person who he or she claimed to be and not any other person. (UIDAI 2017b: 55)

Authentication

Aadhaar is designed to work as a paperless ID, to be valid only when authenticated against the central database. As discussed earlier, application of biometrics at enrolment is useful only if the same is applied at authentication, otherwise it is a free pass to bogus identities. But just as biometric de-duplication is a probabilistic exercise, so is authentication, which therefore cannot provide a guarantee of identity.

The unpredictability of biometric authentication is compounded due to the possibility of an individual's biometrics diverging from the snapshot recorded at enrolment. Some of the factors contributing to this are ageing, manual labour, injury, illness, etc. (Pato and Millet 2010: 27–28; Viswanath 2017c). Neither can these factors be estimated beforehand, nor can they be measured post facto, so the first indication would probably be an authentication failure on the field.

The true picture of biometric authentication is emerging from states where Aadhaar-Based Biometric Authentication (ABBA) has been made mandatory for welfare schemes like the Public Distribution System, National Rural Employment Guarantee Act and Social Security Pensions. In one instance, failure rates of up to 17 per cent were reported from Andhra Pradesh (see chapter 1 of this volume).

The legal position of an individual in the Aadhaar system is extremely weak. The Aadhaar Act, in Section 31(2), makes it the responsibility of the individual to keep their biometric records up to date in the database, as and when there may be changes. Section 28(5) of the same act disallows an individual access to their biometric records in the database. Thus, neither are there any means to cross-verify the recorded biometrics, nor does the identity have any defined validity. The entire burden of uncertainty is therefore borne by the individual (Viswanath 2017a).

Notwithstanding the non-deterministic nature of biometrics, the regulatory framework of Aadhaar continues to consider the original biometrics used for de-duplication as the cornerstone of the unique identity. Regulation 19(a) of the Enrolment and Update Regulations 2016 states that biometric authentication will be done prior to accepting a request for update of biometric information. While the odds may not seem to be too high, considering that there are ten fingers and two eyes, the reality is much harder for those who may have scraped through the enrolment process, teetering on partial or partially obscure biometrics. The crucial question of 'how should a person know that they are due for update' is left for them to grapple with, which may actually trip just about anyone any day (Viswanath 2017c).

As is obvious, waiving the requirement of biometric authentication (even as an exception clause) would be an invitation to fraud, as anyone could then replace anyone else's biometric profile. Therefore, there is a distinct possibility that someone may find themselves permanently locked out of their Aadhaar identity, should biometric authentication fail on all counts.

Thus, from the perspectives of both enrolment and authentication, biometric technology fails the other foundational goal of Aadhaar, that of providing a *guarantee* of identity to all residents of India. Ironically, the worst affected sections are those in whose name the programme was conceived in the first place—the weakest and most marginalised sections of our society.

The extent of the absurdity can be gauged from the fact that the government considered the option of 'proxy authorisation' for mobile SIM linkage to Aadhaar, ostensibly for the benefit of senior citizens who were facing difficulties with biometric authentication (*Times of India* 2017c).

Use of biometrics as an authentication token presents another grave risk, due to the fact that biometric markers are publicly visible and, therefore, can be easily copied. The UIDAI's assertion that the biometrics are stored in their safe custody, under the highest standards of encryption, is therefore a redundant argument, simply because there is nothing 'secret' about biometrics. In the Aadhaar eco-system, biometrics are exposed once at enrolment and subsequently at every authentication. The possibility of compromising the field devices and thereby allow copying of biometrics can never be ruled out. Above all, there is the possibility of copying biometrics completely external to the authorised Aadhaar infrastructure. Agrawal, Banerjee and Sharma (2017) have provided a detailed analysis of the privacy and security issues of Aadhaar.

There are numerous examples to show how easy it is to copy biometrics by external means. In the Uttar Pradesh scam referenced earlier, the gang used cloned fingerprints of authorised enrolment operators in order to log in to the system (*Mail Today* 2017). In another instance, students in Mumbai were able to trick the biometric attendance system in their college by embossing fingerprints on resin films (*Hindustan Times* 2017). Researchers have even been able to synthesise 'masterprints' that could potentially unlock up to two thirds of phones (*New York Times* 2017). The iris scanner on Samsung Galaxy S8 phones has been demonstrably hacked with simple tools that include an infrared camera and a contact lens (*Forbes* 2017).

One of the first instances of the UIDAI trying to secure the authentication end was in response to the case involving Axis Bank, Suvidhaa Infoserve and eMudhra, where the firms were found to be testing out Aadhaar authentication using stored fingerprints (*Times of India* 2017a). The security measures introduced were mandatory registration of the authentication device and encryption of the captured biometric image. But the encryption being in software, the possibility of using stored biometrics still remains, albeit with a little more effort (Sethi and Bansal 2017). The overriding truth is that none of these low-cost methods can prevent the use of external hacks, like fingerprints embossed on resin film.

The only meaningful barrier against fraud is, therefore, regular law enforcement. The curious vulnerability in the case of Aadhaar is that even after someone gets to know that their biometrics have been compromised, there is nothing they can do to secure their identity back, as biometrics cannot be changed at will (unlike passwords). Thus, Aadhaar identity, once breached, is an open secret for life. In other words, the law cannot fix what has been broken by technology (Abraham 2017).

The use of Aadhaar authentication as a sufficient token for such sensitive matters as opening a bank account (*Live Law* 2017), taking a mobile SIM (*Livemint* 2017b), etc. is therefore a matter of grave concern, for both individual and national security. One such case was exposed in Indore, where Reliance Jio SIM cards were fraudulently issued, simply by taking the customer's thumb impression more than once (*India.com* 2017).

The introduction of Aadhaar Enabled Payment System (AEPS) and associated applications like the BHIM-Aadhaar Pay app take the vulnerability a step further, by allowing financial transactions to take place on the sole strength of Aadhaar biometric authentication (*Livemint* 2017a). A few customers of Andhra Bank and Syndicate Bank are reported to have lost money to Aadhaar fraud (*Ultra News* 2017). In Jharkhand, a student was able to embezzle several lakhs of rupees from the savings account of a college, by linking his Aadhaar number to it (*Telegraph* 2017).

In order to mitigate some of the risks and vulnerabilities associated with biometrics, the UIDAI (through its Authentication Regulations 2016) has introduced alternative means of authentication, like OTP on mobile phones. It is another matter that the UIDAI has also allowed the use of the original Aadhaar letter, or a downloaded e-Aadhaar copy, as a sufficient identity document for certain purposes (UIDAI 2017a), without any support in law.

As explained earlier, the availability of non-biometric means of authentication leaves the enrolment step as the single point of vulnerability for introducing fake identities. For bona fide identities, mobile OTP as a single layer of authentication is an extremely weak security layer and hence, not at all suited for sensitive applications. An individual's Aadhaar identity could be compromised simply by taking control of their mobile number, which can be done through means like SIM card cloning or SIM swapping or even by changing the mobile number linked to Aadhaar. The compromised Aadhaar identity then becomes the gateway to everything linked to Aadhaar. A recently exposed scam in Delhi revealed how Aadhaar-linked United Payments Interface apps were used to siphon off money from bank accounts, after replacing the phone number linked to the victims' Aadhaar number (*Scroll.in* 2017).

Security is, therefore, never a one-size-fits-all solution. Every application has evolved security mechanisms as per its own risk assessment. The security processes for banking transactions would naturally be much more stringent than, say, for allowing entry to a public event. The entry of Aadhaar and Aadhaar authentication into varied applications makes it the single point of failure. Curiously though, policy administrators are keen to consider Aadhaar as the 'single source of truth' (Sethi 2017; MPSRDH 2017), which puts honest and law-abiding citizens in an extremely vulnerable position.

Conclusion

The lack of confidence in biometrics as a means of identity has been felt right from the initial days of Aadhaar. Even the UIDAI's Committee on Biometrics, in a December 2009 report, admitted to the unforeseen challenges that may be faced in implementing biometric de-duplication, due to both the quality of the biometrics and the scale of the Indian population. Quoting from the report:

> The Committee however, is also conscious of the fact that de-duplication of the magnitude required by the UIDAI has never been implemented in the world. In the global context, a de-duplication accuracy of 99% has been achieved so far, using good quality fingerprints against a database of up to fifty million. Two factors however, raise uncertainty about the accuracy that can be achieved through fingerprints. First, retaining efficacy while scaling the database size from fifty million to a billion has not been adequately analyzed. Second, fingerprint quality, the most important variable for determining de-duplication accuracy, has not been studied in depth in the Indian context. (UIDAI 2009: 4)

Field reports have corroborated the above, that the problem of poor-quality fingerprints is widely prevalent in the Indian landscape (*FirstPost* 2011). Iris-based authentication was introduced in 2013, when it was becoming increasingly clear that fingerprint-based authentication was too unreliable, this even at a time when there were no available standards in iris authentication technology (*Business Standard* 2013). As can be seen, scientific research and improvisations are going hand in hand.

The fundamental disconnect is that biometrics is well-suited for identification, while the Aadhaar programme attempts to use it as a means of identity. Identification and identity are two entirely different spheres. Identification can happen even without the cooperation of the individual. Biometric technology can add great value to applications like forensics, criminal investigation, surveillance, etc., but even there the enthusiasm must be tempered by an understanding of the limitations of the technology. Even the UIDAI has submitted to the Supreme Court that the biometrics in the Aadhaar database are not suitable for purposes of criminal investigation, principally due to the possibility of false positive matches (*Indian Express* 2014).

On the other hand, identity is a matter of right that is exercised by the individual. There can be no room for uncertainty here. The result of this misplaced application of technology is that only those individuals that can be identified by the state will enjoy their identity. This effectively robs individuals of the sovereignty over their own selves. Mindless improvisations to salvage the situation are creating a fertile ground for fraud. Aadhaar is, therefore, precipitating a situation where criminals may run amok, even while genuine and bona fide citizens are struggling for their identity.

References

Abraham, Sunil. 2017. 'It's the Technology, Stupid'. *Hindu Business Line*, 31 March. Available at http://www.thehindubusinessline.com/blink/cover/11-reasons-why-aadhaar-is-not-just-nonsmart-but-also-insecure/article9608225.ece (accessed 22 October 2017).

Agrawal, Shweta, Subhashis Banerjee, and Subodh Sharma. 2017. 'Privacy and Security of Aadhaar: A Computer Science Perspective'. *Economic & Political Weekly* 52 (37), September, pp. 93–102.

Business Standard. 2013. 'Iris Scan to Add Layer to Aadhaar Authentication', 29 January. Available at http://www.business-standard.com/article/economy-policy/iris-scan-to-add-layer-to-aadhaar-authentication-113010300036_1.html (accessed 22 October 2017).

FirstPost. 2011. 'India's Vanishing Fingerprints Put UID in Question', 24 October. Available at http://www.firstpost.com/politics/aadhar-indias-vanishing-fingerprints-put-unique-identity-in-question-115144.html (accessed 22 October 2017).

Forbes. 2017. 'Samsung Galaxy S8 Iris Scanner Hacked In Three Simple Steps', 23 May. Available at https://www.forbes.com/sites/ianmorris/2017/05/23/samsung-galaxy-s8-iris-scanner-hacked-in-three-simple-steps/ (accessed 22 October 2017).

Hindustan Times. 2017. 'You will be Glued to this: Mumbai College's Students Trick Biometric System', 15 May. Available at http://www.hindustantimes.com/mumbai-news/you-will-be-glued-to-this-mumbai-college-s-students-trick-biometric-system/story-W64f1jdMtecxKDml2DakeI.html (accessed 22 October 2017).

India.com. 2017. 'Reliance Jio SIM Cards Scam: Indore Police Arrests Six Accused, Modus Operandi Revealed', 20 February. Available at http://www.india.com/technology/reliance-jio-sim-cards-scam-indore-police-arrests-six-accused-modus-operandi-revealed-1857021/ (accessed 22 October 2017).

Indian Express. 2014. 'Stop Aadhaar Data Use to Probe Crime: UIDAI to SC', 19 March. Available at http://indianexpress.com/article/cities/delhi/stop-aadhaar-data-use-to-probe-crime-uidai-to-sc-2/ (accessed 22 October 2017).

———. 2017. 'Finance Minister Arun Jaitley Counters Critique: "Yes, we are making Aadhaar mandatory"', 23 March. Available at http://indianexpress.com/article/india/finance-bill-minister-arun-jaitley-counters-critique-yes-we-are-making-aadhaar-mandatory-4581383/ (accessed 22 October 2017).

Live Law. 2017. 'Aadhaar Mandatory for Opening Bank Accounts & for Financial Transactions Above ₹50,000 [Read Notification]', 16 June. Available at http://www.livelaw.in/aadhaar-mandatory-opening-bank-accounts-financial-transactions-%E2%82%B950000-read-notification/ (accessed 22 October 2017).

Livemint. 2017a. 'All Banks Told to Move to Aadhaar Pay by March End', 23 February. Available at http://www.livemint.com/Industry/DHlGQPO1VmmyiE9I9ppEnM/All-banks-told-to-move-to-Aadhaar-Pay-by-March-end.html (accessed 22 October 2017).

———. 2017b. 'Aadhaar to be Mandatory for Mobile Phone Verification', 25 March. Available at http://www.livemint.com/Industry/wyGskI48Ak73ETJ5XW0diK/Aadhaar-now-a-must-for-all-mobile-phone-connections-after-ta.html (accessed 22 October 2017).

Mail Today. 2017. 'UP STF Busts Gang which Hacked Secure Source Code to Crack Aadhaar, Issued Fake Biometric Cards', 11 September. Available at http://indiatoday.intoday.in/story/aadhaar-card-fake-biometric-id-up-stf-uidai/1/1045133.html (accessed 22 October 2017).

Mathews, Hans Verghese. 2016. 'Flaws in the UIDAI Process'. *Economic & Political Weekly* 51 (9), 27 February, pp. 74–78.

MPSRDH. 2017. 'About MPSRDH', *PARICHAI: State Resident Data Hub*, Government of Madhya Pradesh. Available at https://mpsrdh.gov.in/aboutusmpsrdh.html (accessed 20 October 2017).

New York Times. 2017. 'That Fingerprint Sensor on Your Phone Is Not as Safe as You Think', 10 April. Available at https://www.nytimes.com/2017/04/10/technology/fingerprint-security-smartphones-apple-google-samsung.html (accessed 22 October 2017).

Pato, Joseph N., and Lynette I. Millet. 2010. 'Biometric Recognition: Challenges and Opportunities', *The National Academies Press*. Available at https://www.nap.edu/read/12720/chapter/1 (accessed 22 October 2017).

Scroll.in. 2017. 'Sophisticated Aadhaar-related Bank Fraud has Left Police in Delhi and Noida Baffled', 5 October. Available at https://scroll.in/article/852689/sophisticated-aadhaar-related-bank-fraud-has-left-police-in-delhi-and-noida-baffled (accessed 22 October 2017).

Sethi, Aman. 2017. 'Right to Privacy: Data Shows States Using Aadhaar to Build Profiles of Citizens', *Hindustan Times*, 25 August. Available at http://www.hindustantimes.com/india-news/despite-govt-denials-states-building-databases-for-360-degree-profiles-of-citizens/story-qnSLHGyZIXiZiO4ce84UuO.html (accessed 22 October 2017).

Sethi, Aman, and Samarth Bansal. 2017. 'Aadhaar Gets New Security Features, but This is Why Your Data Still May Not Be Safe', *Hindustan Times*, 19 July. Available at http://www.hindustantimes.com/india-news/aadhaar-gets-new-security-features-but-this-is-why-your-data-still-may-not-be-safe/story-RoZJAOUXtWZREr4V4M5TvK.html (accessed 22 October 2017).

Telegraph. 2017. 'Aadhaar Seeding Scam Takes Root', 2 September. Available at https://www.telegraphindia.com/1170902/jsp/frontpage/story_170423.jsp (accessed 22 October 2017).

Times of India. 2012. 'Aadhaar Card Fraud Exposes Registration Process Errors', 30 April. Available at http://timesofindia.indiatimes.com/city/hyderabad/Aadhaar-card-fraud-exposes-registration-process-errors/articleshow/12929354.cms (accessed 22 October 2017).

———. 2017a. 'Probe against Three Firms for Illegal Use of Aadhaar Biometrics', 24 February. Available at https://timesofindia.indiatimes.com/companies/probe-against-three-firms-for-illegal-use-of-aadhaar-biometrics/articleshow/57328109.cms (accessed 22 October 2017).

———. 2017b. 'Gang of 10 Booked for Making Fake Aadhaar IDs in UP', 11 September. Available at https://timesofindia.indiatimes.com/city/lucknow/gang-of-10-booked-for-making-fake-aadhaar-ids-in-up/articleshow/60459388.cms (accessed 22 October 2017).

———. 2017c. 'Govt Plans to Ease Aadhaar-mobile Linking', 11 October. Available at https://timesofindia.indiatimes.com/india/govt-plans-to-ease-aadhaar-mobile-linking/articleshow/61030101.cms (accessed 22 October 2017).

UIDAI. 2009. 'Biometric Design Standards for UID Applications, Version 1.0', UIDAI Committee on Biometrics, December.

———. 2017a. 'Subject: Validity of Downloaded Aadhaar (e-Aadhaar) as Proof of identity – Regarding', Unique Identification Authority of India (Logistics Division), circular dated 28 April, F.No. 14014/8/ 2011-Logistics Vol.II. Available at https://uidai.gov.in/images/uidai_om_on_e_aadhaar_validity.pdf (accessed 22 October 2017).

———. 2017b. 'Sur-Rejoinder on Behalf of Respondents to the Rejoinder Affidavit Dated 21.06.2017 by the Petitioners', *Writ Petition (Civil) No. 342 of 2017*, 3 July.

Ultra News. 2017. 'Andhra Bank, Syndicate Bank Customers Lose Lakhs to Aadhaar Fraud', 5 October. Available at https://ultra.news/t-t/33661/andhra-bank-syndicate-bank-customers-lose-lakhs-aadhaar-fraud (accessed 22 October 2017).

Viswanath, L. 2017a. 'Four Reasons You should Worry about Aadhaar's Use of Biometrics', *The Wire*, 28 March. Available at https://thewire.in/119323/real-problem-aadhaar-lies-biometrics/ (accessed 22 October 2017).

———. 2017b. 'RTI: Low-down on Aadhaar Enrolments (Specifically about Biometrics)', *Bulletman Reporting*, 13 April. Available at https://bulletman.wordpress.com/2017/04/13/rti-low-down-on-aadhaar-enrolments-specifically-about-biometrics/ (accessed 22 October 2017).

———. 2017c. 'RTI: Update of Biometric Information', *Bulletman Reporting*, 13 October. Available at https://bulletman.wordpress.com/2017/10/13/rti-update-of-biometric-information/ (accessed 22 October 2017).

7

INSIDE THE PLUMBING OF TECHNOLOGY PROJECTS

Kiran Jonnalagadda

In 2006, the Government of Karnataka undertook two significant e-governance projects. The first was to computerise the Public Distribution System (PDS), which—among various outcomes—also resulted in India's largest biometric identity database before Aadhaar. The second was a network of 800 'Nemmadi' centres across the state for delivering citizen services, ahead of the central government's Mission 2007 initiative to open a Common Service Centre (CSC) in all of India's 600,000 villages.

I was fortunate to be a participant in both projects, having just arrived at Comat Technologies, the company that won the contracts. Comat is now defunct, but in its final years it provided a reference for the design of Aadhaar.

My experience on the ground highlighted nuances of how technology projects unfold that are not found in official documentation.[1] Robin Williams and David Edge, in *The Social Shaping of Technology* (1996), note that:

> Technology does not develop according to an inner technical logic but is instead a social product, patterned by the conditions of its creation and use. Every stage in the generation and implementation of new technologies involves a set of choices between different technical options. Alongside narrowly 'technical' considerations, a range of 'social' factors affect which options are selected, thus influencing the content of technologies and their social implications.

As I hope to illustrate, these 'social' factors are not limited to a project's scope, and further that the technology project has a reciprocal influence on the conditions of its usage. This chapter has four parts: (i) how technology evolves over the long term; (ii) the underlying agendas in a computerisation project; (iii) how the two clash when operations roll out to the field; and (iv) the implications of this clash for the governance of technology projects.

Intelligent Design

The two tangible components of any modern technology, hardware and software, are both products of intelligent design by humans with explicit intentions. But they are also enormously complex endeavours, beyond the abilities of any individual to comprehend. To build any technology, therefore, we must necessarily collaborate and build on the past work of others. This means the act of intelligent design is subject to evolutionary forces.

About 45 years ago, the Unix operating system introduced the concept of a 'filesystem', a storage area with 'files' organised in 'folders'. Every operating system today is based around a filesystem. When Apple introduced the iPhone in 2007, they decided to wipe the slate clean by removing it. It still exists behind the scenes, because no one is truly capable of such radical change, but Apple removed it from the user interface. For a full decade they have tried to push a paradigm shift, defining the user experience around apps instead of files. Finally in 2017, in what is seen as an admission of defeat, files have reappeared in iOS 11. Between Dropbox, Google Drive and a bevy of competitors, file storage moved to the cloud, but the file and folder paradigm refused to die. A decade of trying by the most powerful technology company in the world was not enough to remove a foundation that had been around for only three prior decades.

This is an important lesson any time someone claims their radical new approach is better. New approaches only take root when enough stakeholders sense opportunity and invest, each exerting a pull in their preferred direction. This suggests that Aadhaar's unusually distinct approach to biometric authentication will not survive unless it evolves to being similar to the rest of the industry.

Computerisation, or the Restructuring of Processes around Technology

Software is routinely commissioned as if it were furniture. The carpenters will come, take the measurements, bang away for a while, and then deliver what you ordered. Clients are routinely confounded to find that it does not work like this. Not only do the programmers seem to be answering an invisible god, the software stops working shortly after they leave. The industry calls this phenomenon 'software entropy' and it has many implications. The more software one builds, the harder it gets to maintain over time. Costs and complexity grow, forcing the introduction of additional stakeholders to bear the load. Software that was originally brought in to automate an organisation's functions grows to become the central activity, with everything revolving around its maintenance. The venture capitalist Marc Andreessen identified the opportunity in this restructuring with the slogan 'software is eating the world'.

A decade ago, as we set out to computerise the PDS and roll out service centres, we were also projecting our idealism on the world. In 2006, mobile networks were transitioning from GPRS to EDGE, the technology we associate with 2G today. iPhone and Android did not exist. Comat's PDS bid called for computerisation only during roll-out and in back-end operations. No computers were expected to be used at ration shops. We thought this was pragmatic, but we—or at least I—did not yet anticipate that the restructuring of processes around technology would extend the technology's influence to spaces where no computers were involved, because these are two distinct things.

It is one thing to empower a worker with a computer and entirely something else to change the worker's job definition using a computer. In many software projects, the client's motivations for better insight and control of their workflows—leakages in the supply chain in the case of PDS—are considered, while the nuances of a worker's workflow rarely are.

Consider, for instance, how we proposed ration shopkeepers to show evidence of having given rations to a beneficiary. Rather than biometric authentication, as has been happening under Aadhaar, we proposed a secure paper-based system. One of the firm's engineers had stumbled on Moni Naor and Adi Shamir's visual cryptography algorithm and found it a suitable candidate. He had been advised to file for a patent on this use and had found the filing process a distraction from figuring out how to actually use it. When I arrived, he was leaving the company, the algorithm was part of the winning bid and a patent had been filed for, but the necessary technology did not exist yet. I got down to the task and produced what I could, given the constraints.

My solution involved 60 transparency sheets, the 'keys', handed out once a month to ration shopkeepers over the five-year duration of the project. When laid on a matching area of the ration card, the key would reveal hidden letters in two out of six boxes, a different pair for each card each month, which the shopkeeper had to note on an Optical Mark Recognition (OMR) sheet. That sheet was going to be evidence of whether the shopkeeper actually saw the ration card when claiming to have handed out rations.

Figure 7.1: Example of pattern to be printed on ration cards, pattern printed on transparency sheets that are handed to ration shop owners, and what they are expected to see when they place the transparency on the ration card

Pattern on ration card	Transparency key	When overlaid
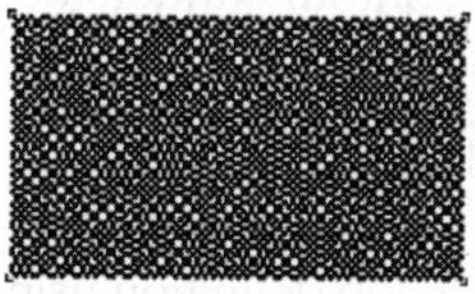		

Source: Author.

This scheme works because it depends on the human eye's ability to ignore noise in a pattern, thereby using a visual 'OR' operation (a dot on either of the sheets is a dot on the combined sheets) to mimic an 'exclusive OR (XOR)' operation (either but not both). XOR is a foundation of cryptography.

But it also depends on the human agreeing to put up with it. I needed the patch on the card to be as large as possible for legibility. I also worried about the codes being guessable. I wanted more letters in the pattern to make it harder, but since I had limited space on the card, smaller letters would reduce legibility and risk shopkeepers refusing to use the method at all.

That risk became a recurring problem. An official complained that the nice-looking ration card was ruined by my ugly black patch. Could it be a different colour? The enrolment team found an unusually large family and did not have enough space to carry all their names. Could I reduce the size of my patch? Both these came at the risk of legibility. A colleague, examining a print run, feared shopkeepers would notice patterns and cheat. My sense of the technology was that both fraud and operator error were to be expected, and we had to tell them apart on the basis of statistical significance. To others, this meant my technology was not deterministic and could not establish evidence of fraud.

Sometime later, I realised that by designing around the assumption that ration cards could only be used at one shop, I had built an inflexible technology that was going to block any reform.

These negotiations revolved around a single theme: despite being the creator of this technology, I was powerless to make it behave in some other manner. We had to design everything else around its limitations. We had arrived in this rut because of a fatal mistake: betting on technology based on a guess that it was viable, before it had been properly refined and its contours understood by everyone whose jobs would now be defined by it.

The Internet Engineering Task Force, which controls internet standards, conducts a very public Request for Comments process where the public is invited to criticise a proposed standard over several months. The assumption is that the promoters cannot possibly be smart enough to have thought about everything. Many technology projects go through similar public review, but often this phase is seen as an inconvenience for the sake of propriety instead of being a fundamental necessity.

But back to our story. While ration disbursal was to have this paper-based verification scheme, the cards themselves were issued based on a fresh citizen enrolment using fingerprint-based biometric de-duplication. There too, well known assumptions like 'fingers have fingerprints unique to one in so many fingers' broke down when we encountered individuals with no prints at all, their fingers having been smoothened out from years of work. We introduced facial recognition as a late-stage requirement to make the de-duplication technology work.

Re-enrolment was not merely a conversion from paper records to computer records. It was also a re-interrogation of the citizen. Was a citizen eligible for subsidies? As ration cards were issued to whole families, did their children reappear in someone else's family? Was a particular dwelling occupied by one family or two? The underlying assumption of the process was that citizens were to be suspected of committing identity fraud unless our technology could prove otherwise. We revised the technology until it worked for a majority and the state then required citizens to submit to it, extending from the majority to universality. While the exercise ostensibly rooted out fraud, it also renewed the risk of exclusion for the marginalised. We had augmented fingerprints with facial recognition because that problem was too large to ignore, but who knows how many problems we had completely failed to notice?

This is a recurring pattern with technology projects. They rarely cover all possible exceptions, and instead depend on the parties using it—in this case government and citizens—making compromises to meet midway, either by offering them incentives or by compulsion. To be precise, it is the technology project, now endowed with some organisational agency and better addressed as a 'platform', that has to offer the incentives to encourage adoption. The business models built around this have spawned a new branch of economics on 'multi-sided platforms'. The economists David S. Evans and Richard Schmalensee have contributed to this field with their books *Invisible Engines* and *Matchmakers*. To encourage adoption, platforms regularly make assurances to one side that compromise the interests of the other, covering this gap until the platform is sufficiently well entrenched to withdraw the compromise. Uber offers incentives to drivers and discounts to customers, covering the shortfall with venture capital. Microsoft famously ignored piracy in developing economies while tightly controlling the Windows platform in developed economies. Or take UIDAI, Aadhaar's steward, who promise privacy to individuals while assuring critical insight to service providers.

Capitalists can afford to concern themselves with only viable customers, but the government is obliged to serve every citizen, and therefore to codify exception handling for anyone who may be excluded. Since these exceptions require discretionary authority, which was the source of the problem that necessitated the overhaul in the first place, any technology deployment only serves to relocate this authority rather than eliminate it. Once again, I hope to illustrate from my experience.

Field Operations

For the service centre project bid later in 2006, we brought in a larger consortium partner. The partner sent two representatives, technically heads of the project, whose only role was to relay updates. The e-governance secretary ignored them and spoke directly to us. This created a delicate balance. While the project contract stipulated a reporting hierarchy, actual lines of communication were now organic, without documentation or accountability. If the bearer of news has no authority, they are not accountable either, allowing such a person to discuss issues frankly. I soon learnt this was not limited to us. Authority and cooperation were to be earned, not commanded. I became the technical head of the project, coordinating between our coalition and the government's, doing whatever it took to make progress.

The first service we delivered from service centres was access to the Bhoomi database of land records, at Rs 15 per authenticated copy of a record. This statement has several layers that need unpacking.

India has two administrative divisions below the state, districts and blocks, with elected representation, but these rungs are politically weak. This gap has resulted in political power becoming concentrated at the state level.

A state-level bureaucrat, Rajeev Chawla, had successfully digitised Karnataka's land records between 1998 and 2002 under the Bhoomi project. Land records were previously maintained on paper by village accountants (VAs), whose discretionary authority was considered problematic. The Bhoomi project soon came to be seen as a success, despite critics pointing out that the legibility it brought to records also legitimised past fraud, among other issues. Mr Chawla credited three factors in a 2005 interview: political will, administrative will and the role of the project officer. He reiterated this in 2012, saying, '(Officials) kind of look at technology to be a panacea for everything, which it cannot be. The political will is the most important thing.' For his efforts, Mr Chawla received an unusually long stint as the e-governance secretary.

In 2006, Nemmadi was going to extend access to Bhoomi from 177 taluk (block) offices to 800 service centres, covering every village cluster in the state. As the private party in a public-private partnership, we ran the front office and did a revenue split with the government, who ran the back office, maintaining the database and providing access to it. My team provided the liaison. Our operation was hinged on a series of because-therefore considerations.

To start with, our contract stipulated a six-month period for setting up most of the 800 service centres. Internet access was a major challenge. Digital Subscriber Line (DSL) was becoming standard in urban areas, replacing dial-up modems, but did not exist in rural areas. There was only one way to get an internet connection in a remote area: via satellite. We invested in nearly 800 VSAT (Very Small Aperture Terminal) dishes at about Rs 75,000 each, plus monthly fees, for a measly 64 kbps per location. Internet by satellite had been a reliable, if expensive, way to overcome ground conditions through the 1990s, mostly used for ATMs, but the technology was rapidly giving way to cheap terrestrial internet.

Our outsized investment was a bet, not on the technology, but on having a monopoly on access to government services for the five years of the contract. This bet turned internet access from being a foundation to instead being a benchmark that everything else was measured against.

Extracting revenue from an impoverished area was necessary to keep its service centre viable, creating the stress points that threatened to fracture the project. Operating a centre regardless of viability was also necessary. The government technically subsidised unviable centres, but the contract went to whoever sought the lowest subsidy (and transaction commissions), so the pressure was entirely on the private partner. (When other states issued service centre contracts, the winning bidder sought a negative subsidy to guarantee their win, and then failed to operationalise.)

Next, when scouting locations for centres, we had a limited choice of retail areas meeting the contractual requirements of size and construction material. Sometimes the choice was influenced by a local Member of Legislative Assembly (MLA) who preferred his or her home village. Landlords would not always allow a heavy VSAT dish—significantly larger than a modern TV dish—to be set in concrete, so they would be weighed down with bricks and subject to dislocation by rain or roving monkeys. That meant dispatching a trained technician from the nearest urban area and downtime of a day or more. Unreliable power and UPS-draining desktop PCs added to our woes. (Energy-efficient netbooks came to market a year later.)

Service centre operators had to meet qualifying criteria, but their candidacy too was influenced by external factors such as landlords preferring their own candidates, political rivalries, or host villages refusing to accept an operator from a neighbouring village. Operators were expected to be proficient at using a computer, but these other factors took greater priority and we had to cover the gap.

For instance, operators had to login to the government website using their unique ID to produce land record certificates. Our field managers found it pragmatic to give these operators accounts tied to their locations rather than to the operators themselves, using standardised passwords (location ID + '123') that substitute operators could easily use when filling in for someone. No variations were allowed because nobody wanted to do any more support for a poorly trained operator with no job commitment. Making their computers and internet work was hard enough.

Some service centre deployments used the 'village-level entrepreneur' model, passing on operational risk to an owner-operator. We preferred having our own skin in the game to be able to extract greater efficiency, and to qualify for an RBI Business Correspondent license. To go from zero to 800 service centres in six months, we found ourselves pursuing a singular goal: reduce the agency of field personnel as much as possible, centralising all authority. We could not afford to tolerate individualism in the quest for uniform service, similar to how Bhoomi itself reduced the agency of VAs, whether they used it to extract a bribe or help a citizen.

It later occurred to me that if projects like ours are meant to extend the reach of infrastructure, attempting to make it uniformly available within an arbitrary deadline, then underlying infrastructure, including human capacity, are crucial to success. Our VSAT investments, for instance, rapidly turned into a liability as DSL internet became available across the state. Internet access affected other parties too. The banks we depended on did not have the 'core banking' required for electronic transfers. We employed money collectors to courier cash around the state, to avoid stiff bank transfer fees and to compensate for a missing local cash circulation economy (which banking correspondents were supposed to solve for us). Our operation would have been a lot more sustainable if only we waited one or two years for these dependencies to fall in place, but instead we had to chase the dramatic gesture of having the chief minister inaugurate uniform access within six months.

Core banking has no obvious correlation to land records until you realise the operational dependency. Missing or unreliable infrastructure made our claim of uniform access hollow. When Aadhaar claims to have given identity to a billion residents, one must question whether the billion are truly able to identify themselves using it and whether the claims reflect political gesturing or reality.

The Geeks shall Inherit the Earth

While we got our service centre front office sorted, there was the matter of the back office. The software had been written by the National Informatics Centre (NIC), the government's software arm, under Microsoft's guidance, but neither bore responsibility for the land record data. Who exactly was responsible? Figuring it out took a while. The most visible artefact, the data centre where Bhoomi was hosted, was operated by a telecom provider at Khanija Bhawan on Bangalore's Race Course Road. The telecom owned the facility and provided the internet connection. The servers within were managed by another service provider. Physical access was off-limits to us. To access the servers, we found ourselves a couple of floors above, in a government office manned by the staff of the Computer Maintenance Corporation (CMC). They were responsible for the software running on those servers, and I knew from our contract that they received some portion of our revenue. But CMC and NIC, the two key players in Bhoomi, did not seem to talk to each other.

The missing piece turned out to be a collection of independent contractors to the Revenue Department, the Bhoomi consultants, who ran liaison for Bhoomi across the state. They took NIC's software to the taluk offices where master servers were located and ensured data synchronisation with the central repository in Bangalore, from which we ran our public access operations. These Bhoomi consultants, individuals with no apparent hierarchy, essentially ran the show. We had to convince one of them to liaison on our behalf to get anything done. The solutions we came up with would never have cleared audit and the need for them had not even been outlined in the contract, but they were fundamental to our operations. As the product of undocumented negotiations where one could refuse to cooperate without consequence, they inevitably reflected the technical proficiency of the lowest-skilled individual involved.

For instance, we produced reporting software but the government had transaction records. To bypass the firewall between us, the entire state's transaction data was posted to a public website with a URL we kept to ourselves.

The artefacts of such past compromises manifested in documented practices too. Our commercial operation was to accept a search request from a walk-in customer at the service centre, presumably a landholder seeking up-to-date evidence of their land title and to provide a print-out in exchange for Rs 15. The tricky part was in providing evidence that a print-out had been exchanged for money and I was amazed to discover how much hinged on this.

Digitisation had removed land records from VAs, but it had not removed their authority. The certificate was not official until the VA signed it. However, since removing their agency was central to the project, the secretary's interim solution to the problem was to require the VA to sign blank paper before anything was printed on it. The secretary had developed a formidable reputation as a man not to be crossed. He was sharp and short of temper. Within the Revenue Department's offices, where we operated from, he inspired fear and compliance. If the secretary wanted VAs to sign blank paper, he got it.

But if VAs were not tracking how many certificates they handed out, who was? Surely not our hastily-hired operators who could pocket any money they did not report? NIC's solution was to use Microsoft's proprietary ActiveX technology to replace the print dialogue in the web browser. Their replacement would record a transaction every time a print was attempted. All prints were assumed to be successful, even if the paper jammed.

The solution to the paper jam problem was to collect that jammed 'waste paper' and physically present it to the government for a refund. However, since this presented the problem of fake waste paper, specially watermarked paper was ordered. This was functionally plain paper, obtainable as a commodity, but the watermarking required a contractual supplier whose ability to supply was also a factor in overall service availability.

This entire apparatus of shunting paper around the state needed to exist because of how one programmer decided to keep transaction records and his or her central authority existed because of a desire to eliminate distributed authority in the hands of VAs.

The land record certificate service broke down often. Irate land owners would occasionally mob a service centre, thrashing the operator because the computer refused to work and the operator could offer no better explanation than 'system is down'. Since responsibility was divided between us, our internet service provider, Bhoomi's server maintainers, the software developers, and the consultants who kept things together, meetings were often finger-pointing affairs with no one willing to own up.

Hereby I encountered the career techie. One of my crew quit explaining that he had to get married. People in his village knew about Infosys and Wipro. Nobody had heard of Comat. To become an eligible bachelor, he needed to secure a job at a prestigious firm. Our cause did not matter to him. Ensuring food security for the poor, spreading access to knowledge, fixing corruption? All those things were just a job. The career techie was on both sides, only sometimes technically proficient, typically apathetic to anything other than the conditions of their employment, and often an unavoidable obstacle. Cooperation was extracted with a combination of empathy and threat display. Managers did their best to bypass them, adding to their resentment.

We had such meetings over and over again, and I felt a growing awareness. While e-governance was ostensibly an effort to improve things for citizens by removing authority from corrupt petty officials and handing it to a noble higher official, in fact the authority was now in the hands of computer programmers. All decisions were based on how good these programmers were at making computers do their bidding, and most of the time these people had a poor appreciation for the consequences of their choices. Since technology is far too vast for any individual to comprehend, programmers were the new priesthood, commissioned to make the technology god happy, but equally also interpreting the will of this god. (This insight changed my career. After I left Comat, my next venture HasGeek set out to educate techies to wield their power responsibly.)

Platforms Need Governance

I left Comat in 2008. The Aadhaar project began in 2009. Many of their design decisions correspond with what I encountered. The most striking of these:

1. A reimagination of the citizen–state relationship centered on a technology platform intended to work for the majority, but not universally.
2. A desire to eliminate local discretionary authority, achieved by projecting this major solution as a universal solution, disclaiming responsibility for the newly excluded.
3. A weak regard for citizen rights in an architecture designed for state and central officials.
4. A technology procurement organisation bestowed with this responsibility (UIDAI), which—like the undesirable discretionary authority it replaced—will defend its own existence above its mission.

Our idealistic plan for accountable governance in 2006 came out severely changed from the rough and tumble of field operations. We heard, on the one hand, from articulate bureaucrats with particular visions of how things should work, and on the other hand, from citizens seeking their entitlements with only a surface understanding of state machinery. This disparity shows in the outcomes. My visual cryptography scheme for holding the state accountable to the citizen, flawed as it was, disappeared in six months. Biometric verification, which holds the citizen accountable to the state, has thrived over the past decade.

As platform operators, it should have been our responsibility to ensure better representation from both sides, but we only saw ourselves as a retail operation, in the business of selling information services. The failure on all sides to recognise the true nature of our operation facilitated a massive centralisation of power and curtailment of citizen rights.

Aadhaar's proponents could do well to learn from the experience of an even larger technology platform. Facebook, with twice the membership, runs its own opaque government regulating the 'citizens' of its social network. Facebook's lack of transparency on how it operates, long justified as its prerogative as a private company, has come under criticism lately for its role in propagating fake news, thereby allowing foreign influence on the United States presidential election of 2016 (particularly via the political consulting firm Cambridge Analytica). Regular government is divided into three branches, the legislative, executive and judiciary, because conflicts and mission creep are inevitable, and a strong system of checks and balances is absolutely necessary. When a platform's toy government threatens a real one, it can no longer be dismissed as a toy.

Platform advocates are fond of citing Lawrence Lessig's aphorism 'code is law' to justify Aadhaar's existence. If technology platforms inevitably tend towards centralised monopolies, they say, it is better to have a public monopoly than a private one, to have the democratically elected Government of India control your identity by literally codifying law in computer code, instead of Facebook or Google. This horrific confusion about how both code and law work is a source of much angst.

Evangelist outfits like the iSPIRT Foundation exist to promote the new platform order, but in the process have become apologists for this authority instead of questioning it. They, UIDAI and the government could all do well to recognise the threat Aadhaar presents.

Note

1. For an academic treatment of the same projects, see Rajadhyaksha 2013.

References

Evans, David S., Andrei Hagiu, and Richard Schmalensee. 2006. *Invisible Engines*. Cambridge: MIT Press.

Evans, David S., and Richard Schmalensee. 2016. *Matchmakers: The New Economics of Multisided Platforms*. Boston: Harvard Business Review Press.

Rajadhyaksha, Ashish, ed. 2013. *In the Wake of Aadhaar*. Bangalore: Centre for the Study of Culture and Society.

Williams, Robin, and David Edge. 1996. 'The Social Shaping of Technology'. *Research Policy* 25 (6), pp. 865–99.

8

Aadhaar's Biometric Tsunami

Will it Sweep Away Privacy, Drown Civil Liberties?

Shyam Divan

The Aadhaar (Targeted Delivery of Financial and other Subsidies, Benefits and Services) Act, 2016 (hereafter, the Aadhaar Act) seeks to harness the magic of biometrics to deliver services to Indian citizens. Simply put, it mandates the world's biggest biometric database while raising serious privacy concerns.

This law validates a biometric collection programme that the government conceived in 2009. The programme has operated for several years under shadowy executive orders that empowered a small department of the government to sweep up biometric information from residents without counselling them on the impact of their actions. The Aadhaar Act is intended to provide a veneer of respectability and a legal prop to this programme. Briefly, it mandates the world's biggest biometric database while raising serious privacy concerns.

The programme, popularly known as the 'Aadhaar' project and now the umbrella statute, was under challenge before the Supreme Court in a batch of petitions. The Supreme Court was to decide on the validity of government actions and the constitutionality of the legislation by 2 October 2018, when the incumbent Chief Justice of India retired.

The Indian Supreme Court is an independent and assertive apex judicial body with a reputation for upholding citizens' rights and checking excessive government interference. The *Aadhaar case* poses special challenges; however, not least amongst them is the dimension of technology that some judges may be shy to grapple with. During the interim hearings in 2015 before the Supreme Court, the Attorney General for India doubted whether Indians had a fundamental right to privacy. Acknowledging nearly 30 judgments that explicitly recognised the right to privacy as a fundamental right, the Attorney General reached out to an early precedent of the Supreme Court containing an observation that privacy rights were not constitutionally guaranteed. Consequently, a three-judge bench of the Supreme Court that was hearing the *Aadhaar case* referred the matter to a larger Constitution bench of at least five judges.[1] On 24 August 2017, a unanimous panel of nine Supreme Court judges rejected the government's stand and held that privacy was indeed a constitutionally protected fundamental right.[2] The first obstacle placed by the state is overcome; several remain.

While the petitions before the Supreme Court bristle with several complex issues, here I propose to outline the programme and alert readers to its potential impact on civil liberties, political rights, privacy and the freedoms that may be endangered. Indeed, this project is potentially so invasive and disruptive that it shakes the foundation of limited government and permanently alters the relationship between citizen and the Indian state.

What is Aadhaar?

The expression 'Aadhaar' means 'base' or 'foundation' in the Hindi language but in Gujarati, and occasionally in Hindi as well, it could also mean 'crutch' or 'support'. This is ironic because these shades of meaning stake out competing visions. While the government seeks to make biometrics the base or foundation for all its programmes and usher in a utopia of seamless services on demand, critics apprehend that Aadhaar will constrict access to services and entitlements apart from working as an electronic leash to tether citizens to a central computer and pose grave threats to national security. In this dystopia, Aadhaar is a crutch on which the citizen must lean.

Aadhaar is the brand and logo of Unique Identification Authority of India (UIDAI), an administrative body created by the Government of India on 28 January 2009. The Aadhaar number is a random, unique 12-digit figure issued to each person who successfully enrols for it. Although until 2016 there was no specific legislative or even administrative notification that permitted UIDAI to collect or use 'biometric information', the government in its role of a benign benefactor aggressively promoted the project, assuring citizens that this would eliminate red tape and petty corruption. UIDAI, headed by a charismatic pioneer of India's software industry, packaged the initiative as a cure for 'ghost' recipients of government pensions and subsidies and an antidote to dubious agents who skimmed away a part of the subsidy before it reached the beneficiary.

The Biometric Connection

Biometrics are distinctive measurable characteristics of a person that may be used to label and mark individuals. Biometric indicators include DNA, palm prints and each individual's distinctive voice and gait.

The biometric information being collected by UIDAI comprises: (1) a facial photograph of the individual; (2) all 10 fingerprints; and (3) a scan of both irises. UIDAI encrypts and stores this information in a vast data bank, the Central Identities Data Repository (CIDR).

Biometric information of an individual is integral to his or her body. The right to bodily integrity is so fundamental that we frequently take it for granted in the rush and tumble of our busy lives. In a system that respects human rights and an individual's privacy, unlike a totalitarian state, eventual control over biometric information ought to remain with the individual. In a hyper-connected, wired world, retaining autonomy and dominion over biometric information is crucial for enjoying privacy, a value that appears to mean less to younger generations.

The Procedure Adopted by UIDAI

The procedure adopted by UIDAI is casual. Briefly, the entire process at the field level is in the hands of private enterprises known as 'enrollers' who operate freely without any government supervision worth the name. They comprise an assortment of trusts, societies, proprietory concerns, partnerships and companies. The biometric information of each enrolee—that set of valuable parameters that we ought to most fiercely guard—is spirited out without any counselling on the benefits and pitfalls of parting with the biometric information. The biometrics are initially captured by private hands before being transmitted to the UIDAI CIDR via a memory stick, courier or by direct uploading. The UIDAI has no pact with the enrolling agencies. The loose relationships linking UIDAI to the collection of biometric data are based on a 'Memorandum of Understanding' between UIDAI and state governments or departments known as registrars. It is these registrars who engage private sector enrolment agencies.

Together with the biometric information, the private agencies also collect demographic information of the enrolee, such as the address and date of birth, and may ask for bank account, mobile number, email address, parents' name and the parents' Aadhaar numbers.

Enrollers are encouraged to maximise enrolment through a fiscal incentive. The enroller receives payment for every fresh enrolment that is 'de-duplicated' or verified by UIDAI.

Upon receiving the biometric information, the process of de-duplication—which is undertaken to ensure that the same individual is not issued two Aadhaar numbers—is carried out by foreign contractors who exercise proprietory rights over the technology that they employ.

Verification

The Aadhaar verification system works online through the mobile telecommunication network. The service provider—say a bank or a supplier of a cooking gas cylinder—reads the customer's fingerprint on a small device. This fingerprint reader may have a GPS locator by which its location can be pinpointed. The biometric identification is confirmed against the data stored by the UIDAI in its central depository and a real-time confirmation is issued about the existence of the person, confirming or denying if she is an imposter. UIDAI expects scores of 'Apps' to be developed that will employ Aadhaar as the verification platform or gatekeeper. There are numerous gates, both visible and invisible, that we walk through every day. Consider these gateways that may be opened through a fingerprint confirmation—unlocking a mobile device; opening the front door to a home, office or any other building, unlocking a car, picking up tickets at a cinema, registering attendance at a school, college or office, withdrawing money from a bank teller, paying for a cab by an Aadhaar-enabled debit card, entering an airport, boarding an aircraft and checking into a hotel.

Aggressive Promotion and Enrolment

After launching the scheme in rural Maharashtra in September 2010, the project gradually extended across the country. Nearly 1 billion individuals have since been enrolled under the scheme. Though the project was supposed to be voluntary, the government carried out a relentless campaign through residential neighbourhoods, educational institutions and businesses to require residents to part with their biometric information and receive an Aadhaar number. Aadhaar was marketed as a single or unique identification that would replace alternative methods such as a driving licence or a voter ID card. Best of all, it was free and, in the government's telling, there was no downside.

The publicity engine of government (and media reports) created an impression that Aadhaar would soon be mandatory and this worked to herd residents to enrol. The aura of governmental sanction persuaded millions of residents to line up at the enrolment centres and part with their personal biometric and demographic information to private operators without any safeguards in place. This continued—virtually unchallenged—for five-and-a-half years.

Soon, government departments began insisting on Aadhaar numbers to register the sale of properties, to certify a marriage and for the payment of salaries. There were reports of a child not being allowed on a school picnic because he did not possess an Aadhaar number. Indeed, the government campaigned for

Aadhaar numbers to be issued at birth and marketed it by saying it was a necessity. The biometric collection of the newborn was postponed by five years.

Concerned about the coercive element of the Aadhaar programme, the Supreme Court of India issued interim orders holding that Aadhaar is voluntary and subject to a few exceptions, government services may not be denied for want of an Aadhaar number.[3]

What the Government Says

Now that the project is supported by the Aadhaar Act, 2016, the government defends its programme at all levels. According to the state, there is nothing wrong with collecting biometric data of all residents, particularly since the programme is 'voluntary'. The Aadhaar number provides an identification for millions of Indians who otherwise were isolated from the economy for the lack of a genuine identity card: an identity that more privileged Indians had in the form of a passport or driving licence. To assuage privacy concerns, the government reassured the public that the UIDAI only provides online verification where the Aadhaar authentication service responds with a 'yes/no', keeping all personal identity information secret.

Citizens' Concerns

The Constitution of India, like other constitutions that set out the basic law for democratic governance, employs an array of checks and balances to ensure an open and accountable government where each wing of the government performs its actions for the benefit of the people, within its sphere of responsibility. The checks and balances are many and amongst them are the respective roles assigned by the Constitution to the legislature, the executive and the judiciary. Provisions in the Constitution, such as the fundamental rights chapter (Part III), circumscribe the authority of the state. These limitations on the power of the state support the notion of constitutionalism or 'limited government'. In this sense, the expression 'limited government' means that each wing of government is restricted by provisions of the Constitution and other laws and is required to operate within its legitimate sphere. Exceeding these limits would render the action of the state *ultra vires* the Constitution or a particular law.

The second and broader connotation of 'limited government' is the idea of a limited government *qua* the citizenry as a whole. This means that there are certain things that the state simply cannot do, because the action fundamentally alters the relationship between the citizen and the state.

The large-scale collection of biometric data including fingerprints and storing it at a central depository, *per se,* puts the state in an extremely dominant position in relation to the citizen. Biometric data belongs to the concerned individual and the state cannot collect or retain it to be used against the individual or to his or her detriment in the future. Further, the state cannot put itself in a position where it has the ability to track an individual and engage in surveillance. The state can neither deprive a citizen of her rights, nor make them conditional to her parting with her biometrics.

The third notion of 'limited government' means that individually, every citizen and collectively, the citizenry are entitled to live, work and enjoy their varied lives without being under the continuous gaze of the state. The Constitution of India is a compact between the people of India and the state. The essence of this compact, as evident from the Preamble to the Constitution, is that Indian society and the Indian nation would foster justice, liberty, equality and fraternity in the widest sense. Every citizen is inherently entitled to secure an education, hold property, engage in social and cultural activity, travel and pursue vocations, recreations and other myriad activities *without* the state knowing about her every move or maintaining a centralised record of these activities. The citizens of India enjoy this rich raft of rights against the state, which are drawn from the Common Law, statutes, the Indian Constitution and a higher order in the form of the 'basic structure of the Constitution'.

A citizen is entitled to enjoy all these rights including social and civil rights, such as the right to receive pensions and benefits under government schemes, without having to part with his or her personal biometrics. An individual's biometrics, such as fingerprints and irises, are the property and entitlement of that individual and the state cannot coerce an individual or direct her to part with biometrics as a condition to enjoyment of rights and entitlements. Every citizen has a basic right to informational self-determination and the state cannot exercise dominion over a citizen's proprietary information, either in individual cases or collectively, so as to place itself in a position where it can aggregate information and create detailed profiles of individuals. The Constitution of India is not a charter for a police state which permits the state to maintain a lifelong log of each individual.

This is why some citizens apprehend that Aadhaar operates like an electronic shackle to bind every citizen from the cradle to the grave.

Moreover, biometrics as a technology is unreliable and at times serves as an instrument of exclusion, depriving persons who are otherwise entitled to financial and other subsidies, benefits and services, from receiving their due.

The accuracy of biometrics is dubious for a variety of reasons. For instance, biometrics of individuals who are engaged in manual labour change over time and the ridges on the fingers of those who are aged, etc. smoothen out and cannot be captured effectively by biometric devices.

The Aadhaar Act is designed to facilitate and encourage private sector operators to create applications that depend upon the Aadhaar platform for the purposes of authentication. This would mean that non-governmental, private sector entities such as banks, employers, any point of payment, taxi services, airlines, colleges, schools, movie theatres, clubs, service providers, travel companies, etc. could all utilise the Aadhaar database and may also insist upon an Aadhaar number or Aadhaar authentication. Consequently, at every stage in an individual's daily life, his or her presence could be traced to a real-time location.

Even assuming that biometrics, such as a fingerprint, are unique, the nature of human and societal interactions is such that individuals leave traces of their fingerprints on several media in the course of a day. These fingerprints can be easily lifted and misused for identity theft. This is quite apart from the danger of some agencies of the government misusing core biometrics and planting them to create a false presence or false interactions by an individual.

Aadhaar does not serve as an identity but serves as a method of identification. Every interaction of the citizen with the state and a service provider requiring identification is sought to be captured and retained by the government at a central base. A whole ecology would develop that would require reference to this central database on multiple occasions during the day. In other words, the Aadhaar Act impermissibly creates the foundation for real-time, continuous and pervasive identification of citizens, in breach of the freedoms guaranteed under the Constitution.

One of the dangers of centralised databases that are connected to the internet is that the information stored on these computers can be hacked and illegally accessed to steal information. Identity theft enables third parties to utilise biometric and demographic information stolen, and enables these parties to electronically impersonate persons while accessing data that is most sensitive or important for an individual. Here are a few instances:

In Brazil, a doctor 'used silicone fingers' to sign in for absent colleagues, ostensibly to game a biometrics-based attendance system (*BBC World* 2013).

A hacker faked a German minister's fingerprints using high-resolution photos of her hands (Hern 2014).

The FBI misidentified one Mr Mayfield as the culprit in the Madrid Bombing Case by incorrectly matching his fingerprints against the suspect's, for which Mr Mayfield later won a civil suit against the FBI in 2006 (Eggen 2006).

The Aadhaar Act, 2016 seeks to sanctify the Aadhaar project. Even when interpreted narrowly, the scope of the Act extends to every 'benefit', 'service' and 'subsidy' defined in sections 2(f), 2(w) and 2(x) of the Act. The scope of these expressions, even at their narrowest, will cover an individual's life virtually from birth till death. For example, the Aadhaar project is issuing numbers to newborn children immediately upon registration of birth, frequently in conjunction with the hospital or maternity facilities. There are several situations where a newborn child or the mother may be in need of the benefit or service that would be covered by the scope of these expressions. Later, children would be entitled to benefits for food, education, scholarships, health interventions, etc. and in each of these situations, the Act envisages authentication through the Aadhaar system. As a person attains adulthood and his or her societal interactions increase, the number of occasions for receiving benefits, services and subsidies are likely to increase. For example, every payment of salary or pension and attendance at a workplace may require Aadhaar authentication.

One major concern is that the Aadhaar lays the framework for real-time surveillance. Simply stated, the biometric capture and authentication procedure operates in the following manner:

(i) Each and every electronic device that is linked to the internet has a unique identification. This is similar to a vehicle registration number, a cellular telephone number or a cheque number, which makes that item uniquely identifiable.

ii) In addition to this generic 'unique identification', when an electronic device is linked to the Aadhaar system's server, the devices electronically exchange information, and at this stage the system will designate a unique identification number to a particular device, which is called its registered device ID. This registered device ID is designed to be the permanent ID in respect of that device *qua* Aadhaar. Illustratively, if a particular authentication device is reading a fingerprint and it is linked to the system, Aadhaar will designate a specific ID to that device at the first interaction and thereafter, whenever that device authenticates an Aadhaar, the transmission will be recognised as emanating from that device.

(iii) The transmission between the external device (now with its registered device ID) and the Aadhaar server will be carried on a network comprising wire and wireless systems. Regardless of whether the message is transmitted through a wire, a unique electronic path attaches to each transmission, which identifies the links through which the message is transmitted and each of these links is uniquely identifiable.

(iv) In a transmission between a registered device (such as fingerprint reader) and the CIDR, it is technically possible to track and trace the electronic route taken by every transmission. This implies that it is possible to electronically track down the location of every registered device in real time. This is because the authentication transaction, comprising a cycle of request and response, can be completed in as little a time period as 3–5 seconds.

(v) Hypothetically, in a situation where Aadhaar authentication is required at the stage of, say, withdrawing money from a teller machine, clocking in at a government office and receiving cooking gas cylinder, it would mean that at each of these stages, the physical location and the broad nature of the transaction would easily be discernible by the state.

The upshot is that should the Supreme Court challenge fail, the state will have a capacity to very easily track down and trace the physical location of every individual seeking authentication with reasonable accuracy and will also have the capacity to assess the broad nature of the activity the person is engaged in. This is a framework of an authoritarian police state. Aadhaar, some fear, will lead to the garroting of civil liberties.

Intimately related to the fundamental principle that a person has full dominion and control over her core biometrics, just as she has over her body and personal autonomy, any collection of personal biometrics can only be done through the individual's free and informed written consent. In contrast, 1 billion Indian citizens have been issued Aadhaar numbers without any counselling on the pitfalls and limitations of the programme. The government claims that by presenting herself for enrolment, consent for use of biometrics is deemed to have been given despite the absence of written consent or counselling.

In addition to these concerns, there is an apprehension that the Aadhaar authentication system could compromise financial and national security. These concerns stem in part from the Aadhaar back office being operated and run by multinational corporations with no particular affiliation to India's national interest. With Aadhaar numbers being embedded in the databases of government departments, telecom providers, banks and other service providers, the potential for identity theft and fraud has increased. If, as its proponents hope, Aadhaar becomes the golden key to unlock an individual's digital world, a hostile hack or malware could severely compromise financial transactions.

India stands at an important juncture with respect to privacy. Lured by the promise of better services, over a billion Indians have parted with their biometrics and ceded information autonomy, without fully understanding the implications of the bargain. While the Supreme Court of India will pronounce on the legality of the Aadhaar project and the Aadhaar Act, the real issue at this crossroad is even more fundamental: In our anxiety to progress and develop, will we surrender the little that is left of the privacy that we enjoy? A decade or two from now, will privacy be viewed as a quaint hangover of the twentieth century or will it remain a core value to be fiercely protected? Much of what we do today and now, in terms of reigning in government and private enterprise who use our biometrics, will decide the contours of invasive technologies and pervasive government. Tomorrow may be too late.

Post-script

On 26 September 2018, the Supreme Court rendered a split verdict (4:1) in the Aadhaar case. The majority downsized the project by curbing its present reach and drastically reduced potential for future application. While upholding most parts of the Aadhaar Act, 2016, the Court struck down the provision that allowed private companies to use Aadhaar authentication to identify consumers. The Court disallowed the forced linking of Aadhaar numbers to bank accounts and cell phones. By shrinking the electronic mesh, the majority hoped to strike a compromise that would contain the power of the state to track and profile citizens, and address serious privacy concerns raised by the petitioners.

The minority held that the legislative procedure followed by Parliament to enact the Aadhaar Act, 2016 was a 'fraud on the Constitution', since the Rajya Sabha was bypassed. Moreover, the minority found that the project was unconstitutional in its entirety. It compromised privacy in the most invasive ways and created the architecture for state surveillance.

Both the state and private corporations will retaliate. Fresh legislation and lobbying will attempt to inflate the Aadhaar balloon back to its ominous, pre-judgment size. Citizens will summon their fundamental rights again. The final battle against Aadhaar awaits.

Notes

1. *K. S. Puttaswamy v. Union of India*, (2015) 8 SCC 735.
2. *K. S. Puttaswamy v. Union of India*, (2017) 10 SCALE 1.
3. *K. S. Puttaswamy v. Union of India*, (2014) 6 SCC 433; (2015) 8 SCC 735; (2015) 10 SCC 92.

References

BBC World News. 2013. 'Doctor "Used Silicone Fingers" to Sign in for Colleagues', 12 March. Available at http://www.bbc.com/news/world-latin-america-21756709 (accessed 11 November 2016).

Eggen, Dan. 2006. 'U.S. Settles Suit Filed by Ore. Lawyer', *Washington Post*, 30 November. Available at http://www.washingtonpost.com/wp-dyn/content/article/2006/11/29/AR2006112901179.html (accessed 11 November 2016).

Hern, A. 2014. 'Hacker Fakes German Minister's Fingerprints Using Photos of her Hands', *The Guardian*, 30 December. Available at https://www.theguardian.com/technology/2014/dec/30/hacker-fakes-german-ministers-fingerprints-using-photos-of-her-hands (accessed 11 November 2016).

9

Aadhaar—Constitutionally Challenged

Prasanna S.

Since 2009, the Aadhaar project, aiming to give to each resident of India a unique 12-digit identification number, has been underway. This project, initially operated under an executive notification dated 2009, was given statutory status following the passage of the Aadhaar Act, 2016 as a Money Bill. Such a central identification system, operating and controlling a central database of personal profiles, raises questions of constitutional importance and they were raised in writ petitions filed in the Supreme Court and high courts from 2012 onwards.

The petitions challenged the constitutionality of the project and later, the Act, on a number of grounds. An exhaustive list of those grounds is as follows:

First, it was argued that the project violated the citizens' right to privacy, which is guaranteed under the Constitution. This is because the project gave the government the power to operate and control a central database of personal profiles, and to capture and store transaction logs for each transaction. It contemplated the re-engineering of virtually every IT system in the country to incorporate the UID number and the identification mechanism provided by the project, thereby profoundly facilitating convergence of all personal data held by almost all players—state and non-state. The potentiality of such a system's use as a tool of mass surveillance by the state was also raised as a related ground.

Second, it was contended that mandatory Aadhaar production and/or authentication contemplated an unreasonable, unconstitutional and unconscionable bargain, where citizens were made to part with their intimate personal data and biometrics for accessing essential rights, such as the right to food and the right to shelter. Even for the purpose of transfer of subsidies, such an unconstitutional condition that has no relation to the subsidy being transferred cannot be imposed. Further, pilot studies and the field experience indicated that such insistence on Aadhaar is actually resulting in widespread exclusion, resulting in people who were otherwise eligible to receive benefits and subsidies not being allowed to access them merely because they either did not have Aadhaar, could not get themselves enrolled,[1] or that the Aadhaar system could not assign them numbers,[2] or they could not get themselves authenticated online because of problems relating to electricity or connectivity at the point of service or problems relating to authentication failures (Government of India 2017: 194).

Third, it was contended that the overall unreliability of biometrics as the basis of the system was irrational, unreasonable and arbitrary and, therefore, manifestly unconstitutional. The petitioners produced documents to show not only how biometrics were unrealiable in practice, but also that biometric technology can never be reliable, even in theory.

Fourth, it was contended that the manner of implementation of the project—from engaging unaccountable private enrolment agencies for collection of data to employing foreign companies that have links from foreign intelligence agencies for providing the biometric de-duplication and authentication algorithms and technology base, was both a personal security, and a national security, violation.

Fifth, it was argued that the exercise was against the principles of federalism to the extent that it contemplated a complete lack of the role of the state government in the area of public welfare and social and economic planning, a field that the state government and authorities have an equal, if not higher, mandate to operate on.

Sixth, not unrelated to the federalism point, was the contention that the Act should not and could not have been passed as a Money Bill, bypassing the Rajya Sabha. A Money Bill under Article 110 of the Constitution of India, unlike other bills, requires only passage through Lok Sabha and the Rajya Sabha's role becomes purely recommendatory. A bill ought to satisfy conditions under Article 110(1) for it to be a Money Bill. The final decision on whether any bill is properly certified as Money Bill rests with the Speaker of the Lok Sabha under Article 110(3).

More importantly, the petitions also contended that such a project fundamentally altered the relationship of a citizen with the state. They argued that a citizen's right to identity, personhood and all other rights derived from being recognised as a person were being made subject to the assertions and claims made by this database system. And that the citizen has no reasonable control over such a database system—both due to asymmetry of information and asymmetry of power.

The array of petitioners before the Supreme Court included Justice Puttaswamy, a retired judge of the Karnataka High Court. His petition was the first to get to the Supreme Court in 2012, which challenged the project predominantly on the ground that it had no legislative basis and that it is unconstitutionally helping illegal immigrants gain citizenship rights. Another petition by Major General Sudhir Vombatkere, an ex-serviceman, and Bezwada Wilson, who leads the *Safai Karamchari Andolan*, the movement to eradicate the practice of manual scavenging and a Magsaysay award winner, laid emphasis on the privacy challenge. Another challenge was mounted by Aruna Roy and Nikhil Dey of the Mazdoor Kisan Shakti Sangathan and the National Campaign for People's Right to Information—their petition emphasised the potential and actual exclusion due to the adoption of Aadhaar for disbursing life essentials and basic subsidies such as rations under the Public Distribution Scheme (PDS), mid-day meal, work and wages through National Rural Employment Guarantee Act (NREGA), pensions, etc. Colonel Mathew Thomas, also an ex-serviceman, started a petition emphasising the theoretical impossibility of using biometrics and the national security concerns with the project. In their petition, the *Beghar Foundation*, an organisation working for the rights of the homeless, emphasised the exclusion the project was causing among the homeless urban poor. Vickram Crishna, who worked in the fields of engineering, design, media and management consultancy for over 30 years, emphasised the mass surveillance aspect of the project. The *Nagrik Chetana Manch*, an organisation working on issues related to transparency and accountability in governance, predominantly challenged the use of Aadhaar identification and the security loopholes in its manner of implementation for banking purposes and how such a step has led to an increase in money laundering, of proportions threatening the economic sovereignty of the nation. Shantha Sinha, a child rights activist, Padma Shri awardee and also a recipient of the Ramon Magsaysay award, and Kalyani Menon Sen, a women's rights activist, dealt with exclusion in detail and sought to debunk the claims of savings that the government was attributing to the adoption of Aadhaar in welfare schemes.

The Supreme Court gave its first order in the matter on 23 September 2013.[3] Among other things, this was a time when the then United Progressive Alliance government had begun implementing the Direct Benefits Transfer (DBT) schemes, including the DBTL (Direct Benefits Transfer of Liquefied petroleum gas) scheme, and these were being actively pursued. For DBTL, the government had made Aadhaar-seeding mandatory even though the scheme was still being said to be 'voluntary'. The Supreme Court, which heard arguments by senior advocate Anil Divan, who had appeared for Justice Puttaswamy and senior advocate Shyam Divan who appeared for Vombatkere and Wilson, concerned that the enrolment to the scheme was being made de facto mandatory even without statutory backing[4] and that Aadhaar cards were also being given to illegal immigrants,[5] directed that:

> In the meanwhile, no person should suffer for not getting Aadhaar Card in spite of the fact that some authority had issued a circular making it mandatory and when any person applies voluntarily, it may be checked whether that person is entitled for it under law and it should not be given any illegal immigrant.

Following the 23 September 2013 order, three public sector oil marketing companies, namely the Indian Oil Corporation, Bharat Petroleum Corporation Ltd and Hindustan Petroleum joined the UIDAI and the Ministry of Petroleum and Natural Gas, and applied to the Court to modify its order and allow them to make Aadhaar mandatory for DBTL. However, this application was not allowed and the earlier order was reiterated on 26 November 2013, even as the Court directed that all state governments also needed to be added as party respondents in the litigation.

Even as these matters were pending in the Supreme Court, the Goa bench of the Bombay High Court passed an order directing the UIDAI to share biometrics of all persons in a locality with the CBI in connection with criminal investigation of a case involving the offence of rape and sexual assault.[6] The UIDAI came rushing to the Supreme Court challenging that order, on the grounds that such sharing was not contemplated under the scheme and would amount to violation of privacy and the terms under which such data was shared by citizens with them. The Supreme Court, in March 2014,[7] restrained the UIDAI 'from transferring any biometric information of any person who has been allotted the Aadhaar Number to any other agency without his consent in writing'. Further, it made it clear that,

> More so, no person shall be deprived of any service for want of Aadhaar Number in case he/she is otherwise eligible/entitled. All the authorities are directed to modify their forms/ circulars/ likes to as to not compulsorily require the Aadhaar Number in order to meet the requirement of the interim order passed by this Court forthwith.

Despite these repeated directions by the Supreme Court, the authorities of central and state governments continued to make Aadhaar a mandatory precondition for various services and purposes. In March 2015,[8] when the matter came up for hearing, the Supreme Court directed thus:

> In the meanwhile, it is brought to our notice that in certain quarters, Aadhar identification is being insisted upon by the various authorities, we do not propose to go into the specific instances. Since Union of India is represented by learned Solicitor General and all the States are represented through their respective counsel, we expect that both the Union of India and States and all their functionaries should adhere to the Order passed by this Court on 23rd September, 2013.

The batch of petitions next came up for hearing before a bench of three judges led by Justice Chelameswar and included Justice Bobde and Justice Nagappan in August 2015 for a final decision on the constitutionality of the Aadhaar scheme. As arguments began, the then Attorney General for India, Mukul Rohatgi, raised a preliminary objection and told the Court that the right to privacy is not guaranteed under the Indian Constitution. Insofar as the petitions against Aadhaar raise questions of infringement of privacy, those questions would need to be referred to a constitution bench.[9] Rohatgi referred to inconsistency in the jurisprudence that had developed on the question of the right to privacy being guaranteed under the Constitution as a fundamental right. He relied on a 1954 eight-judge bench decision of *M.P. Sharma*,[10] and a six-judge bench decision of 1962 in *Kharak Singh*[11] that seemed to record an observation that the right to privacy is not guaranteed under the Constitution given that there was no such explicit right provided for under the Constitution. Rohatgi submitted that the long line of decisions of smaller benches, starting from *Gobind*[12] in 1975 (three judges), had overlooked the binding larger bench decisions in *Sharma* and *Kharak Singh*, in deciding on the basis that privacy was a guaranteed fundamental right. Those appearing for petitioners contested this claim and argued how the jurisprudence of fundamental rights had undergone a tectonic shift following the *Bank Nationalisation*[13] case in 1970 (11-judge bench) and *Maneka Gandhi*[14] in 1978 (seven-judge bench) and therefore, there was no error in any of the decisions starting from *Gobind*. However, the Court ruled in favour of the government on that point and decided that the matters ought to be referred to a constitution bench to give quietus to that controversy.

However, the Court was cognisant of the fact that the scheme continued to operate and flourish, notwithstanding the earlier orders of the Court and thought it fit to give much stronger interim protection to the petitioners, as it directed[15] that:

> Having considered the matter, we are of the view that the balance of interest would be best served, till the matter is finally decided

by a larger bench if the Union of India or the UIDAI proceed in the following manner:

- The Union of India shall give wide publicity in the electronic and print media including radio and television networks that it is not mandatory for a citizen to obtain an Aadhaar card;
- The production of an Aadhaar card will not be condition for obtaining any benefits otherwise due to a citizen;
- The Unique Identification Number or the Aadhaar card will not be used by the respondents for any purpose other than the PDS Scheme and in particular for the purpose of distribution of foodgrains, etc. and cooking fuel, such as kerosene. The Aadhaar card may also be used for the purpose of the LPG Distribution Scheme;
- The information about an individual obtained by the Unique Identification Authority of India while issuing an Aadhaar card shall not be used for any other purpose, save as above, except as may be directed by a Court for the purpose of criminal investigation.

The central government, along with the governments of Haryana, Maharashtra, Gujarat and Rajasthan (incidentally, the ruling coalitions in all these states were headed by the Bharatiya Janata Party, as was the centre), and statutory authorities such as the Securities Exchange Board of the India, the Telecom Regulatory Authority of India, the Central Board of Direct Taxes, the Reserve Bank of India, and the Insurance Regulation and Development Authority of India, unhappy with the 11 August order, applied to the Court to modify the order to allow them to make voluntary use of Aadhaar for their purposes. These applications, filed in October 2015, were initially listed before the same three-judge bench that had referred the petitions to be heard by a Constitution bench. The bench, however, ruled that they had no jurisdiction to entertain the applications as the petitions they had referred were no longer before them and asked the union government and others to get the petitions listed before the Constitution bench instead.

On 15 October 2015, the then Chief Justice of India (CJI) constituted a bench of five judges to hear and decide only the applications for modification of the 11 August 2015 order.

The Constitution bench that was led by the CJI himself and consisted of Justice Nagappan, Justice Eqbal, Justice Arun Mishra and Justice Amitava Roy decided to partially modify[16] the 11 August order to include four more uses—the Pradhan Mantri Jan Dhan Yojana, Mahatma Gandhi NREGA, National Social Assistance Programme (providing for widow and old-age pensions), the Employees Provident Fund and Employees Pension Schemes—in addition to the PDS and LPG schemes that the earlier bench had allowed. Even so, the Court made it clear that Aadhaar shall be purely voluntary till all the cases are heard and decided finally. This order was the sixth[17] time that the Supreme Court made it clear that Aadhaar cannot be insisted upon as a mandatory condition for any purpose whatsoever. However, the Supreme Court's orders continued to be flouted and contempt petitions[18] continued to be filed before the Court. Those contempt petitions were also tagged along with the main matters.

Meanwhile, the Aadhaar (Targeted Delivery of Financial and Other Subsidies, Benefits and Services) Act, 2016 was passed in March 2016 as a Money Bill in March 2016. The Act was fully brought in force in September 2016. Petitions challenging the Act led by existing petitioners Vombatkere and Wilson started hitting the Court in October, on grounds similar to those that challenged the original scheme, in addition to other grounds such as the legality of the Act's passage as a Money Bill.[19] Those petitions were also admitted and tagged along with the original set of cases.

In March 2017, the Finance Act was passed which, among other things, amended the Income Tax Act to add Section 139AA that made it mandatory for all PAN card holders and tax payers to link their Aadhaar with PAN and to specify their respective Aadhaar number in their income tax return. This provision was challenged by three petitions, among whom were also Vombatkere and Wilson. The counsels for the petitioners, senior advocates Shyam Divan and Arvind Datar, argued on grounds other than privacy.[20] It was during the hearings in this case that the Attorney General, on the day he was to leave for Geneva to defend India's human rights record at the Universal Periodic Review, famously argued that Indians do not have absolute rights over their bodies (Choudhary 2017). The hearings, before Justice Sikri and Justice Ashok Bhushan concluded in May 2017 and the judgment, authored by Justice Sikri, was delivered on 9 June 2017.[21] The bench ruled to largely uphold the provision even as it partially stayed the operation of the consequence of not linking PAN with Aadhaar, for those people who did not already possess Aadhaar. The bench, however, made it clear that its decision on Aadhaar-PAN linking was not a final one, as it did not examine provision on grounds relating to Article 21 of the Constitution, including on the anvil of the right to privacy. The issue had been left open until there is a decision in the main challenge.

On 18 July 2017, after repeated requests by the counsels for petitioners led by senior advocate Shyam Divan, a five-judge bench was constituted to hear the cases, particularly the question on the nature of the right to privacy as a first issue. Attorney General K. K. Venugopal[22] reiterated the government's position on that day that the right to privacy was not a fundamental right. The bench, led by Chief Justice Khehar and including Justice Chelameswar, Justice Bobde, Justice Chandrachud and Justice Abdul Nazeer, in view of the government's stand decided to refer the matter to a bench of nine judges, to decide on the limited issue of the right to privacy, including if need be, to overrule the *Sharma* decision of the eight-judge bench that the government was relying on. A bench of nine judges that included Justice R. K. Agarwal, Justice Nariman, Justice Sapre and Justice Kaul, in addition to the aforementioned five, commenced hearing on that limited point on 19 July. The hearings went on for six full days spanning three weeks and concluded on 2 August.

The judgment by the nine-judge bench on the limited point of the nature of the right to privacy was delivered on 24 August.[23] In six separate opinions but by a unanimous decision, the judgment not only upheld the right to privacy as an inalienable, inherent, basic, fundamental right that can be located in Article 21 of the Constitution and other provisions in the fundamental rights chapter of the Constitution, but also enriched and deepened India's fundamental rights jurisprudence. The judgment also cleared the decks for the main case, that is, the challenge against the Aadhaar project to be heard.

The hearings on the main case commenced from 17 January and ended in early May 2018. Meanwhile, the court extended most of the Aadhaar-linking deadlines in its order dated 15 December 2017 as an interim arrangement. Apart from the petitioners, the central government, the UIDAI, some state governments and the Reserve Bank of India, interestingly, corporate interests such as Digital Lenders' association also intervened to 'save' Aadhaar.

Over four months after the case was reserved for judgment, the Supreme Court gave its 1,448-page long verdict. The majority judgment, led by Justice A. K. Sikri, upheld the Aadhaar project and Aadhaar Act insofar as it is used only for welfare subsidies, welfare benefits and welfare services paid out of the Consolidated Fund of India and additionally for linking PAN cards with Aadhaar.

The majority struck down other uses of Aadhaar including private sector use, E-KYC for banks and mobile SIMs, and other uses of Aadhaar not backed by law, such as requirement of Aadhaar for Board examinations or entrance examinations, accessing earned pensions, requirement of Aadhaar for children's education, etc., and held them to be unconstitutional. The disssenting opinion of Justice D. Y. Chandrachud, on the other hand, struck down the entire project and the Act as being unconstitutional, virtually accepting each one of the petitioners' contentions—including that the Act was null and void for being incorrectly certified as a Money Bill. The majority opinion has certainly addressed the petitioners' concerns relating to mission creep, convergence and unlawful profiling caused by Aadhaar being seeded in multiple databases, including private companies. It has, in many ways, clipped the project's wings. It, however, refused to deal with exclusion due to Aadhaar, and it relied on assurances given by the Attorney General and the UIDAI to frame appropriate regulations to ensure no one is deprived of her entitled benefits. It remains to be seen how this plays out on the ground—particularly in a case in which the union government, the UIDAI and the larger eco-system of companies have repeatedly played hide-and-seek with the Supreme Court, with conduct varying from creative interpretation of Supreme Court orders (such as the mobile-linking order) to blatant violations of its directions—something that even the majority judgment acknowledged as unfair and which the dissenting opinion termed as contumacious.

Notes

1 Reasons being physical disability, the enrolment stations being too far away, etc.
2. Among other reasons, also because of biometric de-duplication rejecting the enrolment as a false positive duplicate of an existing Aadhaar holder's biometric.
3. Order dated 23 September 2013 in W.P.(Civil) 494 OF 2012 etc., Supreme Court of India.
4. The scheme was operating under an executive notification dated 28 January 2009. A bill to give statutory backing titled National Identification Authority of India, Bill, 2010 was pending in the Rajya Sabha. The bill was referred to the Parliamentary Standing Committee on Finance. By its 42nd Report in 2011, the Standing Committee, led by Yashwant Sinha, recommended that the bill not be passed and further recommended that the project be discontinued.
5. Justice Puttaswamy's petition raised the concerns that because Aadhaar was so easy to get, illegal immigrants were enrolling for Aadhaar and apprehended that that will be used to illegally claim citizenship. This issue was not raised in other petitions.
6. Order dated 26 February 2014 in CRLWP No.10/2014, of The High Court of Bombay at Panaji.
7. Order dated 24 March 2014 in Special Leave to Appeal (Crl) No(s).2524/2014, Supreme Court of India.
8. Order dated 16 March 2015 in W.P.(Civil) 494 OF 2012 etc., The Supreme Court of India.
9. A Constitution bench, in legal terms, is a bench of the Supreme Court consisting of a minimum of five judges. Under Article 145 of the Constitution, any case involving questions relating to the interpretation of any provision of the Constitution ought to be referred to a Constitution bench.

10. AIR 1954 SC 300.
11. AIR 1963 SC 1295.
12. (1975) 2 SCC 148.
13. (1970) 1 SCC 248.
14. (1978) 1 SCC 248.
15. (2015) 8 SCC 735.
16. (2015) 10 SCC 92.
17. Starting from 23 September 2013, followed by 26 November 2013, 24 March 2014, 16 March 2015, 11 August 2015 and finally on 15 October 2015.
18. Contempt petitions are petitions brought to the Court to complain of, among other things, persons violating the Court's orders. Contempt powers of the Supreme Court are governed by Article 129 of the Constitution of India and the Contempt of Courts Act, 1971.
19. Although the Speaker's decision is final on the question of the certification of a bill as Money Bill, there are past decisions of the Supreme Court, such as in Khihoto Hollohan v Zachillu (1992) SCC Supl. (2) 651, wherein it has been held that the Speaker's decision is beyond appeal, but not beyond review.
20. Grounds relating to privacy were not pressed, as that would have entailed even those petitions being tagged with the pending petitions, resulting in potentially not getting a hearing in time before the provision became effective.
21. (2017) 7 SCC 59.
22. Mukul Rohatgi had declined to continue in June 2017 and senior advocate K. K. Venugopal was appointed to that position on 3 July 2017.
23. (2017) SCC Online SC 996.

References

Choudhary, Amit Anand. 2017. 'Citizens don't have Absolute Right over their Bodies: Government'. *The Times of India*, 3 May.

Government of India. 2017. *Economic Survey 2016–17*. New Delhi: Ministry of Finance.

Ministry of External Affairs. 2017. 'Universal Periodic Review III—India's National Report 27th UPR Session of UNHRC', May.

10

THE PRIVACY JUDGMENT*

Gautam Bhatia

On the 24 August 2017, a nine-judge bench of the Supreme Court delivered its verdict in *Justice K. S. Puttaswamy vs Union of India*,[1] unanimously affirming that the right to privacy is a fundamental right under the Indian Constitution. The verdict brought to an end a constitutional battle that had begun almost exactly two years ago, on 11 August 2015, when the Attorney General for India had stood up during the challenge to the Aadhaar Project and declared that the Constitution did not guarantee any fundamental right to privacy. The three judges hearing the case referred the constitutional question to a larger bench of five judges which, in turn, referred it further to a nine-judge bench. The case was argued over six days in the month of July, during which the Union of India, with many supporting state governments, the Unique Identification Authority of India and Telecom Regulatory Authority of India, repeated the Attorney General's 2015 claim—a claim which, as we shall see, was decisively rejected by the Court.

Six out of nine judges—Justices Chelameswar, Bobde, Nariman, Sapre, Chandrachud and Kaul—delivered separate opinions (Justice Chandrachud wrote for himself and on behalf of then Chief Justice of India Khehar, Justices Aggarwal and Nazeer). Spanning 547 pages, *Puttaswamy* is undoubtedly a historic and

---

* A previous version of this chapter was published as Gautam Bhatia, 2017, 'The Supreme Court's Right to Privacy Judgment–I: Foundations', *Indian Constitutional Law and Philosophy*, available at https://indconlawphil.wordpress.com/2017/08/27/the-supreme-courts-right-to-privacy-judgment-i-foundations/.

landmark verdict of our times, and one of the most important civil rights judgments delivered by the Supreme Court in its history. Apart from affirming the existence of the fundamental right to privacy under the Indian Constitution—for which each of the nine judges must be unreservedly applauded—*Puttaswamy* will have a profound impact upon our legal and constitutional landscape for years to come. It will impact the interplay between privacy and transparency and between privacy and free speech; it will impact state surveillance, data collection, and data protection, LGBT rights, the legality of food bans, the legal framework for regulating artificial intelligence, and many other issues that we cannot now foresee or anticipate. For this reason, the judgment(s) deserves to be studied carefully, and debated rigorously.

In this essay, I will provide a brief account of what was held in the judgment and what it might mean for the future. There are two possible ways of going about this task: *first*, to analyse each judge's opinion separately, discover points of overlap and bases of agreement, and finish with an analysis of the verdict as a whole. The second is to identify some of the core themes that occur throughout the separate opinions and address them separately. In this series, I shall be adopting the latter course of action, that is, a thematic analysis of the verdict and its component judgments.

At the outset, it is important to draw an important distinction between what is found in the *operative order* of the Court, and everything else that is found in the six separate opinions. The operative order is a page-long statement at the end of the verdict, signed by all the nine judges, and it is only this order that is legally binding upon future benches of the Supreme Court and the high courts. There are two reasons for this. The first is that it is this order that answers the two referral questions that were before the Court, and the reason why the nine-judge bench was established in the first place (see next section of chapter). And the second is that with six separate opinions, there is no real 'majority' judgment (Justice Chandrachud's opinion, that commands the support of four judges out of nine, is a plurality, but not a majority). There is likely to be extensive debate over whether there are certain legal propositions that command the support of five or more judges. This is an important debate, because these propositions—and how they are interpreted—will inevitably shape the way that future benches decide concrete privacy cases brought before them.

Notwithstanding that, however, it is important to remember that ultimately, the Court was answering two legal questions put to it by a smaller bench. In the course of answering these questions, it was obliged to traverse wide and extensive legal terrain. However, the very fact that this entire enquiry was conducted in the abstract should caution us against treating the discussion beyond the referral questions as laying down binding propositions of law. Rather, the 547 pages of discussion, in my opinion, are better understood as setting up signposts and guidelines that will assist lawyers, judges and academics in shaping the contours of the right to privacy under the Indian Constitution in the years to come.

To take a few examples, this verdict does not—and could not—decide whether and to what extent the Aadhaar Project is constitutional, whether and to what extent public figures can prevent the publication of unauthorised biographies or biopics, or the circumstances and the extent to which the state can surveil its citizens. What this verdict does do, however, is that it provides the *constitutional framework* within which these cases are to be debated and decided when they come before the courts.

Therefore, let us begin with examining operative order, which expresses the unanimous verdict of nine judges—unquestionably now the law of the land. This operative order lays down four simple propositions of law.

Proposition One: Stands Overruled

Recall that the reason for the initial reference[2] was the state's contention that the judgments of the Supreme Court in *M. P. Sharma*[3] (eight judges) and in *Kharak Singh*[4] (six judges) had held that there was no fundamental right to privacy under the Indian Constitution, and all subsequent judgments to the contrary had been decided by smaller benches. In *Puttaswamy*, four out of the six opinions examined the issue in detail and entirely accepted the petitioners' arguments. On *M. P. Sharma*, Justices Nariman[5] (paragraph 27), Chelameswar[6] (paragraph 7), Bobde[7] (paragraph 5), and Chandrachud[8] (paragraph 26) all agreed that *M. P. Sharma* only held that the American Fourth Amendment[9] could not be incorporated into the guarantee against self-incrimination in the Indian Constitution (Article 20(3))[10]. However, the Fourth Amendment, which was limited to protecting 'the right of the people to be secure in their persons, houses, papers, and effects, against unreasonable searches and seizures' was not, and had never been, exhaustive of the concept of privacy, even in the United States. Consequently, even if *M. P. Sharma* was correct in refusing to find an analogue to the Fourth Amendment in Article 20(3) of the Indian Constitution, that was no warrant for holding that there was no fundamental right to *privacy*—a much broader and more compendious concept. In the words of Justice Bobde:

> M. P. Sharma is unconvincing not only because it arrived at its conclusion without enquiry into whether a privacy right could exist in our Constitution on an independent footing or not, but because it wrongly took the United States Fourth Amendment—which in itself is no more than a limited protection against unlawful surveillance—to be a comprehensive constitutional guarantee of privacy in that jurisdiction.[11]

Proposition Two: Stands Partially Overruled

In *Kharak Singh*, the Supreme Court had considered the constitutionality of various forms of police surveillance upon a 'history-sheeter'. It had upheld reporting requirements, travel restrictions, shadowing and so on (by arguing, in part, that there was no fundamental right to privacy), but had struck down nightly domiciliary visits as a violation of 'ordered liberty'.

The Court's rejection of *Kharak Singh* was based on two prongs. First, it held that the judgment was internally contradictory, because the Court *could not* have struck down domiciliary visits on any other ground but that of privacy; indeed, in doing so, the Court had itself quoted American judgments affirming a right to privacy. As Justice Nariman noted:

> If the passage in the judgment dealing with domiciliary visits at night and striking it down is contrasted with the later passage upholding the other clauses of Regulation 236 extracted above, it becomes clear that it cannot be said with any degree of clarity that the majority judgment upholds the right to privacy as being contained in the fundamental rights chapter or otherwise. *As the majority judgment contradicts itself on this vital aspect*, it would be correct to say that it cannot be given much value as a binding precedent.[12] (paragraph 42; emphasis added)

Justices Bobde[13] (paragraph 6), Chelameswar[14] (paragraph 9), and Chandrachud[15] (paragraph 27) agreed that there existed a 'logical inconsistency' within *Kharak Singh*, in that the Court could not have struck down one facet of police surveillance without invoking the right to privacy. Furthermore, the Justices also agreed that *in any event*, *Kharak Singh's* finding that there was no right to privacy under Article 21 of the Constitution was based on a narrow reading of the phrase 'personal liberty', which in turn was a relic of the judgment in *A. K. Gopalan*[16]. In *A. K. Gopalan*, the Supreme Court had adopted what Justice Chandrachud called the 'silos' approach to Part III of the Constitution, holding that each separate clause dealt with a separate right, and each clause was hermetically sealed from all other clauses. On this reading, 'personal liberty' under Article 21 contained only what remained after subtracting the various freedoms guaranteed in Article 19(1). The 'silos approach', however, had been comprehensively rejected by the Supreme Court in *R. C. Cooper*[17], and in fact, in *Maneka Gandhi*[18], the majority judgment in *Kharak Singh* had been held to be overruled in view of this development. Consequently, as Justice Chandrachud observed:

> The jurisprudential foundation which held the field sixty three years ago in M P Sharma and fifty five years ago in Kharak Singh has given way to what is now a settled position in constitutional law. Firstly, the fundamental rights emanate from basic notions

> of liberty and dignity and the enumeration of some facets of liberty as distinctly protected rights under Article 19 does not denude Article 21 of its expansive ambit. Secondly, the validity of a law which infringes the fundamental rights has to be tested not with reference to the object of state action but on the basis of its effect on the guarantees of freedom. Thirdly, the requirement of Article 14 that state action must not be arbitrary and must fulfil the requirement of reasonableness, imparts meaning to the constitutional guarantees in Part III.[19] (paragraph 24)

Proposition Three: The Right to Privacy is Protected by the Constitution

The rejection of the State's claim based on *M. P. Sharma* and *Kharak Singh* was only half the story. The affirmative case for why privacy *is* a fundamental right remained to be made. At the bar, privacy was argued to be latent within liberty, autonomy and human dignity, apart from being foundational towards ensuring that the freedom of speech, expression, association and religion, remained meaningful. All these arguments figure, in different ways, in each of the six opinions.

Justice Chelameswar, for example, grounded his opinion in the concept of liberty. Defining 'privacy' as comprising of three aspects—'repose', 'sanctuary' and 'intimate decision'—he held that each of these aspects was central to the idea of liberty guaranteed by both Articles 21 and 19[20] (paragraph 36). He then took a series of examples of privacy violations (forced feeding, abortion, telephone tapping and intimate association, to name a few) and grounded them within the broader rights to freedom of the body (Article 21) and freedom of the mind[21] (Article 19) (paragraphs 38–40).

Justice Bobde founded his judgment on 'two values… the innate dignity and autonomy of man'[22] (paragraph 12), which he located in the overarching structure of the Constitution. In addition, he held that privacy was a 'necessary and unavoidable logical entailment of rights guaranteed in the text of the constitution'[23] (paragraph 35). In Justice Bobde's opinion, we find the important insight that to be effectively exercised, the liberties in Article 19(1) (speech, expression, association, assembly, movement) and 21 (personal liberty) require, on occasion, to be exercised *in seclusion*. Privacy, therefore, was 'an enabler of guaranteed freedoms'[24] (paragraph 29) and 'an inarticulate major premise in Part III of the Constitution'.[25] (paragraph 25)

Justice Nariman made an overarching argument, linking the three aspects of privacy (bodily integrity, informational privacy and the privacy of choice)[26] (paragraph 81) with the preamble of the Constitution, which guaranteed democracy, dignity and fraternity[27] (paragraph 82). It was here that the constitutional foundations of privacy could be found. The connection was drawn by him in this manner:

> The dignity of the individual encompasses the right of the individual to develop to the full extent of his potential. And this development can only be if an individual has autonomy over fundamental personal choices and control over dissemination of personal information which may be infringed through an unauthorized use of such information.[28] (paragraph 85)

In other words, individual self-development—which lay at the heart of democracy, dignity and fraternity—was simply meaningless without a right to privacy that guaranteed, at the minimum, security of the body, security of personal information and security of intimate choices.

Very similar reasoning—based on dignity and individual self-determination—was employed by Justice Sapre, who noted that dignity imposes 'an obligation on the part of the Union to respect the personality of every citizen and create the conditions in which every citizen would be left free to find himself/herself and attain selffulfillment'.[29] (paragraph 8) It was also employed by Justice Kaul, who brought dignity and liberty together, noting that 'privacy...is nothing but a form of dignity, which itself is a subset of liberty'[30] (paragraph 40) and 'key to the freedom of thought'[31] (paragraph 52).

These complementary strands of reasoning were brought together by Justice Chandrachud in his judgment. He grounded privacy in dignity[32] (paragraphs 32, 107 and 113) 'inviolate personality...the core of liberty and freedom'[33] (paragraph 34), autonomy[34] (paragraphs 106 and 168), liberty[35] (paragraph 138), bodily and mental integrity[36] (paragraph 168), and across the spectrum of protected freedoms[37] (paragraph 169). Therefore:

> The freedoms under *Article 19* can be fulfilled where the individual is entitled to decide upon his or her preferences. Read in conjunction with *Article 21*, liberty enables the individual to have a choice of preferences on various facets of life including what and how one will eat, the way one will dress, the faith one will espouse and a myriad other matters on which autonomy and self-determination require a choice to be made within the privacy of the mind. The constitutional right to the freedom of religion under *Article 25* has implicit within it the ability to choose a faith and the freedom to express or not express those choices to the world. These are some illustrations of the manner in which privacy facilitates freedom and is intrinsic to the exercise of liberty. The Constitution does not contain a separate article telling us that privacy has been declared to be a fundamental right. Nor have we tagged the provisions of *Part III* with an alpha suffixed right of privacy: this is not an act of judicial redrafting. Dignity cannot exist without privacy. Both reside within the inalienable values of life, liberty and freedom which the Constitution has recognised. Privacy is the ultimate expression of the sanctity of the individual. It is a constitutional value which straddles across the spectrum of fundamental rights and protects for the individual a zone of choice and self-determination.[38] (paragraph 169; emphases added)

There is something of tremendous significance here. Even as it agreed with the petitioners that privacy was a fundamental right, the Court could have chosen to give it a narrow cast and frame. The Court may have limited it to an aspect of dignity or restricted it to a derivative right under Article 21. This would have thrown up difficult initial barriers in future cases, compelling petitioners to shoehorn their claims within the shifting and largely symbolic concept of dignity (and jurisdictions such as Canada provide salutary warnings about how easy it is to constrict rights by pegging them to dignity) or the (diluted) umbrella of Article 21. The Court, however, did the exact opposite. Starting with the basic idea that privacy encompassed the body (and bodily integrity), the mind (and informational self-determination) and intimate choices, all nine judges agreed that privacy was at the heart of individual self-determination, of dignity, autonomy and liberty, and *concretely*, inseparable from the meaningful exercise of guaranteed freedoms such as speech, association, movement, personal liberty and freedom of conscience. Privacy, therefore, was both an overarching, foundational value of the Constitution *and* incorporated into the text of Part III's specific, enforceable rights.

This, in my view, is at the heart and soul of *Puttaswamy*, and the primary reason why this judgment deserves to be a landmark, not only in the annals of Indian constitutional jurisprudence, but across the world. The verdict locates privacy in the grand sweep of democracy and within the core human values of autonomy, dignity and freedom, while also placing it within the realm of the concrete, the flesh-and-blood relationship between the individual and the state. In its attention to the abstract and to the world of concepts, it does not ignore the world in which individuals struggle against coercive state power; and in its care to outline how privacy is concretely meaningful, it does not forget to include it within that constellation of ideas that frame this reality and give it meaning. This is a difficult path to travel. However, all nine judges have demonstrated the intellectual courage required to travel it and the result is a ringing endorsement of the central place of privacy in a modern, constitutional, democratic republic.

Proposition Four: Decisions Subsequent to Kharak Singh Upheld

As the petitioners had repeatedly argued before the Court, there was no need to reinvent the wheel. After *Gobind vs State of MP*,[39] there was an unbroken line of Supreme Court judgments, spanning 40 years, that had repeatedly affirmed the status of privacy as a fundamental right (Justice Chandrachud's judgment examines all the precedent on the point). Petitioners asked the Court to affirm that line of judgments. The Court agreed.

The consequences of this are that the extended discussions in the separate opinions on the scope of privacy, its operation in the public and the private spheres, and its limitations cannot be studied in isolation, but in the context of 40 years of case law. The task of future benches now is to build upon this existing jurisprudence, taking into account, of course, the insights of *Puttaswamy*. This, in conclusion, brings me to an important point. As Apar Gupta (2017) points out:

> While the privacy judgement is a cause for celebration, its full benefit will only come when it is applied to actual state actions that undermine privacy. Adherence to constitutional principle is not an academic exercise, but requires a prompt protection of real rights and liberties. Judicial action should spring at moments when the state oversteps onto the citizen. Few would dispute that determinations on privacy would be of greater benefit when the Supreme Court protects us with foresight rather than retrospect.

The nine-judge bench of the Supreme Court has given us an outstanding foundation for a progressive civil liberties jurisprudence, located in ideas of liberty, dignity, autonomy and privacy. In the times to come, citizens will look to the Court to build upon that foundation and to carry through with the beginnings that it has made in *Puttaswamy*. But in the future, the situations that come before the Court will no longer be abstract, the questions will no longer be purely legal and the pressures will be real, not merely academic. *Puttaswamy* only makes possible what will, in the last analysis, require judicial courage and wisdom to accomplish: meaningful protection of the rights of the individual against the creeping claims of the state. But it is that very possibility—which, if the state's arguments had been accepted, would have been snuffed out at its very inception—that gives us cause to celebrate today.

The Way Forward

In fact, the future relevance of *Puttaswamy* will undoubtedly be contested, given past history. For example, *Maneka Gandhi vs Union of India*[40] is one of the most famous cases in the history of the Indian Supreme Court. It is the crown jewel of our constitutional canon, India's answer to *Brown vs Board of Education*, the case that revolutionised the US Supreme Court's civil rights jurisprudence. It is the judgment that consigned the notorious *A. K. Gopalan* to the dustbin of history, inaugurated an era in which the Constitution's fundamental rights were to be read in an integrated and holistic manner and breathed life into the 'colourless' due process clause of the Constitution.

But Maneka Gandhi did not win her case. Her constitutional challenge to Section 10(3)(c) of the Passports Act failed and the Court accepted the Attorney General's 'assurance' that she would be given a hearing about her passport being impounded. The operative order of the Court, which is rarely quoted, stated:

> Having regard to the majority view, and, in view of the statement made by the learned Attorney-General to which reference, has already been made in the judgments we do not think it necessary to formally interfere with the impugned order. *We, accordingly, dispose of the Writ Petition without passing any formal order. The passport will remain in the custody of the Registrar of this Court until further orders.*[41](emphasis added)

Maneka Gandhi vs Union of India was the repentant Court's *mea culpa* for its abdication during Indira Gandhi's Emergency, the first concrete embodiment of its will to make amends, a precursor to the age of public interest litigation. *Maneka Gandhi* was the point at which the Court abandoned three decades of formalist interpretation and inaugurated a new path where courts would expand the rights of individuals against the state, instead of limiting or contracting them.

But neither the Court's repentance, nor its ringing words about interpreting Articles 14, 19, and 21 together, and not even its inauguration of the substantive due process doctrine, was of any use to the petitioners in the constitutional challenges to the preventive detention provisions of the National Security Act in 1980;[42] or, in 1994, to the constitutional challenges to the Terrorist and Disruptive Activities (Prevention) Act's (TADA) departure from the Code of Criminal Procedure safeguards such as confessions to police officers, upheld on the justification of fighting terrorism;[43] or, perhaps most glaringly, to the constitutional challenge to the Armed Forces Special Powers Act (AFSPA) a few years later.[44]

What then did *Maneka Gandhi* transform exactly? How could the TADA and the AFSPA have been upheld by a Court serious about atoning for what happened during the Emergency? Which anti-civil rights statutes were struck down on the basis of the interrelationship-of-rights theory, or on grounds of substantive due process? To take just three examples, after *Maneka Gandhi*, the Supreme Court continued to uphold book bans,[45] (total) cattle slaughter bans,[46] and 'anti-sodomy' legislation.[47] For all its grand words, *Maneka Gandhi* was more a continuum along a long history of the Court saying many wonderful things, but when it came to the crunch, deferring to the state and finding a 'public interest' that justified the limitation of rights (two exceptions to this general rule are *Selvi vs State*[48] and *Mohd Arif vs Union of India*[49]). The history of the Supreme Court's jurisprudence post-*Maneka Gandhi* warns us, therefore, that what matters more is not grandeur in words, but concrete application.

Justice Puttaswamy vs Union of India has said many wonderful things about the right to privacy. That needs to be acknowledged and praised. However, it is equally important to note that *Puttaswamy* was a case decided in the abstract. The state's arguments were limited to advocating a strict, originalist reading of the Constitution, and the protean nature of privacy—weak arguments at best, even when made by excellent counsel. And in deciding upon the pure proposition of law before it, the *Puttaswamy* bench did all that it could have done in the context of the proceedings before it: declared that a fundamental right to privacy existed, grounded it in Part III of the Constitution and laid down rigorous standards for the state to meet if it wanted to limit the right to privacy.

However, when future benches of the Court are called upon to apply *Puttaswamy*, it will not be quite so straightforward. There will be challenges to dragnet surveillance, where the state will claim that the only way to catch terrorists is to surveil the entire population, and will submit 'evidence' in a sealed envelope to the Court. There will be challenges to DNA profiling laws, where the state will argue that everyone must give up their privacy to help in the national effort to detect and prevent crime. There will be challenges to data collection and data mining, where the state will argue that the loss of privacy is a small price to pay for the gain in efficiency.

This is predictable, because it has happened before, for the last 65 years. The law of sedition was upheld because the Court believed that the state must have the means of 'preserving itself' and freedom of speech was an acceptable casualty. TADA was upheld because the Court felt that police abuse was an acceptable compromise in the fight against terrorism. The Court did not strike down police surveillance in *Gobind*, despite holding that there existed a fundamental right to privacy. In *PUCL*, the Court did not even mandate a judicial hearing as a prerequisite to telephone surveillance under the Telegraph Act. As the Court itself has reminded us many times, in the last analysis, individual interests must 'yield' to larger social interests—and that effectively, it is the state's prerogative to both define the social interest, and to prescribe the means towards achieving it.

But it is the very *point* of individual rights that they prescribe limits upon what the state can do to achieve its goals. In a world without the right against self-incrimination or a right to personal liberty, law and order would be much more efficient. In a world in which the state could ban books and organisations without judicial scrutiny, no doubt counter-terrorism efforts would be facilitated greatly. When you agree that individuals have rights, that there are some things that the state *cannot* do to them no matter how laudable the goal, you agree that there may well be a net loss of efficiency. And you agree because there are other values that exist apart from security, law and order, and efficiency in plugging leaks in welfare programmes. In his book about the Snowden revelations, Glenn Greenwald (2014) puts the point perfectly, when he writes:

> Nations and individuals constantly make choices that place the values of privacy and, implicitly, freedom above other objectives, such as physical safety. Indeed, the very purpose of the Fourth

> Amendment in the US Constitution is to prohibit certain police actions, even though they might reduce crime. If the police were able to barge into any home without a warrant, murderers, rapists, and kidnappers might be more easily apprehended. If the state were permitted to place monitors in our homes, crime would probably fall significantly. If the FBI were permitted to listen to our conversations and seize our communications, a wide array of crime could conceivably be prevented and solved.
>
> But the Constitution was written to prevent such suspicionless invasions by the state. By drawing the line at such actions, we knowingly allow for the probability of greater criminality. *Yet we draw that line anyway, exposing ourselves to a higher degree of danger, because pursuing absolute physical safety has never been our single overarching societal priority.* Above even our physical well-being, a central value is keeping the state out of the private realm—our "persons, houses, papers, and effects", as the Fourth Amendment puts it. We do so precisely because that realm is the crucible of so many of the attributes typically associated with the quality of life—creativity, exploration, intimacy.
>
> Forgoing privacy in a quest for absolute safety is as harmful to a healthy psyche and life of an individual as it is to a healthy political culture. For the individual, safety first means a life of paralysis and fear, never entering a car or an airplane, never engaging in an activity that entails risk, never weighing the quality of life over quantity, and paying any price to avoid danger. (emphasis added)

In its long history, the Supreme Court has invariably favoured the claims of the security state over the rights of individuals. And the crucial point is this: *Puttaswamy, in itself,* is not going to change that. The standards that the Court has laid down—'legitimate purpose', 'necessity', 'proportionality' and 'procedural safeguards'—are commodious ones. For a Court still steeped in the institutional logic that upheld TADA and AFSPA, it is but a short step to argue that (for example) dragnet surveillance is constitutional because, well, anti-terrorism.

There is no doubt that without *Puttaswamy*, we would have been far worse off than we are today. And there is also no doubt that *Puttaswamy* has built a foundation for a new jurisprudence of civil rights. But we must all be equally clear about the fact that the real task will begin now: it will begin with the first bench that is asked to apply *Puttaswamy* to a concrete case where privacy runs up against reasons of state, and it will continue in the months, years and decades to come. The task is not simply to apply *Puttaswamy*, but to use *Puttaswamy* to craft a genuinely progressive civil rights jurisprudence, where the original constitutional compact—that individual rights are *not* subordinate to 'public good', 'social good', 'public interest' (or any other variant of the phrase)—is restored. And that, now, is the responsibility of citizens, of lawyers, and of course, of the judges who will be called upon to adjudicate privacy and liberty claims in the wake of this judgment. For judges, indeed, it is a challenge: to be true to the animating spirit of *Puttaswamy*, and make the hard decision to tell the state that although its aim may be laudable, its motives unimpeachable and its method beneficial, under the Constitution of India, it nonetheless cannot have what it wants.

In that sense, the legacy of *Puttaswamy* is open. It could become what it promises to be—the foundation for a transformative civil rights jurisprudence. Or it could become only a rhetorical lodestar, a beautiful and ineffectual angel, beating in the void its luminous wings in vain.

Time will tell.

Notes

1. *Justice K. S. Puttaswamy vs Union of India*, Writ Petition (Civil) No. 494/2012, decided on 24 August 2017 ('*Puttaswamy*').
2. *K. S. Puttaswamy vs Union of India*, (2015) 8 SCC 735.
3. *M. P. Sharma vs Satish Chandra*, 1954 SCR 1077.
4. *Kharak Singh vs State of UP*, AIR 1963 SC 1295.
5. *Puttaswamy*, supra, para 27 (separate opinion of Nariman J.).
6. *Puttaswamy*, supra, para 7 (seprate opinion of Chelameswar J.).
7. *Puttaswamy*, supra, para 5 (separate opinion of Bobde J.).
8. *Puttaswamy*, supra, para 26 (plurality opinion of Chandrachud J.).

9. Fourth Amendment to the Constitution of the United States.
10. Article 20(3), Constitution of India, states that no person accused of an offence may be compelled to be a witness against himself.
11. *Puttaswamy*, supra, para 5 (separate opinion of Bobde J.).
12. *Puttaswamy*, supra, para 42 (separate opinion of Nariman J.).
13. *Puttaswamy*, supra, para 6 (separate opinion of Bobde J.).
14. *Puttaswamy*, supra, para 9 (separate opinion of Chelameswar J.).
15. *Puttaswamy*, supra, para 27 (separate opinion of Chandrachud J.).
16. *A. K. Gopalan vs State of Madras*, 1950 SCR 88.
17. *R. C. Cooper vs Union of India*, (1970) 1 SCC 248.
18. *Maneka Gandhi vs Union of India*, (1978) 1 SCC 248.
19. *Puttaswamy*, supra, para 24 (plurality opinion of Chandrachud J.).
20. *Puttaswamy*, supra, para 36 (separate opinion of Chelameswar J.).
21. *Puttaswamy*, supra, paras 38–40 (separate opinion of Chelameswar J.).
22. *Puttaswamy*, supra, para 12 (separate opinion of Bobde J.).
23. *Puttaswamy*, supra, para 35 (separate opinion of Bobde J.).
24. *Puttaswamy*, supra, para 24 (separate opinion of Bobde J.).
25. *Puttaswamy*, supra, para 25 (separate opinion of Bobde J.).
26. *Puttaswamy*, supra, para 81 (separate opinion of Nariman J.).
27. *Puttaswamy*, supra, para 82 (separate opinion of Nariman J.).
28. *Puttaswamy*, supra, para 85 (separate opinion of Nariman J.).
29. *Puttaswamy*, supra, para 8 (separate opinion of Sapre J.).
30. *Puttaswamy*, supra, para 40 (separate opinion of Sapre J.).
31. *Puttaswamy*, supra, para 52 (separate opinion of Sapre J.).
32. *Puttaswamy*, supra, paras 32, 107 & 113 (plurality opinion of Chandrachud J.).
33. *Puttaswamy*, supra, para 34 (plurality opinion of Chandrachud J.).
34. *Puttaswamy*, supra, paras 106 & 168 (plurality opinion of Chandrachud J.).
35. *Puttaswamy*, supra, para 138 (plurality opinion of Chandrachud J.).
36. *Puttaswamy*, supra, para 168 (plurality opinion of Chandrachud J.).
37. *Puttaswamy*, supra, para 169 (plurality opinion of Chandrachud J.).
38. Ibid.
39. *Gobind vs State of MP*, (1975) 2 SCC 148.
40. *Maneka Gandhi vs Union of India*, (1978) 1 SCC 248.
41. *Maneka Gandhi*, supra, Order of the Court.
42. *A. K. Roy vs Union of India*, (1982) 1 SCC 271.
43. *Kartar Singh vs State of Punjab*, (1994) 3 SCC 569.
44. *Naga Peoples' Movement for Human Rights vs Union of India*, (1998) 2 SCC 109.

45. *Baragura Ramachandrappa vs state of Karnataka*, (2007) 5 SCC 11.
46. *State of Gujarat vs Mirzapur Moti Kureshi Kassab Jamat*, (2005) 8 SCC 534.
47. *Suresh Kumar Koushal vs Naz Foundation*, (2014) 1 SCC 1.
48. *Selvi vs State of Karnataka*, (2010) 7 SCC 263.
49. *Mohd Arif vs Supreme Court of India*, (2014) 9 SCC 737.

References

Greenwald, Glenn. 2014. *No Place to Hide: Edward Snowden, the NSA, and the U.S. Surveillance State.* New York: Metropolitan Books, p. 207.

Gupta, Apar. 2017. 'Privacy, Dignity, Sexual Autonomy'. *Indian Express*, 25 August.

11

The Relevance of Children's Consent under a Mandatory Aadhaar Regime*

Kritika Bhardwaj

In 2017, the central government made it mandatory for children to provide their Aadhaar numbers in order to continue receiving benefits under vital welfare programmes such as the mid-day meal scheme (Chari, Yadav and Chowdhury 2017). Latest figures indicate that over 95 per cent of India's adult population already has an Aadhaar number (Mahapatra 2017). In contrast, the enrolment figures for children are substantially lower (Krishnan 2017; Press Information Bureau 2016). Linking child-specific schemes with Aadhaar reflects the government's intention to plug this gap and drive up the enrolment of children. However, in pushing this policy, little attention has been paid to the ethical and legal issues associated with mandatory enrolment of children under Aadhaar.

Enrolling for Aadhaar typically involves parting with extensive personal information including all 10 fingerprints and both iris scans. This information is permanently stored in a centralised database. Forcing individuals who lack decision-making capacity to part with biometric information has grave implications, especially in light of the Supreme Court's landmark ruling on privacy, where informed consent and decisional autonomy have been recognised as inherent aspects of the right to privacy.

---

* A previous version of this chapter was published as Kritika Bhardwaj, 2016, 'India is Enrolling Infants and Children in Aadhaar—but What about their Consent?', *Scroll.in*, available at https://scroll.in/article/816815/india-is-enrolling-infants-and-children-in-aadhaar-but-what-about-their-consent.

No Informed Consent

The ability to make logical and rational decisions comes with age and the development of one's cognitive skills. These are not new findings—lawmakers have been alive to children's lack of decision-making capacity for a long time. The need of parental consent for children's medical treatment or the legal invalidity of contracts by minors are examples of how the law deals with this.

In the context of Aadhaar, however, the legal framework has no special safeguards for ensuring informed consent of minors. The Aadhaar (Targeted Delivery of Financial and other Subsidies, Benefits and Services) Act, 2016, (henceforth, Aadhaar Act) stipulates that the Unique Identification Authority of India (UIDAI) should take special measures while issuing Aadhaar numbers to children, but does not specify what these might be. The Aadhaar (Enrolment And Update) Regulations 2016 specify that children below five years are not required to provide their biometrics. Their Aadhaar number has to compulsorily be linked with that of either parent (Regulation 5). Every child is mandatorily required to part with her biometrics at the age of five, and then at again at the age of 15 (Regulation 17).

However, the requirement to link parents' Aadhaar information with that of the child is only required till the age of five. For children between the ages of six to 18, the law makes no room for parents' consent for enrolment. It is surprising that the law also does not allow guardians to exercise important rights on behalf of their wards—that of accessing their information and making corrections to it. Even the enrolment form for Aadhaar requires the signature or thumbprint of the applicant herself, irrespective of the enrolee being a minor. The application form for a minor's passport, on the other hand, requires a parent or guardian's signature.

Pertinently, the Aadhaar Act recognises the importance of informing potential enrolees regarding the use of their personal information and the nature of recipients with whom this information is intended to be shared (Section 3 of the Aadhaar Act). This significant provision is rendered almost invalid in the context of a minor, who may be too young to understand these consequences, rendering her consent meaningless. The Act and its corresponding regulations fail to elucidate how this important right can be safeguarded for those incapable of giving valid consent.

Children's incapacity to consent to the collection of sensitive personal information has been given statutory recognition in several countries. In the context of schools using biometric information, the UK Protection of Freedoms Act mandates that written consent of at least one parent is necessary before schools use biometric information of children. This consent can be withdrawn at any stage. Any objection raised by the child overrides parental consent. Further, it is the school's duty to provide reasonable alternatives to make those services accessible if there is no consent. Similarly, the US has the Children's Online Privacy Protection Act to safeguard children's information online. It requires websites and applications to obtain a parent's consent for children below the age of 13. It allows parents to access this information and request that it be deleted.

One may argue that the absence of choice makes the whole issue of informed consent moot. After all, the resultant exclusion from benefits implies that adults would also be forced to enrol. But it is erroneous to think that informed consent is limited only to choice. Understanding and appreciating the consequences of a decision are inherent aspects of decision-making (Charland 2015). This ability to understand and appreciate is, in turn, linked to capacity—which children demonstrably lack.

Arguably, the current legal framework for the enrolment of minors under Aadhaar also falls foul of the standards set by the Supreme Court in its recent decision on the right to privacy. Cognisant of the fact that privacy is conceptually tough to define, the Court nevertheless emphasised the importance of informational privacy—the facet of privacy entitling individuals to exercise control over the collection, use and disclosure of their personal information. The role of consent and decisional autonomy cannot be understated in the context of informational privacy. Effective informed consent is necessary to ensure that information is collected after giving proper notice and is not used in ways that may discriminate or harm the individual parting with their information. A universal ID with no defined purposes, such as Aadhaar, defies this concept.

It is erroneous to think of the Aadhaar project as a simple technological innovation over existing identification systems. To begin with, the permanence of Aadhaar makes it impossible for minors to opt out upon attaining adulthood, robbing them of any opportunity to decide for themselves. More importantly, however, the nature of the Aadhaar project is drastically different from conventional identification systems and comes with significant social consequences, some of which are discussed below.

Privacy Concerns—Lifelong Trail of Transactions

As mentioned above, the information collected by the UIDAI is stored on a centralised database. Besides the personal information collected by the UIDAI itself, this database also keeps a record of all transactions made using the Aadhaar number (Regulation 26). As a result, every time one uses the number, a new entry gets created against one's record in the system. With children being forced to enrol, this database has the potential to create a detailed profile of each child. The Act allows all of this information to be shared if ordered by a court. Since the information can be stored for six months, detailed information from an individual's childhood could be retrieved later in the absence of the relevant context. In his separate, concurring opinion upholding the right to privacy, Justice Kaul highlighted how old, irrelevant and decontextualised personal information could be discriminatory for an individual.

The ubiquity of biometrics may also cause children to become desensitised to parting with such intimate information, and consequently have a lesser regard for personal privacy (Data Protection Commissioner 2007).

Mandating Aadhaar for children to access crucial schemes such as the mid-day meal scheme is, therefore, an ill thought out, if not illegal, policy decision. Evidence suggests that the mid-day meal scheme has had an immense impact on enrolment, retention and regular attendance of students from socially vulnerable backgrounds (Khera 2013). The lack of credible figures on the extent of leakages in such schemes makes the imposition of a mandatory biometric authentication framework wholly unjustifiable (Khera 2017; Yadav 2017).

Practical Hurdles

Besides concerns related to privacy and autonomy, the enrolment of children under Aadhaar is fraught with practical difficulties.

The pilot project for the enrolment of children under Aadhaar witnessed several problems (Makkar 2015). Enrolment agencies found it tough to capture acceptable images because newborns would not keep still. The absence of distinguishing features between children made the photographs meaningless. Further, many children in India are not named immediately at birth. Despite these issues, several states have made Aadhaar enrolment mandatory for receiving even a child's birth certificate (Rao 2017).

This mindless extension of Aadhaar in a manner that erodes long-standing legal recognition of children's incapacity to consent needs to be revisited. Not only is there a complete lack of justification for mandating Aadhaar in this context, but there is also a complete disregard for legal or procedural safeguards to protect children's interests.

Post-script

On 26 September 2018, the Supreme Court of India delivered its judgment in a batch of petitions challenging the constitutional validity of the Aadhaar project. While the majority, comprising three judges, has upheld the Aadhaar Act, it has significantly curtailed the breadth of the project and introduced several important safeguards.

One of the grounds on which the project had been assailed was the mandatory enrolment of children. It was argued before the Court that children lacked the capacity to consent to enrolment and authentication, and therefore, the mandatory linkage to essential child-related schemes was a violation of their fundamental rights. In support, the petitioners relied on international law related to the rights of children and several Indian laws that foregrounded the privacy interests and wellbeing of children, and made necessary deviations to secure their rights.

The Court accepted this argument and held that the enrolment of children under Aadhaar is entirely voluntary. It further held that even voluntary enrolment can only be subject to consent from the child's parent or guardian. Upon attaining majority, the child would also have the option to opt out from Aadhaar. The Court went on to strike down notifications insisting on Aadhaar for school admissions and schemes like the *Sarva Shiksha Abhiyan* as it observed that children have a fundamental right to education under Article 21A of the Constitution and therefore, the insistence on Aadhaar is not for availing any subsidy or benefit. It clarified that a child's Aadhaar cannot be insisted upon so long as she is capable of proving her identity by alternate documents. In addition, the Court also struck down the regulations authorising the UIDAI to maintain detailed transaction logs for over five years, reducing some of the risks associated with profiling of children.

The judgment leaves some room for concern on the efficacy of the right to opt out as, by upholding Aadhaar's linkage with several essential services and benefits, and documents like the PAN card, it is unclear how a recently turned adult can ever truly opt out of the Aadhaar project. However, that said, there is no denying that the majority's decision on this issue is a serious indictment of the government's mindless extension of Aadhaar into areas where it was not only patently illegal, but also wholly unnecessary.

References

Chari, Mridula, Anumeha Yadav, and Shreya Roy Chowdhury. 2017. 'Not Just Mid-Day Meals: Aadhaar Made Mandatory for 11 More Schemes, Violating Supreme Court Ruling'. *Scroll.in*, 5 March. Available at https://scroll.in/article/830946/not-just-mid-day-meals-aadhaar-made-mandatory-for-11-more-schemes-violating-supreme-court-ruling (accessed 26 June 2017).

Charland, Louis C. 2015. 'Decision-Making Capacity'. *The Stanford Encyclopedia of Philosophy*. Available at https://plato.stanford.edu/archives/fall2015/entries/decision-capacity/ (accessed 26 June 2017).

Data Protection Commissioner. 2007. 'Annual Report of the Data Protection Commissioner'. Available at https://www.dataprotection.ie/documents/annualreports/Ar2007En.pdf (accessed 26 June 2017).

Khera, Reetika. 2013. 'Mid-Day Meals: Looking Ahead'. *Economic and Political Weekly* XLVIII (32): pp. 12–14.

———. 2017. 'No Good Will Come From Linking Aadhaar to Mid-Day Meals'. *The Wire*, 24 March. Available at https://thewire.in/118555/aadhaar-mid-day-meals/ (accessed 26 June 2017).

Krishnan, Suhasini. 2017. 'Aadhaar Eliminated 4.4 Lakh "Ghost Kids" Under Mid-Day Meal: HRD'. *The Quint*, 27 March. Available at https://www.thequint.com/india/2017/03/27/aadhaar-data-shows-44-lakh-kids-under-mid-day-meal-exist-only-on-paper (accessed 26 June 2017).

Makkar, Sahil. 2015. 'PM's Idea to Track Kids from Birth Hits Practical Hurdles'. *Business Standard*, 11 April. Available at http://www.business-standard.com/article/current-affairs/pm-s-idea-to-track-kids-from-birth-hits-practical-hurdles-115041100828_1.html (accessed 26 June 2017).

Mahapatra, Dhananjay. 2017. 'No Aadhaar, No Sops after June 30: Centre to SC'. *The Times of India*, 10 June. Available at http://timesofindia.indiatimes.com/india/no-aadhaar-no-sops-after-june-30-centre-to-sc/articleshow/59077841.cms (accessed 26 June 2017).

Press Information Bureau. 2016. 'UIDAI Generates a Billion (100 Crore) Aadhaars, A Historic Moment for India', 4 April. Available at http://pib.nic.in/newsite/PrintRelease.aspx?relid=138555 (accessed 26 June 2017).

Rao, Maneka. 2017. 'Haryana is Making Babies Enrol in Aadhaar before it will Issue them Birth Certificates'. *Scroll.in*, 1 May. Available at https://scroll.in/pulse/835970/babies-in-haryana-are-being-enrolled-in-aadhaar-before-they-are-issued-birth-certificates (accessed 26 June 2017).

Yadav, Monika. 2017. 'Midday Meals Scheme: Are Corruption Claims Exaggerated?'. *Ideas for India*, 31 July. Available at http://www.ideasforindia.in/topics/governance/midday-meals-scheme-are-corruption-claims-exaggerated.html (accessed 1 November 2017).

12

AADHAAR—FROM WELFARE TO PROFIT*

Usha Ramanathan

In January 2009, when the Unique Identification Authority of India (UIDAI) was set up by executive notification, it was described as 'an attached office under the aegis of the Planning Commission'. The 'initial core team' was to comprise 115 officials and staff, with the officials drawn from central and state bureaucracies. The Director General and Mission Director were to be from the level of the Additional Secretary, Government of India.

Nandan Nilekani was appointed chairperson of the UIDAI on 2 July 2009. He was simultaneously, and in addition, given the rank of cabinet minister. This gave him the status, protocol and privileges of a minister, without having to meet the constitutional requirement that a minister has to be a member of Parliament. Article 75(5) of the Constitution states: 'A Minister who for any period of six consecutive months is not a Member of either House of Parliament shall at the expiration of that period cease to be a Minister'. In any event, since the chairperson of the UIDAI is an office of profit, Nandan Nilekani could not have been both the chairperson and a minister. This device, by which he was given the rank of cabinet minister without the constraints of the position, was used to facilitate lateral induction of corporate leadership into the government.

---

* This chapter draws on two previously published articles: 'Aadhaar Unmasked: Making a Business out of Government Data', *The Statesman*, 18 July 2013; 'What We (Don't) Know about the Companies', *The Statesman*, 12 July 2013.

Then, he was appointed the head of several committees, which allowed him to steer state policy towards the adoption of the UID, while pushing the agenda of cash transfer and the phasing out of subsidies, and advancing corporate business agenda. The committees included the Task Force on Direct Transfer of Subsidies which produced an interim report in June 2011 on kerosene, LPG and fertiliser, and a final report in October 2011. The Task Force also produced an 'IT strategy for PDS and an implementable solution for the direct transfer of subsidy for food and kerosene'. In February 2012, another, similar, report on 'an aadhaar-enabled unified payment infrastructure' for the direct transfer of subsidies on kerosene, LPG and fertiliser, of which Mr Nilekani was the chair, pushed the agenda of UID ubiquity and revamping the subsidy structure.

Nandan Nilekani's appointment in July 2009 and the overlap of project head, cabinet ministerial rank and chair of multiple committees were accompanied by an explicit change in the nature, and ambitions, of the enterprise.

UIDAI, TAG-UP and NIUs: Allowing Private Entry

To recap, the UIDAI, as part of its 'role and responsibilities', was to 'issue necessary instructions to agencies that undertake creation of databases, to ensure standardisation of data elements that are collected and digitised and enable collation and correlation with UID [Unique Identification Number/Aadhaar] and its partner databases'. It was to 'take necessary steps to ensure collation of NPR [National Population Register] with UID'. Registering in the NPR can be mandated under the Citizenship Act, and the Citizenship Rules of 2003. Although biometrics is not within the mandate of the NPR, they have also been collected in the process of building up the NPR database. So, the data mandated to be given to the NPR was being handed over to the UIDAI to become the property of the UIDAI, and we did not even know it!

In the notification was a phrase that said that the UIDAI 'shall own and operate UID database...' This signalled a shift from when the state held data in a fiduciary capacity and limited to the purposes for which the data was being collected. This was an open claim that data was emerging as the new property. (In 2012, a National Data Sharing Policy asserted that the state, and each department that holds data, owns the data that is with it. This can only be termed an appropriation of that which is the right of the people whose personal information it is.)

The National Identification Authority of India Bill (NIDAI), 2010 in its draft form, and as introduced in Parliament in December 2010, gave the first indications of the structure intended for the UIDAI. It bears a remarkable resemblance to what was being worked into the Technology Advisory Group on Unique Projects (TAG-UP) report.[1] There had been no enthusiasm for a statutory framework anyway. Once the Parliamentary Standing Committee on Finance sent the Bill, and the project, back to the drawing board in December 2011, however, the NIDAI Bill went into deep freeze.

In the January 2011 report submitted by the TAG-UP Committee, it described a framework for the handing over of data that is with the government to private companies set up for that purpose. We might have treated the TAG-UP report as another report without a future; except, the budget, in March 2012, set out the Goods and Sales Tax Network to be a National Information Utility. In an indication of how much oversight in policy-making we can expect from Parliament, the concept of a National Information Utility (NIU) was not explained to Parliament, and no one seems to have raised any questions about what it is. So we know, NIUs were a 'class of institutions' that will be 'private companies with a public purpose: profit-making, but not profit maximizing' (Government of India 2011).

Government projects involve two major tasks at the top: policy-making and implementation. Government should make policy, but leave implementation to NIUs. Implementation is weak, and rather than spend time finding correctives, the committee found in this an opportunity for private business interests. So, TAG-UP suggested the setting up of NIUs.

While the TAG-UP committee directly addressed five projects—Goods and Services Tax Network, Tax Information Network, Expenditure Information Network, National Treasury Management

Agency and the New Pension System—it recommended that the suggested framework 'be more generally applicable to the complex IT-intensive systems which are increasingly coming to prominence in the craft of Indian public administration'.

NIUs should have at least 51 per cent private ownership, and government may have between 26 and 49 per cent shares. The advisory group had been tasked to deal specifically with five areas in the customs and tax arenas, but the report expanded the reach of the report 'also (to) other projects that may be launched in the future'. Repeatedly, the report drew on the UIDAI as the model to be followed, and the elements of an NIU were derived from how the UIDAI is structured. The UIDAI to be formally designated as an NIU was then merely a half step away.

The TAG-UP report said that the government would have 'strategic control', that is, it would be focused on how it would achieve the objectives and outcomes, leaving the NIU 'flexible' in its functioning.

And, in a statement that should have produced a great deal of public debate but which has so far been met with a stodgy silence: 'Once the rollout is completed, the government's role shifts largely to that of a customer'. And: 'On the one hand, governments by virtue of their shareholding are owners. On the other hand, the same governments are customers.' As a paying customer, 'the government would be free to take its business to another NIU'; though, given the 'large upfront sunk-cost, economies of scale, and network externalities from a surrounding ecosystem (and what this means is not explained any further), NIUs are ... essentially set up as natural monopolies'. And then, in a salute to the free market vocabulary of choice, it says that 'as a paying customer, the government would be free to take its business to another NIU, if necessary', although 'natural monopolies' that have governmental data as their property are less than unlikely to have competitors.

To ensure a buy-in from the bureaucracy, 'in-service officers' are to be deployed in the NIUs and are to be given an allowance of 30 per cent of their remuneration. Though the report does not say it explicitly, the expectation is that this will find the bureaucrats forging loyalties and developing vested interests.

There is disturbing evidence that the UIDAI provided the basis for the NIU. The report is littered with references to the UIDAI, and suggests that the UIDAI had been functioning as a model for the NIU. The Biometrics Standards Committee set up by the UIDAI in September 2009 and which gave its report in December 2009 declared that the UIDAI intended to 'create a platform to first collect identity details of residents, and subsequently perform identity authentication services that can be used by government and commercial service providers'. The 'UIDAI Strategy Overview', in April 2010, estimated that it would generate Rs 288.15 crore in annual revenue through address and biometric authentication once it reaches a steady state, where authentication services for new mobile connections, PAN cards, gas connections, passports, LIC policies, credit cards, bank accounts and airline check-in, would net this profit. Till then, it was to be funded by the government.

The congruence of the UIDAI and the NIU is further in evidence. As with the UIDAI, 'the project should be rolled out as soon as possible, and iterated rapidly, rather than waiting to roll out a perfect system'.

The January 2011 report of the TAG-UP was followed up with a company being set up to take control of governmental data and to make a business out of it along the lines set out in the TAG-UP report. There have been other reports too, such as the report of the Apex Committee for Electronic Toll Collection Implementation in which RFID and the 'unique identification' of vehicles are part of the recommendations, but this does not directly impact the UID or subsidies, although it does have a bearing on tracking, for instance.

Government as Customer

In sum: governmental data and databases were to be privatised through the creation of NIUs which would then 'own' the data. NIUs would be natural monopolies. NIUs would use the data and the database for profit-making and not profit-maximising, and the definition of these terms were indeterminate.

Government would support the NIUs through funding them till they reached steady state, and by doing what is needed to gather the data, create the database using governmental authority. Once the NIU reaches steady state, the government will reappear as the customer of the NIU. The notion of holding citizens' data in a fiduciary capacity cedes place to the vesting of ownership over citizens' data in an entity which would then have the government as its customer.

This notion of private companies owning our data has not been discussed with state governments, nor with people from whom information is being collected.

Data is the New Property

Technology has created the potential to record, collate, converge, retrieve, mine, share, profile and otherwise conjure with data. Data is the new property. The UIDAI, with its push to enrol the whole Indian resident population, signals the emergence of an information infrastructure facilitated by the government—it finances the 'start up', and uses its authority to coerce people to get on to the database, to be handed over to corporate interests when it reaches a 'steady state'.

Mr Nilekani calls it 'open architecture', that is, applications can be thought up as the business grows; there are no limits or contours within which it should be used. He has repeatedly described the UID as a unique number, which will be universal and ubiquitous; the latter two indicate that, despite being marketed as voluntary, all activities and services are intended to be made dependent on the UID for all persons, ensuring steady business for the enterprise. The UID enrolment form has a column for 'information sharing consent'. This will allow the UIDAI to part with the data, both demographic and biometric, for a price. This explains why there has been so little enthusiasm for a law on the subject.

The UIDAI was imagined as a business entity, governed, if it had to be, by the Companies Act; not bound by a law, and not within the fiduciary responsibility of the state: a project that would be coercive, and find various ways of punishing a citizen for not being on the UID database.

Who has Access to the Data?

In July 2010, UIDAI announced names of the companies that had been selected to implement the core biometric identification system. These companies would design, supply, install, commission, maintain and support the 'multi-modal Automatic Biometric Identification System and multimodal Software Development Kit for client enrolment station, verification server, manual adjudication and monitoring function of the UID application' (*The Economic Times* 2010). These would create the ability to de-duplicate on the basis of biometric information collected during enrolment.

The companies were: Mahindra Satyam (as it then was) partnering with Morpho, HP with L-1 Identity Solutions and a recently set up Indian company 4G Identity, and Accenture with MindTree and Daon. L-1 Identity Solutions was already present and participating in the Proof of Concept (PoC) on enrolment.

These are companies with interesting profiles. A promotional document found on the web, around the time that L-1 Identity Solutions was selected to partner with the UIDAI, speaks of a close connection between the company and the security and intelligence establishment of the US government. 'L-1 provides highly specialised government consulting services that address the most important challenges facing US defence and global security', it announced. 'More than 1000 specialists, most holding top security clearances', it advertises, giving a more specific figure of '93 per cent holding high-level government security clearances'.

In 2007, Tim Shorrock, an investigative journalist based in Washington, took a close look at the connection between L-1 and the CIA in an article he did on the former CIA chief, George Tenet, titled 'Cashing in on Iraq'. Shorrock (2007) wrote:

> Tenet sits on the board of L-1 Identity Solutions, a major supplier of biometric identification software used by the US to monitor terrorists and insurgents in Iraq and Afghanistan… The company with the closest ties with the CIA—and the biggest potential financial payoff for Tenet is L-1 Identity Solutions, the nation's biggest player in biometric identification. L-1's software which can store millions of ID records based on fingerprints and eye and

> facial characteristics, helps the Pentagon and US intelligence in the fight against terrorism by providing technology for insurgent registration (and) combatant identification, the company says. L-1 technology is also employed by the State Department and the Department of Homeland Security…

When L-1 acquired Spec Tal, it got 300 employees with security clearances getting them several agencies with whom Spec Tal had contracts, 'including the CIA, the NSA and the Defence Intelligence Agency'. 'We're in the security business, right? So he's a tremendous asset', Shorrock quotes an executive vice president of L-1 as saying about George Tenet.

Sagem Morpho, which is among the participating companies is the Indian subsidiary of Morpho, is part of the Safran group. Safran is a French defence company in which the French government holds 30.5 per cent shares.

In August 2011, Safran completed its acquisition of L-1 Identity Solutions. It was a $1 billion acquisition. With this, L-1 joins Safran's security business which was until then operating as Morpho, and which together with L-1 was renamed Morpho Trust. Morpho and L-1 had, with this acquisition, merged. So, when Mr Nilekani said that the UIDAI had created a competitive environment, that was not quite accurate.

The L-1 buyover by Safran was held back for about a year between September 2010 and August 2011 till the Committee on Foreign Investment in the US approved the acquisition. Since US contracts make up about 80 per cent of L-1's business, and to protect US national interests, Safran was to establish 'a three-person proxy board' to handle sensitive US contracts—a common feature when security companies are acquired by foreign companies. It was contemporaneously reported that the proxy board was expected to include Barbara McNamara, deputy director of the National Security Agency (NSA) and William Schneider Jr, former Under Secretary of state under Ronald Reagan. India entered into no such arrangements despite the contractual arrangement with L-1 that they would be among the three vendors that would be holding the data—biometric and demographic—of all people enrolling on the UID database.

Accenture is known widely as a consultancy corporation; what is less known is its place in the world of surveillance technologies. Katherine Albrecht and Liz McIntyre, writing about Radio Frequency Identification (RFID) in their book, *Spychips: How Major Corporations and Governments Plan to Track your Every Purchase and Watch your Every Move* (2006), introduced us to the patents and practices of Accenture in the RFID arena. It is interesting that Accenture describes itself as a 'US based business...the global management consulting, technology services and outsourcing company'; no word on surveillance. Yet, in 2004, Accenture was selected by US Department of Homeland Security to design and implement the Smart Borders Project which would be deployed at the land, sea and airports of entry. In November 2012, Accenture was awarded a bio-surveillance contract by the Department of Homeland Security. This proximity and interdependence between foreign governments, including their intelligence agencies, and corporate ventures in surveillance technology is no secret.

A question that has been raised repeatedly in various fora relates to the security of the data. What effect does handing over data to companies that are close to foreign intelligence agencies, or allowing them to handle it, have on the security of the person, and on national security? Laws such as the PATRIOT Act in the US, especially provisions such as section 215, bring all agencies in the country within the control of agencies such as the FBI and the Department of Homeland Security. When the PATRIOT Act became law, section 215 was enacted for a period that would run till 1 June 2015. The sun could set on the clause if it was not endorsed and re-enacted by Congress. A clamour of protest against the extraordinary powers given to the agencies under section 215 finally saw the eclipse of this 'sunset clause', and section 215 was cast into oblivion. It was not renewed. The 2013 Snowden revelations of mass spying by the American establishment stoked debate around the PATRIOT Act and the authority it invested in the national security establishment in the US to launch mass surveillance secretly. In India, it caused no more than a ripple, with a senior Minister even trying to explain it away: 'This is not scrutiny and access to actual messages. It is only computer analysis of patterns of calls and emails that are being sent. It is not actually snooping specifically on content of anybody's message or conversation' (*The Hindu* 2013).

As for Morpho and L-1, the French government is part-owner of these entities. Despite the concerns this should have raised in the UIDAI and within government, there has been silence. The UIDAI's response to a Right to Information (RTI) query is more disturbing still.

In March 2011, Mr Veeresh Malik filed a request with the UIDAI for information, specifically asking for the 'full name, address, websites of the foreign companies which are of US and non-US origin or control'. In an appellate order of 21 July 2011, the Deputy Director at the UIDAI gave the names of three Biometric Service Providers to the UIDAI. These were, (i) Satyam Computer Services/SagemMorpho (ii) L-1 Identity Solutions (iii) Accenture Services. In a startling statement, the authority explained that 'there are no means to verify whether the said companies/organisations are of US origin or not. As per our contractual terms and conditions, only the companies/ organisations ... who are registered in India can bid. Any further information in this regard can be obtained from the UIDAI public domain...' There is nothing more to be got from the UIDAI website.

Colonel Mathew Thomas' RTI query asking for copies of the contracts entered into with the companies was refused by the UIDAI citing section 8(1)(d) of the RTI Act, 2005, which speaks of information including 'commercial confidence, trade secrets or intellectual property', disclosing which would 'harm the competitive position of a third party' to the request. The exception to this provision is if the 'larger public interest warrants the disclosure of such information'. The UIDAI seemed unable to see where the larger public interest lay. Creating a database and handing the data over to companies, and with no discernible protection, should worry a government concerned about the safety of the people and national security, one may imagine; except, the government may have a different vision that keeps this worry at bay.

UID's Commercial Potential

In 2016, around the time that the government decided that it could no longer defer the making of the law (and how the law was made and passed, is another story), radio listeners may have heard advertisements for a company called TrustID offering 'India's 1st Aadhaar based mobile app to verify your maid, driver, electrician, tutor, tenant and everyone else instantly'. The app boasts it can do this in 'less than a minute'. Its punchline—'*Shakalpe mat jaao, TrustIDpe jaao*'—translates to 'Don't go by the face, use TrustID'.

Think about what this means. A private company is advertising that it can use Aadhaar to collate information about citizens at a price. It says this openly, even as a case about the privacy of the information collected for the biometrics-linked government database was still pending in the Supreme Court. That was a time when the court had told the government that it had to severely restrict the uses of the Aadhaar number. Even the Bill that is to govern the project had still not been signed into law and the Bill was still to come up for discussion in Parliament.

This did not surprise anyone who had been watching how the project had been unfolding.

Thus far, the Aadhaar project, which had set out to database the whole population, had been marketed as a means of removing leakage and corruption and ghosts and duplicates in the welfare and subsidy system. The title of the law that was passed by the Lok Sabha—the Aadhaar (Targeted Delivery of Financial and Other Subsidies and Services) Act, 2016—is intended to evoke the idea that this is about the state gaining control over the welfare system. (What happened with the Bill in the Rajya Sabha was made irrelevant by treating it as a Money Bill. This needed a strained reading of the Constitution. It has since been challenged in the Supreme Court, and has been upheld by a process of tortuous reasoning by a majority of the judges on the bench.)

Till 2016, talk about the interest of private companies in the UID database was heard only among those being egged on to create businesses on the UID platform. The 2016 Bill introduced in Lok Sabha, and which was passed into law as a Money Bill, was the first express statement from the government that just about any person or company may draw on the Aadhaar system for its purposes. There were no qualifications or limits on who may use it, nor even why. It depends on the willingness of the UIDAI, which controls the database, to decide who could become a part of the Aadhaar system.

That was the import of section 57 of the Aadhaar Act, 2016. During the debate in the Lok Sabha, Congress MP Rajeev Satav raised a question on clause 57 of the Aadhaar Bill which permits private entities—airlines, telecom, insurance, real estate companies—to use the Aadhaar number. Finance Minister Jaitley did not think it necessary to respond to the question. The government simply chose to ignore the questions raised by the Members of Parliament in the Rajya Sabha and passed the Bill within three hours, rejecting all the amendments that had been proposed in the Rajya Sabha.

Personal data on which businesses can be built is central to the imagination that has spurred the project. Nandan Nilekani, the former UIDAI head who has been the chief spokesperson for the project, called it not an identity, but an 'identity platform' on which apps may be built by any entrepreneur. In 2011, the *Economics Times* reported what Nilekani said in his address to dozens of software developers in Bangalore who were there for a 'UID conference': 'It's really up to the imagination and innovation of the people...In some sense we believe it will be game changing...we don't see this project just as giving someone an ID card. This will create a national-level online identity management platform.'

In 2012, in an interview to McKinsey & Company, Nilekani said:

> But what's equally important is that we expect to see a lot more innovation because of the platform's open API. That's the best way to do this: the government builds the platform but makes it open so that individual creativity and entrepreneurship can build more solutions. Ultimately, what we'd like to accomplish in this role is to create a thriving application ecosystem around the platform. Over the next few years, we'd like to see more apps developed by both the public and private sectors...

At an event held in New Delhi in 2013, he said:

> So that creates platforms.... Now, you have used government benefits to jumpstart this thing. But, once you create the link between the ID and the bank account, you can then start using it for commercial payments...that would then be a business to person thing. The next step would be person to person... (Khosla Labs 2013).

These are just a few illustrations. In fact, several people working with the UIDAI in the initial years left to start ventures that would find ways of leveraging the Aadhaar platform. One instance is Srikanth Nadamuni who joined Khosla Labs, a Bay Area entrepreneurial venture, to expand the uses of Aadhaar.

In June 2015, there was an 'Aadhaar application hackathon' mentored by 'experts from UIDAI, Khosla Labs, AngelPrime and Morpho' to create apps based on the system.

This corporate ambition to exploit the business opportunities of this massive population database has been really what this project is about. It was never about welfare.

Note

1. The Report of the Technology Advisory Group on Unique Projects (TAG-UP) in January 2011 said that the government has a lot of data that it has no ability to manage, so data with the government should be handed over to private companies that would be set up for the purpose, and they would be called National Information Utilities. The government would have between 26 per cent and 49 per cent in the NIUs. They would be natural monopolies. They would be `private companies' acting in the `public interest'; profit making, not profit maximising.

References

Government of India. 2011. 'Report of the Technology Advisory Group for Unique Projects'. New Delhi: Ministry of Finance.

Khosla Labs. 2013. 'On Aadhaar—Fireside Chat with Vinod Khosla and Nandan Nilekani' (video of event held at New Delhi on

4 September 2013). Available at https://www.youtube.com/watch?v=1eLqyQZ7KQ0 (accessed 17 September 2018).

McKinsey & Company. 2012. 'An Interview with Nandan Nilekani'. Available at https://www.mckinsey.com/industries/public-sector/our-insights/an-interview-with-nandan-nilekani (accessed 17 September 2018).

Shorrock, Tim. 2007. 'George Tenet Cashes in on Iraq'. Available at https://www.salon.com/2007/05/07/tenet_money/ (accessed 17 September 2018).

The Economic Times. 2010. 'Accenture, Satyam, L1 Win Deal', 30 July.

The Hindu. 2013. 'It is not Actually Snooping: Khurshid on US Surveillance', 2 July.

13

Public Investments and Private Profits

M. S. Sriram

The Promise

When the Unique Identity (UID) project was announced by the Government of India, it was widely welcomed, though there were early sceptics, who saw through the larger design. It is important to note that the project initially promised to be non-invasive, minimalist and facilitative in nature. The big project that the early proponents of Aadhaar promised was financial inclusion—an area where both identity and transaction trail were most important.

If we were to look at the early presentations made by the then chairman of the Unique Identification Authority of India (UIDAI), Nandan Nilekani, the promise was that it would be a de-duplicated database; it would be available ubiquitously—it was a number and not a card and therefore, even if one lost a document, the identity database would still be intact; and the identity document would be provided at the cost of the exchequer, with no costs to be borne by the user for enrolment, verification or usage. There was also an indication that this was a form of identification given to residents; this could not be used as a right to claim citizenship. Thus, it was a process that could be used just for proving one's identity and nothing more. That is, it would only provide a 'yes' or a 'no' answer to a query and the database could not be accessed by anybody else.

The project also had an interesting system of 'introducer' for people who did not have an extant identity. This was thoughtful and proactively inclusive. There were early sceptics who prophetically read into the larger plan that would unfold (see Ramakumar 2010).

Why was Such a Project Desirable?

Such a project was desirable to provide an easy and hassle-free identification system for the poor. It was desirable because of the following aspects:

- It was unique and de-duplicated;
- It was permanent; even a loss of a document or a movement from one place to the other did not necessitate re-enrolment; and it was accessible at the choice of the resident; and
- It was done at the cost of the exchequer and the expenses incurred by the resident were the transaction cost of reaching the enrolment centre, filling in the form and the time involved in providing the necessary data.

This method of identification was superior to the earlier methods, where the cards or paper could get destroyed, soiled, lost and requesting a fresh document would result in significant transaction costs. The other methods also put the onus on the bearer of the identity to supply certified copies of the identity papers whenever the need arose.

What made Aadhaar agreeable was the promise that this would be an easy process, completely voluntary and the authority would do nothing other than provide a Yes or a No answer based on the database. In a way, it provided the poor one more mechanism—a friendly one—of proving who they were and in case they did not have any extant identity document, through the introducer system, provided them an opportunity to come into the formal financial world.

Coming into the formal world had many opportunities of inclusion. It was acutely felt in the case of financial inclusion where for people without collaterals, an effective and objectively verifiable identity document and data on transaction trails would help them to access many more services than were available at that point. Therefore, riding on the financial inclusion bandwagon was useful, important and desirable.

The Approach

The approach in the initial days of Aadhaar was somewhat inclusive. There were many consultations and several advisory committees which looked at the process of enrolment, the technology, privacy concerns, the issue of safety of data and the legal framework that could work around Aadhaar. While there were pilots that were run, in general, there was a hurry in trying to achieve the enrolment numbers. Very much the way the introducer system was used to get people without extant identity documents, 'registrars' were widely deployed across the length and breadth of the country to achieve the enrolment numbers. The project was rolled out on a mission mode. It appeared that the strategy was to make it so big that it would be difficult to withdraw. Most of the targets that were set in terms of enrolment numbers were achieved much ahead of schedule. The approach of the authority was very succinctly summarised in a book co-authored by Nandan Nilekani, where he writes:

> A true entrepreneur [working within the government][1] would figure out all the government processes and follow them to the letter [Note: it does not say spirit]. He will navigate the byways of bureaucracy, keep his multiple masters happy, get his project mentioned in every important speech and every government document of relevance, get his bills tabled in Parliament and enacted as law, secure his budgets, cooperate with investigating agencies, respond to court orders, answer Parliament questions, tirelessly provide information sought in RTI requests, build a general consensus with multiple interest groups within the government as well as citizen groups outside, find allies who will support him when under attack, and do all this while staying focused on hiring the best team and building an organization that is dedicated towards achieving a well-defined goal. (Nilekani and Shah 2015: xxiii)

The description above was a fair description of how Aadhaar was staffed. The architecture was built with a set of 'volunteers' from the technology world, most of whom worked on a pro-bono basis. Somebody working pro-bono seems to indicate that there are no conflicts of interest and no vested interest. Somewhere down the line, the Aadhaar project demonstrated that pro-bono work could be problematic in two senses. The questions we need to ask are:

First, how do you hold somebody responsible for doing pro-bono work, particularly if this work is for the sovereign, what is the system of accountability? Who are these people answerable to if there are no clear terms of engagement and hierarchy? It is well known that the project was rolled out without a clear legal framework in place and the draft bill proposed by the UIDAI was summarily rejected by the parliamentary standing committee. There were flaws in the project: it was clear that the implementation process took primacy over any other safety and due-diligence processes. It was declared upfront that Infosys would not be involved in any way in the project (since Nilekani was from Infosys) and that the project would be built on an 'open architecture'. This gave a sense of comfort to the public at large, but were there layers in this argument? From a corporate governance perspective, does this declaration by a promoter of a company deny the corporation of potentially bidding in interesting projects that may be immensely profitable to the shareholders of Infosys? Are these commitments in the interests of the minority shareholders? These questions were never asked.

Second, how do you prevent somebody who was privy to the architecture from utilising the knowledge outside of the system once the engagement is over? It is clear that the private sector uses adequate legal cover to draw up non-compete and secrecy clauses. Was this done for the 'volunteers'? If we look at the enterprises promoted by all the former volunteers of Aadhaar project led by iSPIRT, it is evident that the chain of unlocking value of the pro-bono investments made in the project are slowly being realised. That is only the financial bit, but it would be deeply flawed if we look at this only from a financial prism.

Gaining Acceptability

A project of this size and magnitude needs larger acceptance. Two keywords that were put in as bait to gain acceptability for the project were that it would be 'inclusive' and would eliminate 'leakages', or it would weed out corruption.

From a positive note of providing an identity document for somebody who did not have an identity at the cost of the exchequer (important for financial inclusion), it was slowly getting articulated as an eligibility document (for welfare programmes). Eventually, there was also some talk about a revenue model emerging out of the services of identity verification. We need to unbundle the understanding of both the positive aspects of inclusion—largely articulated as financial inclusion and the negative aspect of exclusion through de-duplication and thereby providing a revenue implication for the state.

Financial inclusion was an interesting agenda for the Aadhaar project to get on to. That aspect was being widely articulated and there was a perfect fit in the identity agenda. While there were many aspects why the excluded were not getting included in the formal financial system, the question of identity was made out to be a significant aspect. It is true that having an objectively verified, de-duplicated identity gives comfort to the formal financial system in the modern-day world, where there is much terror financing and money laundering happening, including through small accounts. But we need to ask repeatedly whether identity should have been all-pervasive and centralised.

The argument of corruption and plugging leakages would cut much ice with the discourse of the market-based economy. The argument was that either subsidies were to be done away with, or where they were needed, they needed to be delivered in the most efficient manner. So little wonder that there was more acceptability of the project within the bureaucratic set up and the questions were being raised by the civil society activists.

Financial Inclusion and the JAM Trinity

In addition to the general approach of using financial inclusion as an entry point to establish the potential of a large-scale impact with constant reference being made to the poor, the project gained a greater prominence when this was linked to the mobile technology platform. Parallelly, the new government that took charge in May 2014 also launched an ambitious financial inclusion programme under the name Pradhan Mantri Jan Dhan Yojana (PMJDY), which encouraged every household to have a basic bank account with certain facilities. This scheme was rolled out on a mission mode. While the scheme itself suggested that Aadhaar could be used as one of the identity markers for people to open bank accounts, it was not Aadhaar-centric. Instead, the mission was to open as many bank accounts as possible.

It is now being argued that there are three verticals—the database of identity and verifiability, which is the Aadhaar pillar; the widespread enrolment of households into the banking system through opening a bank account; and the ubiquitous nature of almost everyone having a mobile connection. And thereby comes in the Jan Dhan–Aadhaar–Mobile (JAM) trinity. However, it is apparent that each one of these had a rather independent evolution and an independent logic. None of the verticals grew out of or depended on the other. Therefore, in linking these, there is an artificial welding that is being undertaken.

Let us get back to some basics. While agreeing that there could be merit in a natural evolution of JAM, there is little to be gained by putting this on a mission mode. PMJDY provides an access to a bank account. Whether there would be transactions through the account is a choice of the customer. There could be some loading of transactions into the accounts through mandating that all state-related payments (pensions, scholarships, wage payments, etc.) be done only through a bank account. For this, one needs a bank account that could receive payment mapped to an identity of the beneficiary. Whether this identity document needs to be Aadhaar is a moot point, but let us grant that. This takes care of the payments to be received by the beneficiary from the state. The next question is the form in which the beneficiary should withdraw and use those inward remittances to the account. The idea being mooted here is that the beneficiary (mostly the poor) should move from cash transactions to technological transactions—in this case, the digital platform being provided by the mobile companies.

There are questions on moving away from cash towards digital and mobile-based transactions, particularly for the poor. The issue is that larger transactions have their own logic of the complexity of moving large amounts of cash, the need for traceability of transactions, both for security and for tax compliance purposes. However, smaller transactions on a digital platform are problematic essentially because of the incidence-based transaction charges imposed on the poor. In such instances, it is better to use cash. Therefore, while the integration of databases is an idea that needs to evolve based on the use case, the imposition of any technology and any manner of transactional mode on the people, particularly on the poor, is undesirable.

We need to look at each of these from what they set out to achieve, what could be the potential, rather than to straightjacket them into one form of a prescriptive transactional mode. In any case, we have consistently argued that an identity document is essential to start the relationship (open an account), but all through the history of banking, we have been using identity proxies (signature, pin, password and biometrics) for transactions. With the instability of technology, it is important that we continue to retain the choices.

Growth and Cuts in Consultations

As the project started achieving scale and more and more people were getting enrolled, the consultations reduced and the project became a closed-door project. The battle lines were drawn—those in favour of the project were volunteering and doing pro-bono work, and those against were the civil society activists with no place on the table. Enrolment was happening at a frantic pace with no architecture to verify authentication failure at scale in real settings. Irrespective of the due diligence exercised on the registrars and the protocols for data collection and storing, there were instances where hurried enrolment meant that many of the verifiable parameters (10 fingers, iris and photograph) were not collected accurately.

Figure 13.1: Image of an Enrolment Acknowledgement

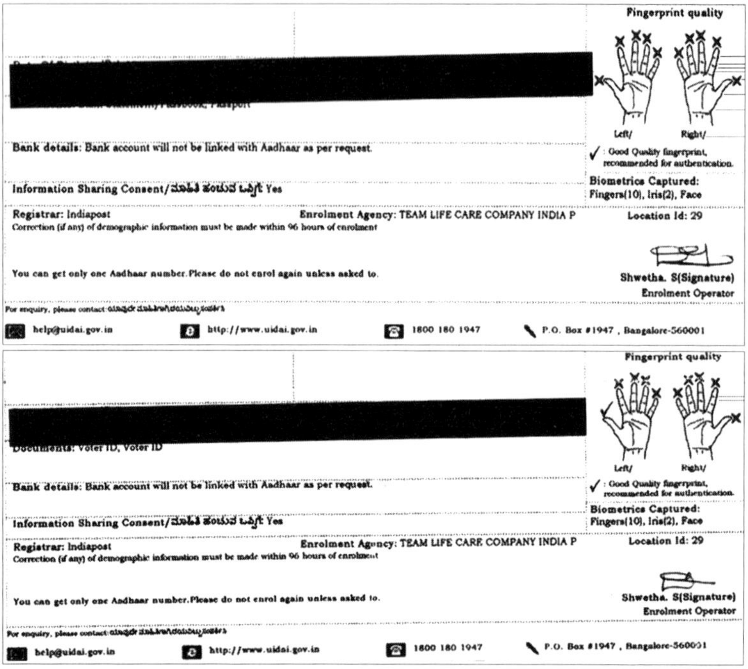

Source: Copies collected from known recipients in the enrolment centre; identity markers are masked to keep their privacy intact. Reproduced with permission.

For instance, let us look at Figure 13.1, where the acknowledgement form indicates that in one instance, nine of the 10 fingerprints are not good for verification and in the other, all the fingers are not good for verification. Still, these persons have received an Aadhaar number. How does this person verify his/her identity on a real-time basis if the fingers did not yield a 'yes' answer? More fundamentally, were the 19 fingerprints that had a cross mark on them good enough to be de-duplicated with the database?

What we had in the process was a fait accompli, a project that is too big and too prestigious to fail. At this stage, dissent was dismissed and disregarded. Engagement stopped and the authorities went into their echo chambers reiterating that they were right and how this could explode into a wonderland of opportunities.

Problems with the Conception of a Linkage with a Centralised Database

Let us discuss both the identity and entitlement issues separately. Identity is necessary to establish a trail that there is no impersonation. This establishment of identity is done through identity proxies—a signature, a password, a personal identification number or a biometric stored at the level of the institution providing a service. Every time an entitlement for a person with a specific identity is to be dispensed, the trail that it was indeed the person who availed of the entitlement has to be established through identity proxies. In the past, this was done through storing these proxies at an accessible and decentralised level. The establishment of identity happened through an identification document, a copy of which was also stored at the decentralised level. Issue of identity documents was also done through a process of verification by several agencies—an employer identification based on the proximity of working and the frequency of contact; a passport based on a police verification of both the identity and the address; a voter's identification based on the place of residence and de-duplication; a landline telephone bill establishing the place of residence through frequency of delivery. Several other identity documents were also acceptable like the Income Tax permanent account number or a driver's license, which were themselves based on a source document that established the identity. This was not biometrically de-duplicated data and therefore, it was possible that a person could have, say, multiple PAN cards or multiple drivers' licences and also multiple residence proofs. However, none of these identity documents, if used correctly, could be impersonated. So, it was possible to have ghost/duplicate identities, but it was not possible to have impersonation given that there were adequate identity markers in the documents.

For the purposes of transacting with any entity, establishing this identity at the time of enrolment and using an identity proxy for every transaction instance was good enough. It was not necessary to verify the identity with a de-duplicated centralised database, since this could be established at the time of enrolment and periodically, if needed.

Beyond establishing an identity, the question of eligibility for entitlement is a function of other tests, whether it is a pension or a subsidy or a classification under the category of below/above poverty line. Therefore, identity is essential for addressing the entitlement issue, but not sufficient. The problem is that the leakages and ghosts ('identity fraud' discussed earlier) that have been talked about are sorted to the extent that the person with the same identity is claiming the benefits twice over, or the identity documents are forged or fabricated.

However, it does not sort out the leakage because of an ineligible but genuine person ('eligibility fraud') getting the benefit. The extant system has the potential to err on both sides—provide benefits to somebody not eligible and deny benefits to somebody eligible, largely due to misclassification and not due to the identity. With the biometrics that are not robust in terms of robustness of enrolment and authentication, the problem of denial of services for somebody with the right identity is real just because the machine fails to authenticate a fingerprint or an iris. This denial is a serious issue and there have been ample studies to indicate the extent of exclusion due to the failure of technology. The localised identity proxies provided multiple mechanisms to sort out the issue of identity, whereas a centralised biometric database provides no recourse. The discretion that could be exercised after due diligence is not to be found in the centralised database.

In addition, there is a larger issue of accountability. In the extant schema, the localised databases assumed responsibility and liability for any mistake. However, now the contract between two parties is being dictated by an involuntary authentication with a centralised database which does not assume adequate liability. While Aadhaar gives the sense that it is a robust database due to the process of de-duplication, it does not do physical verification of the address (as is done in the case of passport) and exclusively relies on technology for the back-end processes. This technology is not failsafe, as is evident.

Changing Goalposts

From advocating that the Aadhaar database would be just a verification database to making it the centrepiece of information and moving of goalposts has happened too quickly for comfort. This is happening from two levels and its pervasiveness is unsettling.

The government issued advisories on the linkage of Aadhaar with the following activities. It is now mandatory for opening of any type of bank account, and in particular for accounts that transact more than Rs 50,000. The contract of a bank account is between a depositor and the bank, and identity is necessary for ensuring that the person is who she claims to be. Since people can open multiple bank accounts, there is no element of ghosts and duplicates, as long as the identity is positively established. In the case of opening a bank account, including a Jan Dhan account, Aadhaar is being moved as the essential document while the other identity proxies are treated as additional documents. While the Aadhaar Act indicates that the mandate of Aadhaar (passed as a Money bill) is essentially to avail of benefits from the state, the opening and transacting with a bank does not entail availing any benefits from the bank, including for Jan Dhan accounts, where the overdraft facility is available only if the linkage is done. The same is being applied to filing of Income Tax returns, to maintaining provident fund accounts, getting LPG connections, school admissions, death certificates, investments in mutual funds and so on. Aadhaar is virtually mandatory, though it was initially envisaged as voluntary.

The private sector, on the other hand, is using the Aadhaar platform to build 'Apps'. iSPIRT, a not-for-profit organisation, has been exclusively set up to incubate and encourage entrepreneurs to build apps on Aadhaar. In fact, the institution being not-for-profit is in itself a problem, because while it is not accountable to the state because it falls under the private sector, it is also not accountable to the markets (beyond the limited and closed shareholder community) because it is not-for-profit. This is a peculiar instance, wherein being a not-for-profit is in itself a problem and cannot be seen as a non-interested party.

The platform with the name Indian Software Product Industry Roundtable (iSPIRT) was set up with the objective of influencing policy-making of the state and catalysing market players to work on the Aadhaar platform. iSPIRT is an amalgam of 30 interested product companies and individual entrepreneurs coming together as a platform.[2]

iSPIRT, is a set of individuals, all 'volunteers', mostly people who worked on the Aadhaar platform, working closely with the policy formulation with the state, with little accountability. They are a think tank, they get consulted, but they are independent and therefore the disclaimer to their advise would be for the recipient (in this case, the state) to exercise caution. But these sets of individuals are embedded in many ways in the state apparatus as a think tank which eventually exerts influence on the policy. That the work is done pro-bono puts a sheen of objectivity which could be questioned. (Thaker (2018) reports that the work was not pro-bono.)

On the other hand, there is a commercial potential of Aadhaar, and to understand this, it is essential to go through the famous WhatsApp presentation made by Nandan Nilekani,[3] which uses the Aadhaar platform for commercial enterprises. Here enters another initiative by the same set of actors. This initiative, called IndiaStack, builds applications (both commercial and non-commercial) on the Aadhaar platform, arguing that Google Maps would not have been possible without the internet and therefore, the Aadhaar platform is a valid platform to build commercial applications. The IndiaStack website indicates that it evangelises the applications to solve much of the difficult policy problems pertaining to service delivery through a technology-enabled architecture, working on a pro-bono basis.[4]

Both these initiatives represent a conflict of interest, and also represent a weak accountability structure with too much of data being accessed. No wonder that it is commonly touted by this group that 'Data is the New Oil' and would be the key to prosperity in the future.

Clearly, when we look at these two initiatives, we are no longer looking at inclusion/provision of an identity, and checking of leakages and corruption as an argument. The argument is of building a new marketplace based on data.

Problems with the Project as it Stands

At the level of seeking benefits from the state, the foremost issue that needs to be addressed is that the authentication mechanism has not been tested at scale at the number of transactions envisaged from a centralised server. Given the large number of authentication failures that are happening, it appears that there is no significant recourse, leading to the exclusion of a statistically significant number of people. The only alternative to this would be a manual override, with some safeguards. The moment we provide for a manual override, we defeat the argument that technology is a superior, failsafe and objective mechanism. Therefore, while this system is not significantly positive on inclusion, it is significantly negative on exclusion.

The digital footprint memory is permanent and every case of violation of the norm, whether intentional or unintentional, is recorded on the database. The poor and vulnerable are bound to have a large number of unintentional violations (like loan defaults) which will not only be permanently there in the database, but might also be used for profiling the citizens for provision/denial of market-based services. This phenomenon can be termed as the 'tyranny of the transaction trail'. This can happen not only in financial services, but in character verification that organisations like TrustID had promised.

While we have discussed unwarranted exclusion, the database and the layers that are being talked about could also lead to unintended inclusion. The number of online lenders that go by the name Earlysalary, Lendoo, etc. are mapping multiple data points including social media profiles to offer financial services to people who might not intend to borrow, leading to an external incentive for a consumptive financial behaviour that might lead to deep indebtedness. Aadhaar only helps this data to get centralised, the targeting sharper, and as of now, provides little recourse.

Increased Transactions Costs for the Poor

The lofty ideal of getting more and more people into the formal sector is welcome as a principle. Formal systems provide a greater amount of transaction trails, greater data and help in sharper policy-making. However, the enthusiasm to get people into formal systems is putting a great burden on the poor in terms of transactions costs. Let us take LPG subsidy as an example. The issue with the LPG subsidy was that of de-duplication and weeding out ghost subscribers. This could have been done easily by re-verification of Aadhaar-based identity which de-duplicates the customer. Having done this, there could have been objective mechanisms of tagging the customer (say, income tax payer) to examine whether they are eligible for a subsidy. Having done this, the LPG could still be supplied to these specified customers at a subsidised rate and the oil companies could have claimed the subsidy from the state in bulk on the basis of underlying eligibility documents. Instead, a transaction which is cash neutral has now been converted into a three-step process: (i) generate and have enough cash for an upfront payment of market prices of LPG; (ii) based on the billing, the oil marketing company transfers the subsidy amount to the customer with a certain lag; and (iii) this amount has to be withdrawn from the nearby bank/ATM/BC in order to be used. Something that was cashless in the first instance has been turned into a cash outflow and inflow transaction under the argument of 'cashless'. The customer has to find time and travel to the proximate banking point in order to get the subsidy.

Let us take another example of use of cash versus digital transactions. As we stand, the cost of printing and circulating the currency is being undertaken by the state apparatus and it is like a public good, available free for the citizen. There is a sense of equity in this because taxes are collected from people who ought to pay taxes, but the facility of using cash is universal. However, the moment cash moves to a digital format, there is a large back-end of settlement for digital transactions, which involves connectivity, authentication machinery, switches and the other paraphernalia, most of which is in the private sector and these transactions would have to be compensated for the services provided. While for large transactions, the compensation (in terms of NEFT/RTGS/IMPS fees) can be justified (for example, it reduces transaction complexity), it does not apply to very small transactions that the poor undertake. In a way, by moving from a cash-based economy to a cashless economy, the state is moving something that was in the public realm to a private realm. The cost that was borne by the exchequer is now sought to be transferred to the user. This is an iniquitous move. The increase in cost is involuntary as against the voluntary use of digital means of transaction for the sake of convenience that most customers do, when they use a card or a mobile wallet.

Public Investments for Private Profits

The argument of IndiaStack is a clear example of private application developers using public infrastructure (Aadhaar). In a physical world, this is like the hawkers on the footpaths and streets built by the state. The difference is that usually, street vendors and hawkers, by the very nature of the job, are most likely to be from the poorer sections of the society; while in case of Aadhaar-based apps, the users of this public property are going to be well-funded business houses or entrepreneurs who have the potential to generate abnormal rents on the basis of using a public architecture. It is even more scary if the state charges the users of this architecture and converts it into a revenue model, because the state then would be playing around with the data of the poor residents. 'Data is the New Oil'—sounds very ominous and scary.

We have made the Aadhaar argument till now as a privacy argument. It is indeed so. However, if we were to consider the points discussed above, we need to shift the argument to that of vulnerability. The poor are being put in a significantly vulnerable position and this architecture looks very iniquitous even in design. It needs to be debated widely and needs more small-level experimentation before it is sledge-hammered into the daily lives of the citizens.

Notes

1. Phrases in parenthesis are of the author of this paper.
2. 'iSPIRT: Why We Exist'. Available at http://www.ispirt.in/who-we-are/Why-we-exist (accessed 2 November 2017).
3. 'Disruption in Financial Services: Nandan Nilekani at TiE LeapFrog'. Available at https://www.youtube.com/watch?v=aGM5TvAUF00 (accessed 2 November 2017); and 'Indian Banking—In a Time for Change—Nandan Nilekani'. Available at https://www.slideshare.net/ProductNation/indian-banking-in-a-time-for-change-nandan-nilekani-64679460 (accessed 2 November 2017).
4. 'About—IndiaStack'. Available at http://indiastack.org/about/ (accessed 2 November 2017).

References

Nilekani, Nandan, and Viral Shah. 2015. *Rebooting India: Realizing Billion Aspirations*. New Delhi: Allen Lane.

Ramakumar, R. 2010. 'What the UID Conceals'. *The Hindu*, 21 October. Available at http://www.thehindu.com/opinion/lead/What-the-UID-conceals/article15786909.ece (accessed 19 October 2017).

Thaker, Aria. 2018. 'The New Oil'. *The Caravan*, 1 May.

14

Is Aadhaar like the Social Security Number?

*Srujana Bej**

India's national identity programme 'Aadhaar' assigns a unique identification number to every resident in the country, accumulates demographic information and operates as the world's largest biometric database (see Unique Identification Authority of India n.d.). To secure the acceptance of Aadhaar amidst bona fide privacy and surveillance concerns, the Unique Identification Authority of India (UIDAI) has equated Aadhaar to the United States of America's Social Security Number (SSN) (Pandey 2017). However, Aadhaar is markedly disparate from SSN because the former functions as an absolute identity number, authenticates identity, collects biometric data and links multiple databases through 'seeding' (convergence) to create dossiers of personal information on citizens (Yadav 2016). Importantly, personal information in SSN is protected by legislation specifically enacted for the purpose of guarding informational privacy. On the other hand, Aadhaar operates in a legal framework that is yet to regulate the ownership of personal information and protect it from potential misuse, collection and dissemination.

Inherently Different Inclinations towards Privacy

SSN carries limited personal information about individuals. At the time of applying for a SSN, the following personal information is

* I would like to thank Reetika Khera for her guidance and helpful comments.

collected—full name at birth, other names used, place and date of birth, mailing address, citizenship status, ethnicity, race, sex, parents' names, parents' SSNs, telephone number, signature and details of any previous SSNs assigned. No biometric information is collected—SSN neither carries information of an individual's fingerprints nor facial photographs.

At the outset, the US government rejected storing individuals' fingerprints in SSN because fingerprint identification was associated with criminal activity in the collective consciousness at the time (Puckett 2009). Later considerations to include biometric information and facial photograph in SSN have also been rejected by the Social Security Administration (SSA). The SSA's 1997 Report to Congress on Options for Enhancing the Social Security Card cautions against including biometric information and facial photograph in SSN on the ground that this would 'increase its usage for non-SSA purposes (e.g., proof of identity), thereby generating more lost or damaged cards needing replacement and, perhaps, creating incentives for counterfeiting' (Social Security Administration 1997). Furthermore, the report advises against incorporating biometric identification in SSN on the grounds that it 'is not universally accepted in our society', 'would require a high level of physical security to ensure electronic information was not tampered with or misused in any way' and 'would add considerable cost to issuing cards when compared to the current process'. The demand for photographs was rejected as it would require updation throughout the individual's life and issuance of new cards. The report concludes that the costs and administrative burdens would exceed potential benefits.

In the following years, the SSA received recommendations from the Office of the Inspector General to integrate biometric matching technology into SSN to address fraud and waste in SSN-based welfare delivery (Office of the Inspector General 2000). In its response, the SSA prioritised privacy concerns, questioned the coerciveness of biometric technologies, asserted that the regulatory legislation does not anticipate the use of biometric identification and emphasised the possibility that biometric matching technologies could disadvantage genuine beneficiaries in the absence of adequate checks (ibid.).

The use of SSN as a personal identifier is relatively sporadic. The SSN is required when applying for a passport, federal education grant, student loan, driver's license, learner's permit, non-driver identification card and in most states, a marriage license. SSN is mandatory for government tax records and employers collect the SSN of employees to properly account for taxes. Additionally, the SSN is used in the records of law enforcement agencies, filings before the Tax Court and in the compilation of master jury lists by courts to remove duplicates and convicted felons. The SSN is also required for bankruptcy procedures, delivery of benefits to veterans and collection of alimony and child care support payments. Although beneficiaries under the Social Security Act are required to provide their SSN, the SSA allows benefit claimants the alternative of providing sufficient additional information such as date of birth, parents' names and birthplace instead. In the private sector, the SSN is usually required by banks, lending institutions, universities, standardised test administering agencies and stakeholders in the healthcare industry (Komuves 1998). However, individuals are not obliged to provide their SSN to private businesses unless the transaction is required to be notified to the Internal Revenue Service or is subject to federal Customer Identification Program rules (Hickok 2015). Of paramount importance with regard to privacy is the fact that despite these uses, the SSN does not have the capacity for storing such additional information of use (Social Security Administration n.d.). Thus, in its use, the SSN broadly resembles the Permanent Account Number (PAN) in India.

At the time of enrolling for Aadhaar, an individual's name, date of birth, gender, address and parent or guardian's name is collected. Aadhaar also collects biometric information—an individual's 10 fingerprints, two iris scans and a digitised facial photograph—during enrolment. While this may *quantitatively* seem to be less information than that collected when applying for SSN, the information collected by Aadhaar is *qualitatively* far less conducive to privacy for the following reasons:

First, the collection of biometric information facilitates invasive surveillance into an individual's life and the commercial exploitation of personal data (Scientific American 2014).

Second, Aadhaar is seeded across multiple government and private databases. This seeding lays bare the private lives of individuals for government agencies and private companies to track and exploit, as one unique number accorded to an individual unveils diverse amounts of personal information about that individual across databases (Ramanathan 2015). Seeding eases the way for governments and corporations to converge data and create meticulous dossiers of personal information on individuals (Hickok and George 2015).

Third, Aadhaar is increasingly growing ubiquitous in the Indian citizen's ordinary life. It is becoming mandatory for opening bank accounts, using a mobile number, filing income tax returns, applying for PAN, applying for driver's license, investing in mutual funds, withdrawing amounts from the Provident Fund, registering deaths and making cash transactions above Rs 50,000. Aadhaar is also essential for a host of government services and benefits.[1] Aadhaar has additionally been made mandatory—without justification—for accessing maps published by the Survey General of India, gaining admission into Delhi government schools, etc. A broad range of private sector companies has also begun to harness Aadhaar in numerous ways that threaten individuals' privacy (Rajshekhar 2016). Furthermore, the government actively pursued the integration of Aadhaar in devices and services produced by global technology firms such as Microsoft Corp., Samsung Electronics Co., Apple Inc., and Google Inc. (Sharma and Alawadhi 2016). Evidently, the mushrooming Aadhaar is intrinsically irreconcilable with privacy, whereas SSN can operate in numerous spheres within the ambit of respecting the inviolability of individuals' privacy.

Comparing Legislative Safeguards for SSN and Aadhaar

Personal information collected in SSN is regulated and protected by the Privacy Act of 1974. In fact, the legislative process of the Privacy Act was prompted by concerns over the risks to individuals' privacy from the creation of a centralised storehouse of data by the federal government's extensive record-keeping practice through SSN (Hanus and Relyea 1976). Thus, the Congressional Findings and Statement of Purpose of the Privacy Act explicitly states that 'the right to privacy is a personal and fundamental right protected by the Constitution of the United States'. Furthermore, it recognises that 'the privacy of an individual is directly affected by the collection, maintenance, use, and dissemination of personal information by Federal agencies'.

The Privacy Act regulates the collection, maintenance, use and dissemination of personal information in all federal government agencies' systems of records that contain any identifying particulars of individuals, including the SSN. Through Section 552a(m)(1), the Act also applies to government contractors and any employees of government contractors performing any of the activities associated with maintaining the systems of records (including collection, use and dissemination) for federal agencies or to accomplish a function of the federal agencies. The section imposes recordkeeping and disclosure restrictions on such government contractors and their employees. In the event of violations by government contractors, the private cause of action for a civil lawsuit lies only against the federal agency.

First, Section 552a(e)(1) of the Privacy Act broadly regulates the collection of data. It authorises agencies to collect, use and disseminate only as much information about individuals as is relevant and necessary to accomplish the statutory purpose of data collection. Data collection must specifically be required and authorised by either legislation or executive orders. For example, the Social Security Independence and Program Improvements Act of 1994 specifically allows SSN to be collected for its use in jury selection.[2]

With particular respect to SSN usage, Section 7(a)(1) of the Privacy Act provides that it is unlawful for any federal, state or local government agencies to deny individuals benefits, rights or privileges conferred by the law on account of refusal by individuals to disclose their SSN. Only two exceptions are allowed to this general rule by Section 7(a)(2)—either Congress must have provided specific permission by statute for the disclosure of SSN or there must exist a statute or regulation operating prior to 1 January 1975 requiring the disclosure of SSN for such benefit, right or privilege.

When making any request for the disclosure of SSN, government agencies are bound by Section 7(b) of the Privacy Act. They must inform the individual whether such disclosure is mandatory or voluntary, state what use will be made of the information and cite the legislation or executive order which authorises them to make this request of SSN disclosure from individuals. In *Greidinger v. Davis*,[3] the state agency did not provide timely notice in accordance with Section 7(b) at the time of requiring SSN disclosure for the registration of voters. The Court held that the Privacy Act had been violated. The provisions of Section 7 limit the scope of disclosure of SSN and attempt to impose a moratorium on the use of SSN as a personal identifier (Mayer 1978).

In case of other personal information collected by federal government agencies, Section 552a(e)(3) of the Privacy Act ensures that an individual's consent to disclosing such personal information is voluntary and intelligent. At the time of collection of information, agencies must inform the individual of the statute or executive order which allows the collection of information, whether providing the information is voluntary or mandatory, the intended use of the personal information, the regulated routine uses which may be made of the information and the penalties or effects on the individual upon refusing to disclose the requested information. Thus, in *Cooper v. FFA*,[4] where the SSA was disclosing social security records to the Transportation Department, the Court held that such disclosure was improper because the notice of use provided at the time of collecting the personal information was insufficient.

Second, Section 552a(b) of the Privacy Act strictly prohibits the disclosure of personal information without the written consent of the concerned individual. Though the Act permits 12 specific exemptions to this general rule, it delineates their application and generally clarifies the exemptions so as to not allow for adverse exploitation. For instance, Section 552a(b)(4) provides an exemption allowing disclosures to be made to the

Bureau of Census only for the purpose of planning or carrying out a census or survey or related activity which is pursuant to the provisions of Title 13 of the US Legislative Code.

The only contentious exemption is that under Section 552a(b)(3) which allows the disclosure of personal information of individuals for 'routine uses'. However, this exemption is not unregulated as routine use is defined under Section 552a(a)(7) of the Privacy Act as 'the use of such record for a purpose which is compatible with the purpose for which it was collected'. Furthermore, Section 552a(e)(4)(D) regulates the routine uses exemption by requiring that the disclosing agency publish each routine use of the records in the system, the categories of users and the purposes of such use in the Federal Register. Thus, the routine uses exemption must meet both tests. The Office of Management and Budget has noted that the concept of compatibility requires that the uses of disclosure be functionally equivalent, necessary and proper (United States Department of Justice 2015).

In *Britt v. Naval Investigative Service*,[5] the Naval Investigative Service disclosed records describing a then pending criminal investigation of the individual to the individual's employer (the Immigration and Naturalization Service). The Court held that such disclosure was not provided for under the routine uses exemption because the purpose of the disclosure (ascertaining the suitability of the individual for employment) was not compatible with the criminal law enforcement purpose with which the information was originally collected. In *Krohn v. Department of Justice*,[6] where the Federal Bureau of Investigation sought a routine uses exemption, the Court held that such routine use did not qualify for exemption as it was impermissibly vague and could be construed so broadly as to encompass all legal proceedings. Nonetheless, critics have raised concerns that the routine uses exemption grants governmental agencies the opportunity to circumvent the general non-disclosure rule under Section 552a(b) as government agencies are not prohibited from deeming whether a use is routine use or not and because there is no independent oversight of such decision-making (Azrael 1984).

Third, Section 552a(i)(1) of the Privacy Act imposes criminal liability on government employees who knowingly and wilfully make disclosures to persons or agencies not entitled to receive such information. Section 552a(i)(3) imposes similar penalties on individuals who solicit or obtain personal information from government agencies under false pretences. Further, Section 552a(e)(10) legally obliges government agencies to establish 'appropriate administrative, technical and physical safeguards to insure the security and confidentiality of records'. Government agencies must also protect records against any threats or hazards that could endanger the security or integrity of the records or cause substantial harm, inconvenience, embarrassment or unfairness to the individuals concerned. In *Schmidt v. US Department of Veterans Affairs*,[7] the court considered it important to examine whether the government agency had intentionally violated Section 552a(e)(10) by failing to install patches on its systems that trace users' access to SSNs.

Section 552a(c)(1) of the Privacy Act mandates agencies to maintain an account of disclosures made—along with details of the date, nature and purpose of each disclosure—to any person or agency, other than intra-agency and Freedom of Information Act disclosures. In *Clarkson v. Internal Revenue Service*,[8] the Court found that the disclosure of records by Internal Revenue Service to its criminal investigation unit did not require accounting since it was an intra-agency disclosure.

Additionally, Section 552a(c)(3) of the Privacy Act grants individuals the right to access these accounts of disclosures, except for the disclosures made for law enforcement requests. In *Stanley v. Department of Justice*,[9] the Court held that the plaintiff was entitled to access the US Attorney-compiled list of persons in the Internal Revenue Service to whom disclosures of grand jury materials about him were made.

Fourth, Section 552a(d)(1) of the Privacy Act provides individuals the right to seek access to their personal information in government records. Foreseeing that government databases may contain incomplete, false or inaccurate information, Section 552a(e)(6) of the Privacy Act imposes the responsibility that the government agency make reasonable efforts to ensure that such record is 'accurate, complete, timely and relevant'.

Section 552a(e)(5) of the Act adds that an agency must maintain all records used by it to make any determinations about individuals with 'such accuracy, relevance, timeliness and completeness as is reasonably necessary to assure fairness to the individual in the determination'. Individuals also have the right to request an amendment under the Privacy Act (Section 552a(d)(2)). Within 10 working days of receiving such a request, the government agency must acknowledge receipt of the request in writing and either make the correction or inform the individual of its refusal to amend the information. There is a review procedure that individuals can initiate when an agency refuses to make the requested amendment (Section 552a(d)(3)). If all else fails, individuals may bring a civil suit against the government agency under Section 552a(g)(1)(A).

Fifth, to prohibit the creation of secret or covert systems of records, Section 552a(e)(4) of the Privacy Act requires every government agency that maintains records of personal information to publish, upon establishment or revision, a notice of the existence and character of such records in the Federal Register and its attendant website. These notices must outline the procedures by which an individual can gain access to records and challenge their content. Among other things, the notices must also clearly state the categories of individuals about whom records are collected, the categories of records maintained in the system, the routine uses of the records, and the categories of users and purpose of such uses. Section 552a(i)(2) of the Act imposes criminal penalties on agency employees who wilfully maintain record systems without meeting these necessary notice requirements of the Act.

To sum up, although not perfect, the Privacy Act still sets reasonable safeguards to protect the personal information of individuals. It limits the collection and maintenance of data, requires agencies to maintain accurate and relevant records, mandates the publishing of a guide to all record systems in order to inform individuals of the uses of such information, grants individuals access to record systems and protects the records from unauthorised use. Crucially, the Act gives individuals the rights of notice, access and challenge and thereby establishes due process rights (Sullivan 2003).

In stark contrast is India's scant Aadhaar (Targeted Delivery of Financial and Other Subsidies, Benefits and Services) Act of 2016 (the Aadhaar Act). Unlike the Privacy Act, the Aadhaar Act neither mentions the right to privacy nor refers to the term privacy. This is significant as any legislation granting compelling powers to an actor effectively provides a *carte blanche* for the use (or abuse) of such power by that actor. Therefore, the legislation must also carry limits to the exercise of power and set known, reasonable expectations of interference for all affected actors *vis-à-vis* the authoritative actor. Rights are the medium through which reasonable expectations are set, made known to affected actors and breaches are redressed (Michel 2009). Furthermore, only by elevating privacy to a right will individuals be able to stand up to the government's interest in obtaining their personal information. As the Aadhaar Act immensely empowers the government to collect, store and use the personal information of citizens without adequate restraints or redressal mechanisms, it is fair and necessary to ask for a right to privacy from the Aadhaar Act.

The Aadhaar Act rules that no information on race, religion, caste, tribe, ethnicity, or language can constitute demographic information. However, the Act does not impose any limitations on the demographic personal information that can otherwise be collected by the government, or with which Aadhaar details can be merged ('seeded'). Thus, information that is not relevant to or necessary for statutory purposes can also be collected by the government. There is also no requirement on government agencies to ensure that the information collected is maintained in a manner fair to individuals when using such information to make determinations about the individuals.

Section 7 of the Aadhaar Act provides that the use of Aadhaar number can be made mandatory to receive certain government subsidies, benefits or services. No specifics have been enumerated on which government schemes may or may not be included under the scope of this section. The Aadhaar Act does not address privacy concerns relating to the collection of information or risk of disclosure by the enrolment agencies (Marda 2015). Further, the prohibition against disclosure of information appears farcical with the inclusion of the easily manipulated, vaguely worded exception of national security in Section 33(b), especially given that there is no requirement of a formal record of justification for invoking the same (Kak and Malik 2010). Contrary to international data protection practices, the Aadhaar Act is also silent on how long the personal information of citizens can be stored.

Section 8 of the Aadhaar Act allows private companies to request the authentication of an Aadhaar number but fails to stipulate the minimum requirement that needs to be met in order to be eligible to make such requests. Further, apart from excluding core biometric information (fingerprints and iris scans), the Act fails to regulate how much personal information can be disclosed upon receiving authentication requests (Drèze 2017). Capitalising on this lack of regulation, private companies have begun to use Aadhaar in creative ways to derive profits from the personal information of citizens (Rajshekhar 2016).

The Aadhaar Act does not provide individuals notice on breach of their personal information. Under Section 29, the Act prohibits individuals from accessing their own core biometric information. Furthermore, Section 6 of the Act places the responsibility of ensuring accuracy of personal information collected and stored through Aadhaar on the concerned individual and not on the government. This effectively grants impunity to the government for the maintenance of inaccurate records and consequent determinations based upon such records.

Finally, the Aadhaar Act fails to unequivocally prohibit seeding or the creation of dossiers of personal information on citizens. This legislative ambiguity empowers the government to aggregate information on individuals across record systems, seemingly in complete legality as no express law is violated.

In conclusion, the Aadhaar Act does not establish safeguards to check that personal information is used only for its intended purposes by authorised persons with the intelligent and informed consent of the individual. Whereas the Privacy Act adopts a wisely cautious approach towards the ability and willingness of government agencies to protect the privacy of individuals, the Aadhaar Act places blind trust in the government's capability and willingness to protect records of personal information of individuals (Grewal et al. 2016). Thus, despite the Aadhaar Act, individuals continue to remain extremely vulnerable to abuse.

Can Aadhaar be Redeemed?

One may conclude from this chapter that the enactment of a strong informational privacy law will prohibit the potential misuse of Aadhaar. However, the enactment of a conceptually sound legislation *per se* does not guarantee protection to individuals unless accompanied by meaningful and timely enforcement of the law. Despite the establishment of a relatively protective informational privacy regime in USA, government agencies have succeeded in eroding the Privacy Act by manipulating provisions or exploiting loopholes (Shattuck 1984).

Furthermore, the enactment of the Privacy Act has failed to deter identity thieves from misusing the SSNs of millions of Americans. The SSN is the key element in nearly every identity theft case. It enables criminals to access victims' existing financial accounts and open fraudulent accounts to take loans, make credit purchases and falsely obtain government benefits (Webb 2005). Since the SSN contains permanent, unchanging information such as an individual's name and birth date, the likelihood of repeated identity theft of the same victim exists even after they obtain new identity documents (Rusch 2008).

The expanding use of SSN for a range of financial transactions and economic activities has contributed to making identity theft among America's fastest growing crimes. The collection and storage of SSNs by monopolistic financial institutions and credit rating agencies—which are unaccountable, profit-making enterprises—has also increased the likelihood of data breach and misuse of SSN. The 1972, 1974 and 1981 Amendments to the SSA to criminalise the misuse of SSN and the 1998 Identity Theft and Assumption Deterrence Act to address the criminal misuse of personal information have failed to check identity theft.

The Indian state also has a questionable track record in protecting and respecting citizens' privacy (Datta 2017). Given bureaucratic attitudes of selective enforcement and legal amnesia, there is little reason to believe that any government will uniformly and meaningfully enforce the informational privacy law and protect individuals. Besides, legislations can always be quietly amended subsequently to undermine their intended purpose and courts are often approached after harm has occurred.

The most alarming ramification of Aadhaar is that, by its very nature, it subverts the political status of citizens *vis-à-vis* the government by grossly undervaluing and infringing privacy. The concept of privacy is a constitutive value of society itself because it provides citizens a bulwark against excessive government interference in facets of personal, social, political and religious life (Solove 2007). The erosion of privacy leads to individuals' exclusion from control over their own lives and the use of their personal information (Cohen 2000). This engenders a deep asymmetry in the power relation between citizens and the government, leaving the former vulnerable to abuses, errors and indifferences of the latter. Therefore, privacy is a *sine qua non* for the welfare of society. It cannot be trivialised by being pitted against imagined values of governmental efficiency. Characteristic of national identity systems around the world, Aadhaar demeans the political identity of citizens by transforming personhood from an inherent quality to an entry in bureaucratic databases (Sobel 2002). Aadhaar thus imperils the future of a constitutional, dignity-based democracy far more than it provides any benefits to citizens.

Notes

1. This includes food grains under the Targeted Public Distribution system, school meals, LPG subsidies, pension payments under the National Social Assistance Programme, Central Sector Scholarship

schemes, cash assistance under the national Tuberculosis programme, payments under the national rural employment guarantee scheme, disability cash benefits, cash assistance for rehabilitated bonded labourers, housing subsidy for workers in the beedi, iron ore or limestone industry, subsidies for constructing latrines, compensation for the victims of Bhopal Gas Tragedy, assistance in rescue and rehabilitation of victims of sex trafficking, benefits for children between the ages of six and 14 under the Sarva Siksha Abhiyan scheme, training programmes arranged by the National Career Services, rehabilitation assistance for women victims of unfortunate circumstances under the Swadhar Greh scheme, healthcare benefits for pregnant women, crop insurance benefits for farmers, benefits under the supplementary nutrition programme, benefits under the National Apprenticeship Promotion scheme, financial support under the national mission for women empowerment, benefits under the National Rural Livelihood Mission, welfare services under the soil health management scheme, benefits under the National Social Assistance programme, etc.

2. See Section 205(c)(2)(E)(ii) of the Social Security Act (42 U.S.C. 405(c)(2)).
3. 782 F. Supp. 1106 (E.D. Va. 1992).
4. No. 3:07-cv-01383, slip op. at 15-19 (N.D. Cal. Aug. 22, 2008).
5. 886 F. 2d 544 (3d Cir. 1987).
6. 628 F. 2d 195 (D.C. Cir. 1980).
7. 218 F.R.D. 619 (E.D. Wis. 2003).
8. 811 F. 2d 1396 (11th Cir. 1987).
9. 835 F. 2d 216 (9th Cir. 1987).

References

Azrael, Miriam Lapp. 1984. 'Lost Privacy in the Computer Age: Computer Matching Programs are Turning Uncle Sam into Big Brother'. *University of Baltimore Law Forum* 14 (2): pp. 18–25.

Cohen, Julie E. 2000. 'Examined Lives: Informational Privacy and the Subject as Object'. *Stanford Law Review* 52 (5): pp. 1373–438.

Datta, Saikat. 2017. 'The End of Privacy: Aadhaar is Being Converted into the World's Biggest Surveillance Engine'. *Scroll.in*, 24 March.

Drèze, Jean. 2017. 'Hello Aadhaar, Goodbye Privacy'. *The Wire*, 24 March.

Grewal, Jaspreet, Vanya Rakesh, Sumandro Chattapadhyay, and Elonnai Hickok. 2016. 'Report on Understanding Aadhaar and its New Challenges'. *Centre for Internet and Society*, 31 August.

Available at http://cis-india.org/internet-governance/blog/report-on-understanding-aadhaar-and-its-new-challenges (accessed 10 May 2017).

Hanus, Jerome J., and Harold C. Relyea. 1976. 'A Policy Assessment of the Privacy Act of 1974'. *The American University Law Review* 25 (3): pp. 555–93.

Hickok, Elonnai. 2015. 'Aadhaar Number vs the Social Security Number'. *Centre for Internet and Society*, 21 July. Available at https://cis-india.org/internet-governance/blog/aadhaar-vs-social-security-number#_ftnref15 (accessed 27 May 2017).

Hickok, Elonnai, and Rohan George. 2015. 'Supreme Court Order is a Good Start but is Seeding Necessary?'. *Centre for Internet and Society*, 29 August. Available at https://cis-india.org/internet-governance/blog/supreme-court-order-is-a-good-start-but-is-seeding-necessary (accessed 23 May 2017).

Kak, Amba Uttara, and Swati Malik. 2010. 'Privacy and the National Identification Authority of India Bill: Leaving Much to the Imagination'. *NUJS Law Review* 3 (4): pp. 485–510.

Komuves, Flavio L. 1998. 'We've Got Your Number: An Overview of Legislation and Decisions to Control the Use of Social Security Numbers as Personal Identifiers'. *The John Marshall Journal of Information Technology & Privacy Law* 16 (3): pp. 529–77.

Marda, Vidushi. 2015. 'Data Flow in the Unique Identification Scheme of India'. *Centre for Internet and Society*, 3 September. Available at http://cis-india.org/internet-governance/blog/data-flow-in-unique-identification-scheme-of-india#_ftn6 (accessed 27 May 2017).

Mayer, Stephen. 1978. 'Privacy and the Social Security Number: Section 1211 of the Tax Reform Act of 1976'. *Rutgers Journal of Computers and the Law* 6 (2): pp. 221–64.

Michel, Christian. 2009. 'Why We Have Rights'. *Mises Institute*, 11 March. Available at https://mises.org/library/why-we-have-rights (accessed 26 May 2017).

Office of the Inspector General. 2000. 'The Social Security Administration is Pursuing Matching Agreements with New York and Other States Using Biometric Technologies', Audit Report. Maryland: Social Security Administration. Available at https://oig.ssa.gov/sites/default/files/audit/full/pdf/9841007.pdf (accessed 25 May 2017).

Pandey, Ajay Bhushan. 2017. 'Criticism Without Aadhaar'. *The Indian Express*, 13 May.

Puckett, Carolyn. 2009. 'The Story of the Social Security Number'. *Social Security Bulletin* 69 (2): pp. 55–74.

Rajshekhar, M. 2016. 'How Private Companies are Using Aadhaar to Try to Deliver Better Services (but There's a Catch)'. *Scroll.in*, 22 December.

Ramanathan, Usha. 2015. 'Decoding the Aadhaar Judgment: No More Seeding, not till the Privacy Issue is Settled by the Court'. *The Indian Express*, 12 August.

Rusch, Jonathan J. 2008. 'Identity Theft: The Scope of the Problem'. *United States Attorneys' Bulletin* 56 (2): pp. 1–5.

Scientific American. 2014. 'Biometric Security Poses Huge Privacy Risks'. *Scientific American,* 1 January. Available at https://www.scientificamerican.com/article/biometric-security-poses-huge-privacy-risks/ (accessed 26 May 2017).

Sharma, Aman, and Neha Alawadhi. 2016. 'UIDAI Wants to Make Mobile Phones Aadhaar-enabled, Holds Discussion with Smartphone Makers'. *The Economic Times*, 29 July.

Shattuck, John. 1984. 'In the Shadow of 1984: National Identification Systems, Computer Matching, and Privacy in the United States'. *Hastings Law Journal* 35 (6): pp. 991–1006.

Sobel, Richard. 2002. 'The Demeaning of Identity and Personhood in National Identification Systems'. *Harvard Journal of Law and Technology* 15 (2): pp. 319–87.

Social Security Administration. 1997. 'Report to Congress on Options for Enhancing the Social Security Card'. Maryland: Social Security Administration. Available at https://www.ssa.gov/history/reports/ssnreport.html (accessed 25 May 2017).

———. n.d. 'History of SSA 1993–2000', Government of United States of America. Available at https://www.ssa.gov/history/ssa/ssa2000chapter6.html (accessed 25 May 2017).

Solove, Daniel J. 2007. '"I've Got Nothing to Hide" and Other Misunderstandings of Privacy'. *San Diego Law Review* 44 (4): pp. 745–72.

Sullivan, Julianne M. 2003. 'Will the Privacy Act of 1974 Still Hold Up in 2004? How Advancing Technology Has Created a Need for Change in the "System of Records" Analysis'. *California Western Law Review* 39 (2): pp. 395–412.

Unique Identification Authority of India. n.d. 'About Aadhaar', Government of India. Available at https://uidai.gov.in/your-aadhaar/about-aadhaar.html (accessed 8 May 2017).

United States Department of Justice. 2015. 'Overview of the Privacy Act of 1974'. Washington, D.C.: United States Department of Justice.

Available at https://www.justice.gov/opcl/overview-privacy-act-1974-2015-edition (accessed 23 May 2017).

Webb, John K. 2005. 'Prosecuting Social Security Number Misuse: Attacking Identity Theft at Its Source'. *United States Attorneys' Bulletin* 53 (1): pp. 1–15.

Yadav, Anumeha. 2016. 'Despite the Comparisons, India's Aadhaar Project is Nothing like America's Social Security Number'. *Scroll.in*, 20 December.

15

Identity and Development

Questioning Aadhaar's Digital Credentials

Gus Hosein and *Edgar Whitley*

Aadhaar is frequently presented as a leading digital identity scheme that will help enable a truly digital, developed Indian economy (Wadhwa 2017). The Unique Identification Authority of India (UIDAI) describes Aadhaar as 'a strategic policy tool for social and financial inclusion, public sector delivery reforms, managing fiscal budgets, increase convenience and promote hassle-free people-centric governance'. In particular, UIDAI suggests that the Aadhaar identity platform 'is one of the key pillars of the "Digital India", wherein every resident of the country is provided with a unique identity' (UIDAI 2017a). The UIDAI collects biometrics and then uses computer systems to analyse an individual's biometrics (face, fingerprint and iris) and ensure that no individual is allocated more than one Aadhaar number (UIDAI 2017a).

In parallel to this narrative of India shifting towards a digital future, there is one that emphasises ongoing practices based on analogue record keeping (Abraham et al. 2017; Rao 2017). Academic studies are increasingly documenting the 'social struggles accompanying shifts in management systems from paper-based record-keeping to biometrical e-governance' (Rao 2017: 127) and the 'practical feasibility of digitisation' (Masiero 2016: 9), especially in rural areas.

For example, following the introduction of demonetisation policy on 8 November 2016, there were widespread reports of 'note cheats' buying bulk photocopies of Aadhaar documents from shops selling SIM cards and from education institutions

(Reddy 2016) and using them as proof of identity for bank transactions. Similarly, Singh and Jackson (2017) report how a colour-printed and laminated letter confirming an Aadhaar number was considered to be 'original'. Indeed, the UIDAI had to issue official guidance warning that it was not necessary to pay to have the Aadhaar letter laminated (Press Information Bureau 2016).

This chapter draws on current thinking around what constitutes a good digital identity scheme (BCS Identity Assurance Working Group 2016; Bernat 2011; Nyst et al. 2016a) and the World Bank's principles for identity schemes in a digital era (2017) to help unpack the specific claims around Aadhaar as a *digital* identity scheme, particularly in terms of identification, authentication and authorisation. Questioning Aadhaar's digital credentials will help explain the relationship between the immediate development benefits attributed to Aadhaar and the longer-term developmental opportunities that a truly digital identity scheme can enable whilst not undermining public trust.

Development Benefits Arising from an Effective Identity Scheme

Effective identification systems are increasingly seen as a key part of the development agenda (Dahan and Gelb 2015) and this has resulted in a specific Sustainable Development Goal (SDG) around the provision of a legal identity for all by 2030 (United Nations 2017: 17). Not having an official identity condemns millions of people to being undocumented and, in turn, marginalised, because so many activities—from opening a bank account to attending school to selling goods 'up the value chain', not to mention voting or moving within or between countries—now legally require proof of identity (Pokharel and Niroula 2015; Sriram 2018).

However, as noted in chapter 1 of the present volume, having a unique identity only addresses some aspects of social protection with other elements being related to (politically defined) attributes associated with an identity or even fraudulent activities that are unrelated to identity claims. Similarly, Sriram (2018) notes that the requirements for 'know your customer' (KYC) checks are, in part, a consequence of a particular model of financial inclusion that singles out remittances and payments.

This decentring of the role of identity in development becomes more pronounced in the context of a digital identity scheme and this is explored further in the next section.

Defining Digital Identity Schemes

The domain of identity is often broken up into three activities: identification, authentication and authorisation.

Identification is the process of *establishing information about an individual* and may involve examining 'breeder documents' such as birth certificates and consulting alternative sources of data to corroborate the identity being claimed.

Authentication is the process of *asserting an identity* previously established during identification. This typically involves presenting or using an authentication credential (that was bound to the identity during identification) to demonstrate that the individual owns, and is in control of, the digital identity being asserted.

Finally, authorisation is the process of *determining what actions may be performed or services accessed* on the basis of the asserted and authenticated identity (see Table 15.1).

Table 15.1: Three Aspects of an Identity

Stage	*Key question*
Identification	What do we know about you?
Authentication	How do we know it is you?
Authorisation	What can you do?

Source: Drawn by Authors based on data from Nyst et al. 2016a.

From these definitions, Nyst et al. (2016a) define a digital identity scheme as one where 'identification, authentication and authorisation are **all** performed digitally' (sec. 4.2; emphasis added). This strict definition of what makes an identity scheme digital provides a perspective for understanding the current status and scope of Aadhaar for development.

Identification in Aadhaar

With India lacking an existing universal identification baseline from birth registration (UNICEF reports that only 71.9 per cent of births are registered in India), Aadhaar was designed with a focus on ensuring biometric uniqueness and with demographic identification playing a secondary role in establishing the identity. This also explains why all residents can be enrolled and can receive an Aadhaar number, yet the system says nothing about citizenship.

The biometric de-duplication process seeks to ensure that no person (set of biometrics) can be allocated more than one Aadhaar number and this has resulted in the world's largest biometric database. Before an Aadhaar number is issued, the biometrics of the enrolee are checked against all the biometrics already recorded in the system. This is typically done by comparing the (digital template representations of) enrolled biometrics against (digital template representations of) all the previously submitted biometrics.

Aadhaar collects face, fingerprint and iris biometrics because of fears that too many false matches would occur when using fingerprints alone for de-duplication, particularly for a country the size of India.

Alongside the biometric enrolment and de-duplication process, Aadhaar also collects demographic data, such as name, date of birth and address. Where an individual has no existing identification documents, this demographic data will be self-asserted and verified on the basis of a known 'introducer' who has an Aadhaar number. In other cases, the data will be taken from existing documents. It is reported that 99.97 per cent of enrolees had at least two existing identification documents and did not need to rely on alternative, 'introducer' systems to support their identity claims (Khera 2018).

The quality of this demographic data is, therefore, dependent on the quality of the issuing processes for these breeder documents (GOV.UK 2014, annex B). The UK GOV.UK Verify scheme scores the quality of the identity evidence presented at enrolment, that is, the different forms of breeder documents and information used and performs active anti-fraud checks (for example, to ensure that a breeder document has not been reported lost or stolen) (GOV.UK Verify 2014; Whitley 2017). It is unclear how much, if any, active checking of demographic documentation is involved in the Aadhaar enrolment process. Indeed, if no adequate birth records are available, a default value of 1 January has been used in Aadhaar demographic data (Azad 2017; PTI 2017). For example, recent guidance issued to enrolment staff simply notes a requirement to ensure that the original document presented as proof of identity 'is scanned for every enrolment' (UIDAI 2017b).

Whilst biometric de-duplication should ensure that even low quality demographic data in Aadhaar can only be associated with a single person, there are significant consequences to the limited checking of the data, not least in terms of news reports of Aadhaar numbers being allocated to coriander plants (Dharur 2012) and Hindu gods (PTI 2014).

Authentication in Aadhaar

Once an Indian resident has an Aadhaar number, there are a number of different ways in which they can authenticate themselves. Some processes are still relying on physical inspection of a (possibly laminated) letter listing the person's Aadhaar number (Caribou Digital 2017). Failing to authenticate a digital identity can result in many of the kinds of fraud and leakages that Aadhaar is intended to address.

If a process requires some form of authentication, then Aadhaar offers five authentication levels of increasing sophistication and integrity (Abraham et al. 2017, appendix 2.2). The simplest form of authentication involves checking demographic data. In this situation, an individual's Aadhaar number and demographic data are checked to see whether they match the data held on the Central Identities Data Repository (CIDR).

A second form of authentication involves sending a one-time PIN to the mobile phone that has been linked to the

Aadhaar number. This provides reasonable confidence that the person presenting the Aadhaar number is the person associated with the mobile phone associated with the number.

The third form of authentication involves presenting biometrics and checking against those held on the CIDR. If the submitted Aadhaar number is associated with the submitted biometric on the CIDR, then the identity is authenticated.

Higher levels of authentication involve combining the PIN and biometric methods. Each of these forms of authentication requires the installation of appropriate authentication devices (to collect biometrics or enter demographic data for checking) and connecting them to the CIDR (this includes provision of suitable power and internet connectivity). Moreover, as Table 15.2. shows, even appropriate authentication methods do not mitigate all the identification risks.

Table 15.2: Authentication Methods in Aadhaar

Authentication method	*Risks*
None	No link between use of Aadhaar number and the person it is formally associated with
Demographic check	Limited knowledge required to undertake impersonation fraud
One-time PIN	Only confirms that person has access to mobile phone associated with Aadhaar number
Fingerprint biometric	Failure to acquire fingerprint/failure to match fingerprint. Needs fingerprint reader/electronic point of sale (ePOS) system to be connected to CIDR
Iris biometric	Failure to acquire iris/failure to match iris. Needs iris reader to be connected to CIDR
Multiple biometric	Failure to acquire some/all biometrics. Needs to be connected to CIDR. Multi-modal biometrics may not reduce false non-match rates.

Source: Drawn by Authors.

For most transactions, authentication returns either a Yes or No response. It is also possible for authentication to return the associated demographic data as e-KYC data after a positive authentication. This data can then be used to populate the records of other computer systems (such as for new mobile phone connections).

Authorisation in Aadhaar

An increasingly large number of Indian government services are now requiring an Aadhaar number before they can be used.

In most cases, residents can 'seed' the service with their Aadhaar numbers (Khera 2018). For example, in order to reduce leakages arising from ghost accounts, the existing records for a social programme can be digitised (if not already available electronically) and each beneficiary's record matched and linked to their associated Aadhaar number (Abraham et al. 2017: 58). Those records that are not linked to an Aadhaar number can no longer be used and can, in due course, be deleted from the system, although authorisation to access the service may impose additional attribute requirements beyond possession of an Aadhaar number.

The second authorisation approach arises when the Aadhaar holder is known to be 'new' (or cannot be matched to an existing record held by the service provider). In such cases, with the consent of the individual, it is possible to share relevant demographic details from the CIDR (name, address, date of birth, etc.) to populate a new record using an e-KYC authentication. This record is then automatically linked to the new service user's Aadhaar number.

It is important to differentiate between seeding a social protection system with an Aadhaar number and simply using the Aadhaar number as a unique identifier ('key').

An example of an Aadhaar number being used simply as an identifier can be seen in the 2017 announcement that provision of an Aadhaar number will be required for registration of a death (Jain 2017). In this case, the Aadhaar number is not being used for authentication purposes, but rather will help 'in recording the identity of the deceased person' and 'will obviate the need for producing multiple documents to prove the identity of the deceased person' (Jain 2017).

Progress in seeding social protection accounts remains mixed, ranging from 82 per cent of 187 million beneficiaries of LPG subsidy, 72 per cent of 667 million PDS beneficiaries to 51 per cent of recipients of cash transfers to vulnerable populations through the National Social Assistance Programme (NSAP) (Abraham et al. 2017, fig. 5.3). There is also significant variation in seeding levels between states (Abraham et al. 2017, fig. 5.4).

Unpacking Aadhaar's Digital Identity Credentials

Some of the challenges that Aadhaar currently faces are specific to its intended role as a digital identity system, particularly when one takes a strict definition of a digital identity system.

Identification Challenges

Aadhaar's emphasis on biometric de-duplication at enrolment can have a significant effect on removing ghost accounts in existing social welfare systems. These erroneous duplicate or faked accounts can significantly distort the allocation of social welfare protections.

Aadhaar's approach accepts that the demographic data associated with an individual, including their entitlement to social welfare protections, may well be problematic (inaccurate, poorly recorded, fraudulently created, etc.). As a result, it effectively creates a new baseline digital identity that accepts 'we don't know (or cannot prove) who you are and we don't know for certain what you've done in the past, but from now on this is your digital identity and we will tie all your transactions across all outlets to this digital identity' (Makin 2017: 9).

Linking each individual to a single Aadhaar number and then using this number to seed the appropriate social welfare system records means that individuals should not be capable of making multiple claims for the same benefit. Depending on the number of false accounts in existence, this form of data cleansing could enable savings.

This data cleansing arising from linking social welfare records to (de-duplicated) Aadhaar numbers will, however, only offer a one-time benefit as future additions to the social welfare system records should then have their own unique Aadhaar number, preventing the creation of new ghost accounts. The size of these one-time benefits will provide additional evidence of the extent to which identity problems influence social welfare fraud and inefficiencies.

The use of biometrics (both at initial enrolment and, more significantly, at authentication) can raise its own problems. UIDAI studies from 2012 suggest fairly low 'failure to acquire' rates for biometrics, especially when using 'best finger detection', reporting 1.87 per cent of study participants unable to provide sufficiently high-quality fingerprints and who were then 'not included in further authentication tests' (UIDAI 2012: 24). Of these, 89.8 per cent (that is, 1.68 per cent of all participants) were identified as having 'intrinsically poor quality fingerprints', with the remaining individuals having problems matching to their original enrolment fingerprints.

Abraham et al. (2017, fig. 5.7), however, report failed transaction rates, even after multiple attempts, ranging from 5 to 15 per cent. Whilst it is possible that some of these failed matches are appropriate (that is, attempts at fraudulently claiming social protections using someone else's Aadhaar number), the scale of the problem suggests a significant role for biometric failure (Magnet 2011).

When an individual is allocated an Aadhaar number, this is a recognition that they are biometrically unique within the CIDR. However, as noted above, there is little information about the quality of the demographic data collected and also, there is no obvious attempt to audit the quality of the CIDR data recorded alongside the Aadhaar number that drives so many consequential system uses.

Many identity systems use state-issued documents such as birth certificates, issued as part of the civil registration process, as one of the breeder documents confirming demographic data. Birth (and death) registration plays a vital role in the provision of vital statistics (including population counts [Jain 2015]). More generally, a well-functioning civil registration and vital statistics system is generally associated with better health outcomes (Phillips et al. 2015). However, Aadhaar's focus on biometric uniqueness over birth registration data raises the prospect that support for birth registration (and associated vital statistics) might fall over time.

Other digital identity systems illustrate how demographic data provided on enrolment can be checked and how the quality of the data can determine its uses. The GOV.UK Verify scheme scores the strength of the biographical identity evidence (for example, did the issuing source do any identity checking itself? Are the personal and evidence details confirmed as valid by the issuing source?). It also scores the outcome of identity verification (such as confirmation of the applicant's ownership of the claimed identity) and the outcome of any counter-fraud checks and assessment of the activity history associated with the identity evidence (GOV.UK 2014, chapter 5).

By combining these individual scores, it is possible to determine an overall level of assurance for the biographic identity evidence provided. An identity evidence package that draws on sources that are confirmed as valid and with no counter-fraud indicators might be given higher assurance than an identity evidence package that does not score so well. This level of assurance in the identity evidence package can then be matched against the level of assurance required to complete a particular transaction. For example, higher level of assurance might be needed to open a bank account (OIXUK 2017), while a lower level of assurance might be sufficient for an individual to view (but not alter) his or her data held by a government service provider.

Authentication Challenges

Different levels of assurance can equally be associated with different requirements for authentication (a transaction that requires a lower level of assurance would have less stringent authentication requirements than one at a higher level of assurance and might not need biometric authentication).

Even without consideration of different levels of assurance around Aadhaar identities, without suitable authentication, the leakages in social welfare that Aadhaar is supposed to address may well continue. If a service can be accessed without *proper* authentication, for example by presenting a photocopy of an Aadhaar card or, even better, a supposed 'original' Aadhaar card suitably laminated, misallocation of resources will continue.

Managing the roll-out of suitable authentication devices is known to be a challenge for bank card authentication devices and this will equally be the case for Aadhaar biometric authentication devices.

Authorisation Challenges

The link between authentication and authorisation is perhaps the key challenge for Aadhaar to become a truly digital identity system. Requiring an Aadhaar number to create (or seed) a service provider's database immediately addresses the issue of fake accounts. Without proper authentication, however, fraud amongst the remaining (legitimate) accounts may continue. For example, whilst dead people will not be able to provide live authentication biometrics, if authentication is limited to visual inspection of an Aadhaar card or even sending a one-time PIN to a registered mobile phone for authentication, it will not prevent others from misusing that Aadhaar identity. This also highlights the role of linking back from death registration to the CIDR.

These kinds of issues require careful consideration of the underlying processes, processes that will frequently be required to be completely redesigned. The growing number of services that seem to simply require an Aadhaar number (whether suitably authenticated or not) strongly suggests that this process review and redesign is not being undertaken, and is likely to result in excessive and unnecessary linkability across a variety of public and private sector services. It is also likely to increase public distrust in Aadhaar and frustration that the new digital India is becoming as unnecessarily bureaucratic as the India of old.

The consequences of such cross-sector traceability and misuse are widely recognised in other countries, to the extent that some explicitly forbid the use of a single identifier and even use sophisticated cryptographic methods to break the linkages across uses (Otjacques et al. 2007; Whitley 2017). Proper authentication and authorisation offers some mitigation of these risks but without

Table 15.3: Aadhaar as a digital identity system

Stage	*Response*	*Opportunity*	*Risk*
Identification ('What do we know about you?')	You are biometrically unique	• Remove ghost accounts	• Biometric exclusions
	We know these demographic things about you	• Better service by using e-KYC capabilities to share demographic data with service providers	• No attempt to determine quality (assurance) of data • De-emphasis on Civil Registration Vital Statistics (CRVS)
Authentication ('How do we know it is you?')	We checked your biometrics and/or we sent a one-time PIN to your registered mobile device	• Range of authentication methods available	• No authentication undertaken • Unnecessary creation of audit trail of authentication records
Authorisation ('What can you do?')	You need an Aadhaar number to benefit from this public service	• Control over who is entitled to benefit from public service	• Creeping mandatory use • Mismatch between using Aadhaar number as an identifier and as basis for authorisation

Source: Drawn by Authors.

it, concerns about privacy and surveillance will remain and grow (Khera 2017; Munshi 2016).

Table 15.3 presents a summary of the opportunities and risks that emerge when Aadhaar is viewed as a digital identity system. The table provides researchers with some useful analytical heuristics when evaluating the economics of Aadhaar (Mishra 2017):

- When it is claimed that Aadhaar has resulted in social protection savings, are these savings simply a consequence of biometric de-duplication?
- When Aadhaar demographic data is being used to seed new services, how important for the process is the quality of the underlying data?
- When Aadhaar is being used, are appropriate authentication methods being employed?
- When services 'use' Aadhaar numbers, are they simply using the number as a unique identifier or does the Aadhaar number imply authorisation?

The table also suggests a range of more detailed questions that can form the basis for empirical studies of Aadhaar in practice:

- What mechanisms are put in place for the biometrically excluded? Are biometric performance rates improving over time?
- What are the consequences of poor-quality demographic data in the CIDR? If errors are found, how easily are updates to the CIDR propagated to other systems that use Aadhaar numbers?
- In what circumstances do authentication activities, beyond visual inspection/entry of an Aadhaar number, take place? Does the task warrant the use of a stronger form of authentication? If it does, what are the barriers to this authentication taking place?
- What are the emerging privacy risks associated with the growing audit trail associated with successful Aadhaar authentications?

- Might Aadhaar authentication records be used as proof of residency within India, perhaps in relation to claiming Indian citizenship?
- What evidence is there for process redesign around the use of Aadhaar as an authorisation mechanism?
- What effect is the creeping compulsion to use Aadhaar having on public trust in the scheme?
- What is the split between Aadhaar acting as a unique identifier and Aadhaar acting as the basis for authorisation to access public services?
- What are the consequences of regional variation in Aadhaar deployment, biometric authentication devices, etc. on the development goals that Aadhaar is seeking to address?

One of the intellectual inspirations behind the LSE identity project (2005) was the recognition that there are always multiple, often competing, perspectives on complex social problems such as reliable identification systems. These differing perspectives imply choices that must be made, ideally on the basis of well informed analysis and due process consideration of the alternatives (Whitley and Hosein 2008).

In the context of digital identity systems, such choices can have profound consequences for citizen trust and the reliability of the service. For example, although Aadhaar is currently targeted at services used by the poorest in society, there are clear plans to associate its use with mobile phone-enabled services (setting aside the fact that even ownership of mobile phones may be an issue at times for the target population). In such a context, it is possible to see the effect of design choices found in (currently expensive) high-end phones. These phones increasingly offer biometric readers to enhance the consumer experience from unlocking the phone to making payments. However, to ensure consumer trust (and because it is not necessary for the proposed functionality), the biometric capture devices are designed to not share the biometric data (template or image) with a central server, that is, the biometric data do not leave the device.

Thus, a design choice that Aadhaar could have made, and could still make, would be to utilise this form of biometric technology to enable high-quality authentication *without* connecting to the CIDR. That is, the phone could be used to share a confirmed Aadhaar number with a relevant service on the basis that the number is known to be linked to the person unlocking the phone, using their biometrics.

Another design choice might involve not having, or requiring, a single identifier to be used across many different services. Instead, service-specific identifiers might be used (Otjacques et al. 2007; Whitley 2017).

Such approaches would be privacy-enhancing as they would allow services to operate on the basis of confirmed (de-duplicated) and authenticated Aadhaar identities without generating an audit trail (and privacy risks) of Aadhaar transactions and the associated surveillance capitalism (Munshi 2016; Zuboff 2015). Moreover, they would support high-quality digital identity transactions that could, over time, also help improve the quality of the identity evidence package based on the originally supplied demographic data (Nyst et al. 2016b).

References

Abraham, R., E. S. Bennett, N. Sen, and N. B. Shah. 2017. 'State of Aadhaar Report 2016–17'. *IDInsight*. Available at http://stateofaadhaar.in/wp-content/uploads/State-of-Aadhaar-Full-Report-2016-17-IDinsight.pdf (accessed 20 September 2018).

Azad, S. 2017. 'All Residents of this Village Born on January 1, Say Aadhaar Cards'. *Times of India*. Available at https://timesofindia.indiatimes.com/city/dehradun/all-residents-of-this-village-born-on-january-1-say-aadhaar-cards/articleshow/61254173.cms (accessed 20 September 2018).

BCS Identity Assurance Working Group. 2016. 'Aspects of Identity Yearbook 2015–16: How to Recognise a Good Online Identity Assurance Scheme'. Available at https://policy.bcs.org/sites/policy.bcs.org/files/Aspects%20of%20Identity_2015-16_A4%204pp_WEB.pdf (accessed 20 September 2018).

Bernat, L. 2011. 'National Strategies and Policies for Digital Identity Management in OECD Countries'. *OECD*. Available at http://dx.doi.org/10.1787/5kgdzvn5rfs2-en (accessed 20 September 2018).

Caribou Digital. 2017. 'The Identities Research Project'. Available at https://www.identitiesproject.com/ (accessed 20 September 2018).

Dahan, M., and A. Gelb. 2015. 'The Role of Identification in the Post-2015 Development Agenda'. *Centre for Global Development.* Available at http://pubdocs.worldbank.org/en/149911436913670164/World-Bank-Working-Paper-Center-for-Global-Development-Dahan-Gelb-July2015.pdf (accessed 20 September 2018).

Dharur, S. 2012. 'Coriander, s/o Pulav, Gets Aadhaar Card in Andhra'. *The Tribune.* Available at http://www.tribuneindia.com/2012/20120416/main6.htm (accessed 20 September 2018).

GOV.UK. 2014. 'Identity Proofing and Verification of an Individual'. Available at https://www.gov.uk/government/publications/identity-proofing-and-verification-of-an-individual (accessed 20 September 2018).

GOV.UK Verify. 2014. 'GOV.UK Verify: IPV Operations Manual (redacted), No. 2.3.1'. Available at https://www.gov.uk/government/publications/govuk-verify-ipv-operations-manual-redacted (accessed 20 September 2018).

Jain, B. 2015. 'Aadhaar Count in 13 States Higher than their Populations'. *Times of India.* Available at http://timesofindia.indiatimes.com/india/Aadhaar-count-in-13-states-higher-than-their-populations/articleshow/46731777.cms (accessed 20 September 2018).

———. 2017. 'Aadhaar Number Made Mandatory for Registration of Death'. *Times of India.* Available at http://timesofindia.indiatimes.com/india/aadhaar-number-made-mandatory-for-registration-of-death/articleshow/59915885.cms (accessed 20 September 2018).

Khera, R. 2017. 'The Different Ways in which Aadhaar Infringes on Privacy'. *The Wire.* Available at https://thewire.in/159092/privacy-aadhaar-supreme-court/ (accessed 20 September 2018).

———. 2018. 'Impact of Aadhaar in Welfare Programmes'. In *Dissent on Aadhaar*, ed. Reetika Khera. Hyderabad: Orient BlackSwan.

LSE Identity Project. 2005. 'LSE Identity Project (Main Report)'. *London School of Economics and Political Science.* Available at http://identityproject.lse.ac.uk/identityreport.pdf (accessed 20 September 2018).

Magnet, S. A. 2011. *When Biometrics Fail: Gender, Race and the Technology of Identity.* Durham: Duke University Press.

Makin, P. 2017. 'Anti-Money Laundering, Know Your Customer, and Curbing the Financing of Terrorism'. *FSD Africa.* Available at http://www.fsdafrica.org/wp-content/uploads/2017/03/17-03-30-AML-Report.pdf (accessed 20 September 2018).

Masiero, S. 2016. 'Digital Governance and the Reconstruction of the Indian Anti-poverty System'. *Oxford Development Studies.*

Aavailable at http://dx.doi.org/10.1080/13600818.2016.1258050 (accessed 20 September 2018).

Mishra, S. 2017. 'The Economics of Aadhaar'. *Livemint.com*. Available at http://www.livemint.com/Home-Page/s22gUzxOULwQxqukfcBMiM/The-economics-of-Aadhaar.html (accessed 20 September 2018).

Munshi, S. 2016. 'Usha Ramanathan Offers the Most Radical Hypothesis of the Note Ban Yet'. *CatchNews.com*. Available at www.catchnews.com/india-news/usha-ramanathan-offers-the-most-radical-hypothesis-of-the-note-ban-yet-1479754933.html/fullview (accessed 20 September 2018).

Nyst, C., S. Pannifer, E. A. Whitley, and P. Makin. 2016a. 'Digital Identity: Issue Analysis', no. PRJ.1578. *Consult Hyperion for Omidyar Network*. Available at http://www.chyp.com/wp-content/uploads/2016/07/PRJ.1578-Digital-Identity-Issue-Analysis-Report-v1_6-1.pdf (accessed 20 September 2018).

———. 2016b. 'Digital Identity: Issue Analysis Executive Summary', no. PRJ.1578. *Consult Hyperion for Omidyar Network*. Available at http://www.chyp.com/wp-content/uploads/2016/07/PRJ.1578-Omidyar-Network-Digital-Identity-Issue-Analysis-Executive-Summary-v1_2-1.pdf (accessed 20 September 2018).

OIXUK. 2017. How Digital Identities Which Meet Government Standards Could be Used as Part of UK Bank's Customer On-Boarding and KYC Requirements'. *OIXUK*. Available at http://oixuk.org/wp-content/uploads/2017/02/How-Digital-Identities-which-meet-Government-Standards-could-be-used-as-part-of-UK-Banks%E2%80%99-Customer-On-boarding-and-KYC-Requirements-FINAL.pdf (accessed 20 September 2018).

Otjacques, B., P. Hitzelberger, and F. Feltz. 2007. 'Interoperability of E-Government Information Systems: Issues of Identification and Data Sharing'. *Journal of Management Information Systems* 23 (4), pp. 29–52.

Phillips, D. E., C. AbouZahr, A. D. Lopez, L. Mikkelsen, D. de Savigny, R. Lozano, J. Wilmoth, and P. W. Setel. 2015. 'Are Well Functioning Civil Registration and Vital Statistics Systems Associated with Better Health Outcomes?' *The Lancet* 386 (10001), pp. 1386–94.

Pokharel, N., and S. Niroula. 2015. 'How a Legal Identity Leads to a Better Life'. *Open Society Foundations*. Available at https://www.opensocietyfoundations.org/voices/how-legal-identity-leads-better-life (accessed 20 September 2018).

Press Information Bureau. 2016. 'UIDAI Cautions Public against Sharing of their Personal Information with Unauthorized Agencies for

Printing PVC (Plastic) Aadhaar Card'. *Ministry of Communications.* Available at http://pib.nic.in/newsite/PrintRelease.aspx?relid=138755 (accessed 20 September 2018).

PTI. 2014. 'Aadhaar Card for "Lord Hanuman"'. *The Hindu.* Available at http://www.thehindu.com/news/national/lord-hanuman-gets-aadhaar-card/article6401288.ece (accessed 20 September 2018).

———. 2017. 'January 1 Birth Date in Aadhaar Cards for 250 Pokhran Villagers in Rajasthan'. *The New Indian Express.* Available at http://www.newindianexpress.com/nation/2017/may/24/january-1-birth-date-in-aadhaar-cards-for-250-pokhran-villagers-in-rajasthan-1608624.html (accessed 20 September 2018).

Rao, U. 2017. 'Writing, Typing and Scanning. Distributive Justice and the Politics of Visibility in the Era of Biometric Governance'. In *Media as Politics in South* Asia, eds S. Udupa, and S. D. McDowell. New York: Routledge, pp. 127–40.

Reddy, L. V. R. 2016. 'Hyderabad: Note cheats Use Aadhaar Card Copies'. Available at http://www.deccanchronicle.com/nation/current-affairs/171116/hyderabad-note-cheats-use-aadhaar-card-copies.html (accessed 20 September 2018).

Singh, R., and S. J. Jackson. 2017. 'From Margins to Seams: Imbrication, Inclusion and Torque in the Aadhaar Identification Project'. Presented at the CHI 2017, May.

Sriram, M. S. 2018. 'Public Investments and Private Profits'. In *Dissent on Aadhaar*, ed. Reetika Khera. Hyderabad: Orient BlackSwan.

UIDAI. 2012. 'Role of Biometric Technology in Aadhaar Authentication: Authentication Accuracy'. Available at https://stateofaadhaar.in/wp-content/uploads/UIDAI_Role_2012.pdf (accessed 20 September 2018).

———. 2017a. 'About Aadhaar'. Available at https://uidai.gov.in/your-aadhaar/about-aadhaar.html (accessed 20 September 2018).

———. 2017b. 'Roles and Responsibilities of Enrolment Staff'. Available at https://uidai.gov.in/images/annexure_b_roles_and_responsibility_of_enrolment_staff.pdf (accessed 20 September 2018).

United Nations. 2017. 'Progress towards the Sustainable Development Goals: Report of the Secretary-General'. Available at http://www.un.org/ga/search/view_doc.asp?symbol=E/2017/66&Lang=E (accessed 25 September 2018).

Wadhwa, V. 2017. 'India is Building the Infrastructure for a Truly Digital Economy'. *Singularity Hub.* Available at https://singularityhub.com/2017/01/26/india-is-building-the-infrastructure-for-a-truly-digital-economy/ (accessed 20 September 2018).

Whitley, E. A. 2017. 'GOV.UK Verify: Development, Operation, Governance and Prospects'. *Centre for Global Development.* Available at http://personal.lse.ac.uk/whitley/allpubs/cgd2018.pdf (accessed 20 September 2018)

Whitley, E. A., and I. R. Hosein. 2008. 'Doing the Politics of Technological Decision Making: Due Process and the Debate about Identity Cards in the UK'. *European Journal of Information Systems.* 17 (6), pp. 668–77.

Zuboff, S. 2015. 'Big Other: Surveillance Capitalism and the Prospects of an Information Civilization'. *Journal of Information Technology* 30 (1), pp. 75–89.

Post-script

Reetika Khera

In the course of preparing this book, there have been significant developments in the Aadhaar project. All the contributions were written in late 2017, over a year before the Supreme Court delivered its judgment on the constitutional validity of Aadhaar.[1] The hearings on the Aadhaar project concluded in early 2018 and the judgment, delivered on 26 September 2018, will not put an end to this debate. The main arguments and concerns listed in the contributions here remain relevant to the future project and to other countries that may go (or be goaded to go) down this path in the future. This post-script attempts at recapitulating the main developments in 2018 and giving a sense of what lies ahead.

The Final Hearings

Starting in mid-January 2018, the hearings on the Aadhaar matter finally began. The hearings were delayed because of the government's 'googly' in 2015, when it claimed that the question of whether privacy is a fundamental right needed to be confirmed by a nine-judge bench. It is widely perceived that the request for a nine-judge bench to reaffirm (or reject) the right to privacy as a fundamental right was mere court craft to delay the hearings so that Aadhaar would then be 'too big to fail'—a *fait accompli*.

There is at least one sense in which this move may have backfired for the government. In mid-2017, a nine-judge bench was constituted to deliberate on whether the right to privacy is a fundamental right. That bench delivered a unanimous and path-breaking judgment in favour of the petitioners. The right to privacy judgment will have implications not just for the

Aadhaar case, but also other matters. The judgment deepens our understanding of the meaning of privacy, especially in the digital age. It provided a boost to those who were going against the tide initially by questioning the project.

There is another reason why the delay in the final hearings may have been helpful. Until 2015, the main constituency harmed by Aadhaar were the rural poor, the beneficiaries of social support. They were easily ignored. Since 2016, the government began to make it compulsory almost everywhere, without much justification and some private sector firms also began demanding it. This meant that the better-off began to grapple with Aadhaar's substandard eco-system. They encountered all the problems that earlier affected the marginalised sections of Indian society—misspelt names, wrongly seeded numbers, incorrect dates of birth, deactivation of numbers, demands to re-enrol biometrics, lack of accountability, etc. During the hearings, one of the judges commented on how the requirement of fingerprint authentication made it difficult for his mother to get her pension. Even the damage to welfare from Aadhaar has begun to be understood more widely. This has been possible partly because independent studies have documented the harms from the coercive use of Aadhaar in welfare.

These developments resulted in a big change in the public mood with respect to Aadhaar. In 2015, an adverse judgment or any restraint on Aadhaar imposed by the Supreme Court might easily have been portrayed as yet another instance of judicial over-reach. By 2018, there were enough 'influencers' (as the Aadhaar media strategy documents call them), early supporters of the project, who became concerned about the turn of events since 2016. Therefore, in the final hearings in early 2018, the government found it tough to make the case that Aadhaar is essential for welfare, its key argument after the right to privacy judgment.

Though already debunked in public debate and in Court, an oft-repeated line by the government, in its defence of Aadhaar, was that it plays an important role in ensuring right to life and the rights under Article 21 of the Constitution. This assertion was made without any evidence about how the two are linked. In the final hearings, the Attorney General's main line of defence was that the Court must 'balance' the right to life of millions, which he claimed is guaranteed by Aadhaar, with the right to privacy.

There are several problems with this line of argument. Aadhaar is a direct assault on the 'right to life' of many in the sense that pre-existing benefits (rations, pensions, etc.) have become contingent upon Aadhaar. Independent research and government data suggest that the number of affected people is in millions. Earlier, to get rations, people were only at the mercy of the dealer. Now, they are at his mercy and at that of electricity supply, point of sale machines, servers and fingerprint authentication. If any of these does not work, they must send another family member or return themselves another time. At the time of going to print, Indian media had reported over 20 hunger deaths precipitated by denial due to Aadhaar. It is bizarre that while Aadhaar harms the poor, it was packaged as 'empowering' the poor before the Court.

Further, Justice Chandrachud's privacy judgment in 2017 rejected the Attorney General's argument that 'the right to privacy must be forsaken in the interest of welfare entitlements' (215). He stated that the idea that one is 'subservient' to the other 'has been urged in the past and has been categorically rejected' and went on to emphasise the complementary nature of the two rights: 'Civil and political rights and socio-economic rights do not exist in a state of antagonism.'

An important aspect of the final hearings was that the government was forced to cede some ground. Rakesh Dwivedi, appearing for the Unique Identification Authority of India (UIDAI), said that the Court should first make 'small repairs' if they find that laws are defective, instead of striking it down and proposed restrictions that may be applied to some sections of the Aadhaar Act. Thus, when it argued that the right to privacy needs to be 'balanced' against the right to life, it was perhaps the first time, even inadvertently, that the government acknowledged that the right to privacy is compromised by the Aadhaar project. One of the judges pulled up the government for forcing people to link their Aadhaar numbers with mobile phones by claiming that it had been mandated by a Supreme Court order. This was a major embarrassment for the government. Further, the government had to reveal the high rates of biometric failure and exclusion resulting from such failures to the Court. On data sharing, authentication logs etc., Rakesh Dwivedi pleaded that the Court 'should be like a doctor, save the patient', openly admitting that there was something wrong with the Aadhaar project. He claimed that, in contrast with the laws in the European Union that provide data protection, Aadhaar was about 'no flow of data', even as lawyers representing corporations with business interests argued just after him to save Aadhaar, as their businesses depended on data flows related to Aadhaar!

The government's ability to misrepresent and misinterpret the petitioner's arguments in order to avoid addressing the issue raised by the petitioners was both remarkable and perplexing. One gross misrepresentation was with respect to how Aadhaar infringes on the right to privacy. For instance, when the issue of profiling and tracking that the Aadhaar project enables was raised, the government kept repeating how little information the UIDAI has, even though it has been clearly demonstrated that the dangers arise not so much from how much information the UIDAI collects and stores, but from the fact that the Aadhaar number is now in so many databases with little or no restriction over its use there.

Similarly, the government appears to have wilfully misrepresented the concern with exclusion and denial resulting from Aadhaar. In its defence, the government repeated how the enrolment ID can be used or that there are exemption mechanisms, when in fact, the enrolment is not the source of exclusion—linking and authentication are—and when the so-called exemption mechanisms at all three stages are actually not functional on the ground.

The Aadhaar Judgment

On 26 September 2018, the Constitution bench of the Supreme Court delivered a split verdict on Aadhaar (4:1, in favour of it). There were three separate opinions—Justice Sikri, writing for the Chief Justice of India and Justice Khanwilkar (the 'majority opinion'), one by Justice Bhushan (the four of them are referred to as the 'majority judges') and one dissenting opinion by Justice Chandrachud. The majority opinion (and the majority judges) upholds the constitutional validity of the Aadhaar project.

The main challenge to the Aadhaar project in the Supreme Court was on the ground that it violates the right to privacy, a fundamental right under the Constitution of India. Along with other sections of the Act and Rules framed by the government, Section 7 allows the state to mandate use of Aadhaar, to store it, to collate databases at the backend and to develop a 360-degree profile of individuals. This creates the danger of mass surveillance by the government. Section 57, on the other hand, allows private entities (phone companies, mobile wallets, food and taxi aggregators, etc.) to demand Aadhaar. Businesses can sell anonymised (or even de-anonymised) metadata to the growing data broking industry. Our personal (meta)data has immense commercial value, to mine for targeted advertising and for screening purposes (such as for health or car insurance, loans, etc.). These two clauses together allow Aadhaar to be seen as a project that enables mass government and corporate surveillance and, therefore, are a threat to the right to privacy.

The majority judges decided to go with the government's claims on the question of whether the Aadhaar project constituted legitimate state aim and on the question of proportionality. Justice Chandrachud rejected large parts of both those claims, coming down especially heavily on the question of proportionality.

Section 57

Yet, the majority judges did strike down Section 57 as unconstitutional, because it fails the test of proportionality (Supreme Court of India 2018: 434). Justice Sikri says that they find 'some portion of Section 57 as offending and declared that unconstitutional' (282); that portion is outlined as 'which enables body corporate and individual to seek authentication' (293). This means that the privacy invasion by private entities inherent in this section is seen to be excessive (410).[2] Striking down Section 57 provides protection—temporarily, at least—from commercial use of our personal data. This is a big blow to entities such as

India Stack, whose products use Aadhaar at the core of their business, to provide 'presence-less, paperless and cashless service delivery'. After the judgment, unsurprisingly, the CEO of 'Aadhaar Bridge', launched by Khosla Labs, was disappointed and said that they are looking for the data protection law to restore their access to the central ID repository for the purpose of ID verification.

Sections 7 and 8

Section 7 allows the government to require Aadhaar authentication 'for receipt of a subsidy, benefit and service'. In its arguments, the government pitched the Aadhaar project as one which required balancing between the right to privacy and the right to life. The majority opinion accepts the welfare assertions of the government, while acknowledging the petitioners concerns regarding exclusion:

> The entire aim behind launching this programme is the 'inclusion' of the deserving persons who need to get such benefits. When it is serving much larger purpose by reaching hundreds of millions of deserving persons, it cannot be crucified on the unproven plea of exclusion of some. We again repeat that the Court is not trivialising the problem of exclusion if it is there. (389)

Later, they state that 'the objective of the Act is to plug leakages' and that 'we have already held that it fulfils legitimate aim' (386). This provided the ground to uphold, by and large, Sections 7 and 8.

The main relief under Section 7 is for children and students (for school admissions) who are given an opt-out facility upon attaining adult age. National eligibility tests such as NEET are also exempt. But that is it. In spite of all the evidence on exclusion, hardship and denial from welfare programmes resulting from the compulsory integration of Aadhaar in these programmes (see chapter 1), the majority opinion decided to accept at face value the claims and assurances made by the government—that Aadhaar was a tool of inclusion, that it had helped combat corruption—and that therefore, in this case, it satisfied the proportionality test. On the question of exclusion, while the majority expressed concern, they also naively accepted the government's assurance that no one shall be denied their benefits. The profiling concerns with respect to Section 7 did not convince the majority judges. This is the most disappointing aspect of the Aadhaar verdict.

It is puzzling that the obvious misrepresentations about the role of Aadhaar in welfare have not become known more widely. This appears to be the outcome of the deep social and economic divide in Indian society. Those who benefit from these programmes and who understand why Aadhaar cannot improve inclusion do not have a voice in the media or policy-making. This allowed anecdotes (repeated ad nauseam) to become the basis for taking big decisions.[3] Contrary to the rhetoric of evidence-based policy-making, what we have seen in this case is anecdote-based policy-making. The opinion of the majority judges also betrays this deep divide—caste and class—in society.

On Section 7, Justice Chandrachud is partially sceptical of legitimate aim, and scathing on proportionality (more below) and several other aspects of the project.

Aadhaar Act as a Money Bill

There were two questions before the constitutional bench—one, whether the Lok Sabha Speaker's decision regarding the classification of a Bill as a Money Bill is open to judicial review and two, whether the Aadhaar Act can be introduced as a Money Bill. All judges ruled that the Speaker's decision regarding the classification of a Bill as a Money Bill is open to judicial review. As Justice Chandrachud put it, barring it 'would render a certification of a Bill as a Money Bill immune from scrutiny, even where the Bill does not, objectively speaking, deal only with the provisions set out in Article 110(1)' (Supreme Court of India 2018: 136).

While the majority judges proceeded to uphold the classification of the Aadhaar Act as one (taking an unusual route to justify such a classification—the application of the 'pith and substance' doctrine), Justice Chandrachud rejected the use of the 'pith and substance' doctrine in this case.

> The doctrine of pith and substance is mainly used to examine whether the legislature has the competence to enact a law with

> regard to any of the three Lists provided under the Constitution. It cannot be applied to sustain as a Money Bill, a Bill which travels beyond the constitutional boundaries set out by Article 110. (176)

The majority judges felt that by striking down Section 57 the Aadhaar Act as Money Bill can be salvaged, but Justice Chandrachud argues that 'even Section 7 is not within the ambit of Article 110(1)(e)', whereas Section 57 'can by no stretch of logic by covered under Article 110(1)'. Justice Chandrachud deems this 'an abuse of the constitutional process' and that it 'constitutes a fraud on the Constitution' (178–79). The majority judgment in this matter is unfortunate, as it opens the door to future misuse by governments with possible long-term consequence of undermining the authority of the Rajya Sabha.

Justice Chandrachud's Dissent on Aadhaar

Contrary to the majority judges, who accepted the government's assertions as facts as also the government's assurances where they had concerns (especially on welfare and exclusion), Justice Chandrachud rejected several such assertions, stating that the government failed to establish these as facts. He rejected the claims of minimal data collection and storage, drawing on Professor Manindra Agrawal's report on 'differential privacy', highlighting the potential to profile individuals. In his opinion, the Aadhaar Act fails on several counts—it fails 'to protect the individual right to informational privacy', fails 'in its legislative design to establish and enforce an autonomous regulatory mechanism', fails to 'demonstrate that a less intrusive measure other than biometric authentication will not subserve its purposes', it fails to 'justify its actions and to demonstrate why facilitating the targeted delivery of subsidies...automatically entails a sacrifice of the right to privacy when both these rights are protected by the Constitution' and fails 'to consider that there were much less rights-invasive measures that could have furthered its goals'. The way forward against the Aadhaar project lies in Justice Chandrachud's opinion.

Will Things Fall Apart?

The early dissenting voices pointed to the privacy and civil liberties challenge inherent in the Aadhaar project. They have now been joined by several others from diverse fields. Lawyers, financial experts, technologists, economists, etc. writing critically about Aadhaar have helped us understand the multiple weaknesses of the programme—in design (such as fragility of the technology, biometrics, data security, etc.), implementation (how procedures are undermined) and its implications for vulnerable sections of society (problems in enrolling, accessing socio-economic entitlements, etc).

In the early years, media helped create the illusion of a general consensus about Aadhaar. On the rare occasion that someone wrote a critical opinion piece about Aadhaar, it was dutifully followed by gushing editorials about the need for Aadhaar. That too is beginning to change. For instance, editorials critical of the Aadhaar project were written in major English dailies, possibly for the first time in 2017. What continues to be missing, and therefore a disappointment, is the lack of good reporting on the issues in implementation and the hardships that people—especially the rural poor—are facing.

It is not surprising that when the media pays greater attention to the problems, public sentiment also turns.[4] The coercive turn, for the middle class and the elite, since 2016, has contributed to the change in public sentiment. Indeed, the 'fire' that until then primarily affected the rural poor, spread to the middle and upper middle classes (after the compulsory linking of bank accounts, mobile phones and PAN to Aadhaar). People are beginning to ask 'what is the logic of making Aadhaar compulsory for competitions for school children, or for banking?' in the same vein that we had been questioning its role in welfare.

The Aadhaar project was initiated by the second government of the United Progressive Alliance (2009–14; often referred to as UPA-2), headed by the Congress party. For much of that period, the Bharatiya Janata Party (BJP), which currently leads the National Democratic Alliance (NDA) government, was a vociferous critic of the project. Famously, the current Prime Minister tweeted on 8 April 2014 that, 'There is no vision, only political gimmick'. Several prominent leaders of the BJP questioned the project in those years.

Revealingly (and predictably?), once the BJP came to power, by all records, all it took was one meeting of the Prime Minister with Nilekani to completely reverse its position. So much so that it has, like the previous UPA-2 government, ignored the restraining orders of the Supreme Court. Moreover, as mentioned earlier, the NDA government that came to power in 2014 used a controversial route to ram the Aadhaar Act through Parliament in 2016.

Until the time of writing, no major political party had taken a clear stand against Aadhaar. The Trinamool Congress is possibly the only exception—its MPs even demonstrated outside Parliament against Aadhaar. While leaders of the Communist Party of India (Marxist), Aam Aadmi Party and Biju Janata Dal made public statements against Aadhaar, state governments run by these parties also violate Supreme Court orders. For instance, in Kerala, a proposal for Aadhaar-linked biometric attendance was mooted in October 2017. The Congress, as political parent of the project, finds itself in a bind, unable to own or disown it. The main defence has been that what they had in mind was a 'benign' version of the project—even though they were warned of the grave pitfalls by their own advisors when the project was initiated.

That political parties support it when in power and oppose it when they are out hints at just how much is at stake for the governments of the day. The betrayal by political parties, however, is hard to reconcile with electoral politics. Given the widespread hardship caused by the project in welfare programmes, why are political parties not competing with each other to rake the issue? One can only hazard guesses as to why this is not happening. One possibility is the capture of political parties by corporate interests and another is that the scale of the problem has not become apparent to political parties. Politicians ought to have two channels of learning about these issues—one, direct feedback from their electorate and party workers and two, through media reports. As mentioned earlier, the media has failed to report the scale of the problem and the fact that politicians remain innocent of these problems hints at the disconnect from their electorate and party workers.

The tall claims of Aadhaar's robust technology and its faultless implementation have begun to fall apart. Large-scale fraud at the enrolment stage has been highlighted in several cases (the government reported to Parliament that 49,000 enrolment agencies were blacklisted due to malpractices). As people link their mobiles and bank accounts, another vulnerability—fraud at the user-stage—has come to the fore. Even if data are secure (as the UIDAI claims), with the Aadhaar-enabled Payments System (AEPS), the Aadhaar project has created a vulnerability to identity fraud, even identity theft. The idea behind AEPS is, as PM Modi put it, 'your thumbprint is your bank'. Fingerprint impressions, however, can be easily reproduced. For instance, Hindustan Times reported that 200 students in Mumbai replicated their fingerprints on a widely used resin to fudge biometric attendance. Easy harvesting of biometric traits and publicly available Aadhaar numbers increase the risk of banking fraud (Brandon 2016; Kazmin 2017). In the light of the emerging financial technology infrastructure, which rides on Aadhaar and biometrics, the 'DataLeaks' scandal mentioned earlier is significant. *Even* without any data breach, the emerging AEPS architecture opens the door to identity theft, an alarming breach of privacy.

Ordinary people are already paying the price for this. Living life in the Aadhaar eco-system, as envisioned by its drivers, requires digital, tech and legal literacy. For the many who are barely literate, this is a tall ask. Since 2017, there have been nearly 200 news reports of people swindled of their savings, their Aadhaar number being misused (for example, to get a new phone connection), etc. and authentication failure when they draw their monthly rations, pensions or wages is undermining their rights.

Aadhaar's Identity Crisis

In this book, I have suggested that the primary purpose of the programme was never really to improve inclusion and welfare administration as projected. Welfare was the sugar-coating to facilitate an essentially commercial project. These commercial activities required a digital ID infrastructure such as Aadhaar, which was built using public money. The dressing up was necessary to speed up enrolment and stall the possibility of the privacy concerns preventing the project from taking off.

One hint that this was never about welfare comes from the fact that there were hardly any social policy-makers involved in the design of the Aadhaar eco-system. The UIDAI was dominated by technologists who have now left government and are setting up businesses that will tap the Aadhaar eco-system. These commercial interests and the conflict of interest issues with the project are only just beginning to be documented. For instance, Krishn Kaushik (2017) found that those who build the Aadhaar infrastructure as 'volunteers' are now using the Aadhaar platform to build businesses.

An early industry report on the Aadhaar project envisaged that over 2010–15, business opportunities worth USD 20 billion and 350,000 new jobs would be created, outlining some of the sectors where these opportunities would lie (for example, consulting, business process reengineering, hardware, etc). 'By the sixth year, the commercial pie would be worth US$10bn annually' (CLSA Asia-Pacific Markets 2010). Thus, during the final hearings of the Aadhaar matter, some businesses that built on the Aadhaar platform intervened in the Supreme Court arguing that, 'access to the Aadhaar eco-system…is critical' and declaring Aadhaar illegal will cause them 'grave and irreparable harm'.

Perhaps the most revealing narrative appears in Aiyar's (2017) biometric history of the Aadhaar project. The early motivation was a robust Know Your Customer (KYC) process. Tellingly, in his book, the use of Aadhaar for welfare appears in chapter 4, titled 'Push for the Pull'. He describes how 'the need to create a push for the pull' was recognised early, because unlike other government programmes that 'are typically behind the curve on wants and needs…there is no need for the system to convince people to queue up'. With Aadhaar, however, 'there was no explicit compulsion to get in the queue' (81–83). Contrary to the welfare argument in Court, in fact it was to improve the speed of enrolment.

To create demand for Aadhaar, an Awareness and Communication Strategy Advisory Council was set up. The council, comprised essentially of marketing gurus, divided the country into three segments—India I, largely urban, who would ask, 'why should they queue up for one more identity card'; India II, small-town India; and India III, largely dependent on the government to survive. 'From India III came an insightful lesson—that there may be no demand for a unique identity but there is truckloads of demand for economic assets' (Aiyar 2017: 84). It was also recognised that good communication was not enough to 'hyper-propel enrolment', and that the 'critical catalyst required for acceleration was utility, and the seeding of the idea of unique identity and Aadhaar into the heart of the discourse on public expenditure and delivery of public services'... 'crafted through the corridors of policy at every level of government' (Aiyar 2017: 87).[5]

The Aadhaar debate in India has significance internationally too. Digital IDs are a key component of the growth of the commercial opportunities arising from new technological advancements. Much of the optimism around digital IDs such as Aadhaar stems from a rose-tinted view of the possibilities of big data, with ever-improving data-mining techniques.

Early insights on the possible harms from digital technologies comes from Daniel Solove's (2004) book, *The Digital Person*. 'Computerized personal record-keeping systems, in the hands of policy and intelligence agencies, clearly extend the surveillance capabilities of the state' (computer scientist Abbe Mowshowtitz, quoted in Solove 2004: 31). Solove argues that while the 'Big Brother' metaphor serves well to highlight many concerns with databases, it is inadequate. Data may not be collected with malignant objectives, yet they 'can result in unintended harmful social effects', including self-censorship (35). Instead, he argues that 'Kafka's The Trial best captures the scope, nature and effects of the type of power relationship created by databases' (37), because it 'captures the sense of helplessness, frustration and vulnerability one experiences when a large bureaucratic organization has control over a vast dossier of details about one's life' (38). He suggests that bureaucracies exist in private organisations too, and that the problem 'emerges from subjecting personal information to the bureaucratic process with little intelligent control or limitation' so that we no longer meaningfully participate in decisions about our information (39). While Big Brother exerts power through surveillance, *The Trial* illustrates that 'unbalanced in power can have debilitating effects upon individuals—regardless of the bureaucracies' purposes (which may, in fact, turn out to be quite benign)'. It disempowers people, makes them vulnerable without a 'diabolical motive or secret plan for domination' (Solove 2004: 41).

One example of this, in early 2018, was the revelation from Canadian whistleblower Christopher Wylie about how our personal data was mined by Facebook and Cambridge Analytica. The episode demonstrated that once we create a digital footprint, we no longer are able to prevent its misuse. This is partly because either consent is inadequately built in, and where it is, is poorly understood and sometimes, even when it exists and is exercised, there can be violations. It has made evident the harmful side of the new technologies such as data mining, machine learning and artificial intelligence.

Finally, we should be aware that at least some of the hype around big data is industry-driven. Kitchin's (2014) critical examination suggests that business interest is an important driver of big data, where business is 'preoccupied with employing data analytics to identify new products, markets and opportunities rather than advance knowledge per se'.[6] An illuminating example of this is Cathy O'Neil's (an industry insider) book, *Weapons of Math Destruction*. Even with the best of intentions, algorithms can get it wrong, but the opacity of algorithms enhances their power (O'Neil, 2016). Assumptions, based on flimsy evidence, get hard-wired into algorithms. Not only are some algorithms suspect, the data they process can be bad too. 'Garbage in, Garbage out' is a recurring theme in O'Neil's work. Worse, she suggests that there is some evidence that they can be intentionally misused, or abused.

The Aadhaar project is a perversion of the constructive purpose of technology to be subservient to the needs of society.

Instead, society is being reordered—through coercion—to serve the needs of technologies controlled by corporations and government. This potential of the Aadhaar project to centralise control and concentrate power in the hands of the state and corporations is what constitutes the biggest threat.

Notes

1. Some chapters have been updated to incorporate insights from the final judgment.
2. Justice Sikri's opinion keeps the door open for a law to be framed where the purpose of identification is clearly laid out, but also asks for that law to be subject to judicial scrutiny.
3. For instance, Nilekani (2009) wrote 'One academic tells me, "the number of BPL [Below Poverty Line] ration cards circulating in Karnataka is more than the state's entire population, let alone the number of BPL families"' (368). In fact, according to official data for December 2011, the projected population of Karnataka in 2000 was 520 lakh and the total number of BPL cards in circulation was 87.5 lakh. The total number of ration cards was 148 lakh. But this statement by Nilekani acquired a life of its own.
4. Personally, one indicator of the changing mood is that instead of getting abusive emails and comments, people call and write to say that I am not critical enough and that my documentation of the problems is incomplete.
5. Aiyar outlines various strategies used—from ensuring Aadhaar is mentioned in every major political speech to having itself 'embedded' in government committees (91).
6. Kitchin's discussion juxtaposes business with academia. However, what is at stake with the current conception of the Aadhaar project is the need of corporations and the state's desire to increase its own power on the one hand, and social or political aspirations of ordinary people, on the other.

References

Aiyar, Shankkar. 2017. *Aadhaar: A Biometric History of India's 12-Digit Revolution.* Chennai: Westland Publications.

Brandon, Russell. 2016. 'Your Phone's Biggest Vulnerability is your Fingerprint'. *The Verge*, 2 May.

CLSA Asia-Pacific Markets. 2010. 'What's in a Number? Integer, Identity, Inclusion'. *Special India Report*, May 2010.

Kaushik, Krishn. 2017. 'Aadhaar Official Part of Private Firms that use Aadhaar Services for Profit'. *Indian Express*, 5 October.

Kazmin, Amy. 2017. 'India's Biometric ID Scan Make Sci-fi a Reality'. *Financial Times*, 27 February.

Kitchin, Rob. 2014. 'Big Data, New Epistemologies and Paradigm Shifts'. *Big Data and Society* 1 (1), April–June, pp. 1–12.

Nilekani, Nandan. 2009. *Imagining India: Ideas for the New Century*. New Delhi: Penguin.

O'Neil, Cathy. 2016. *Weapons of Math Destruction: How Big Data Increases Inequality and Threatens Democracy*. New York: Crown.

Solove, Daniel. 2004. *The Digital Person: Technology and Privacy in the Information Age*. New York: NYU Press.

Supreme Court of India. 2017. *Justice Puttaswamy (Retd) and Anr vs. Union of India and Ors*, Writ Petition (Civil) No. 494 of 2012, 24 August.

Supreme Court of India. 2018. *Justice Puttaswamy (Retd) and Anr vs. Union of India and Ors*, Writ Petition (Civil) No. 494 of 2012 and connected matters, 26 September.

List of Contributors

Anumeha Yadav is an award-winning journalist who works on the effects of economic and social policies on rural India.

Edgar A. Whitley is an Associate Professor of Information Systems at the London School of Economics and Political Science, UK.

Gautam Bhatia is a lawyer and a PhD candidate at the University of Oxford.

Gus Hosein is Executive Director of Privacy International, a London-based charity.

Jean Drèze is Visiting Professor, Department of Economics, Ranchi University.

Kiran Jonnalagadda is co-founder and CTO of HasGeek, and is based in Bangalore.

Kritika Bhardwaj is an advocate practising in New Delhi who assisted some of the petitioners in the *Aadhaar case* before the Supreme Court.

M. S. Sriram is Visiting Faculty at the Centre for Public Policy, Indian Institute of Management, Bangalore.

Prasanna S. is a New Delhi-based lawyer who assisted some of the petitioners in the *Aadhaar case* before the Supreme Court.

Reetika Khera is Associate Professor of Economics and Public Systems at the Indian Institute of Management, Ahmedabad.

Shyam Divan is a Senior Advocate in the Supreme Court of India. He appeared for the petitioners in the *Aadhaar case.*

Srujana Bej studies law at the National Academy of Legal Studies and Research University (NALSAR), Hyderabad.

Sunil Abraham is with the Centre for Internet and Society.

Usha Ramanathan is an independent law researcher who works on the jurisprudence of law and poverty.

Viswanath L. is a Bangalore-based engineer working in the fields of multimedia technologies and embedded systems.

Name Index

Subject Index